Age Discrimination
in
Employment Law

Age Discrimination
in
Employment Law

Joseph E. Kalet

Legal Editor

Labor Relations Reporter

The Bureau of National Affairs, Inc., Washington, D.C.

Library of Congress Cataloging-in-Publication Data

Kalet, Joseph E., 1951–
   Age discrimination in employment law.

   Includes index.
   1. Age discrimination in employment—Law and
legislation—United States.   I. Title.
KF3465.K35   1986   344.73′01394   86-9675
ISBN 0-87179-500-0   347.3041394

Printed in the United States of America
International Standard Book Number: 0-87179-500-0

Contents

Preface

A word is not a crystal, transparent and unchanged; it is the skin
of a living thought and may vary greatly in color and content
according to the circumstances and time in which it is used.

Oliver Wendell Holmes,
U.S. Supreme Court Justice

Towne v. Eisner, 245 U.S. 418, 425 (1917)

Since the passage of the Wagner Act in 1935—the first statute attempting to protect workers in the workplace from unfair employment practices—the courts have attempted to grapple with the word "discrimination." It comes in as many shapes and sizes as the imagination can devise. Congress has attempted to prevent discrimination on the basis of union affiliation, race, sex, religion, handicap, and so on.

But the grayest, and thereby the most troublesome, area of employment discrimination involves employment decisions based on the individual's age. From hiring to training, to promotion to involuntary retirement, employers are making decisions that affect individuals' lives based on a characteristic that they involuntarily assume: age. Such immutable characteristics as sex or race are clearly defined, for the most part, and adjudication usually turns on the employer's conduct. In age discrimination, there may be a question whether a 48-year old "aggrieved person" is in fact *old enough* to prove that his replacement by a 42-year old employee constituted age discrimination. In addition to examining the employer's conduct, the court may be required to examine the employee's status within the protected age group under the Act.

Additionally, employment decisions may be supported or masked by economic considerations. The courts have uniformly stated that an employment decision may not be based on economic considerations; otherwise, this would enable employers to use an economic basis to justify an improper employment decision.

Finally, increased age invariably brings with it diminished physical and/or mental capacity. Where safety is an issue, courts have wrestled with mandatory retirement rules for air line pilots, and others, on the basis of diminished physical/mental ability to perform. This has led to an infusion of scientific and medical data into the courtroom, further complicating ADEA enforcement.

As with most areas of law, the focus of issues shifts with time, from procedural to substantive, from proving a case to the remedy that should be applied. Relatively unresearched in any text were such issues as discovery and EEOC-supervised settlements in age discrimination cases. Other areas could easily constitute an entire book standing alone, such as proving an age discrimination case via statistics.

The hybrid nature of the Age Discrimination in Employment Act—part Title VII of the Civil Rights Act of 1964, part Fair Labor Standards Act of 1938—has left many unanswered questions as to the meaning of "selective incorporation" where the statute and its legislative history are silent. Splits in the federal Circuit Courts illustrate the problem and exacerbate the difficulty for attorneys attempting to advise clients on age issues, such as how to implement a reduction-in-force without running afoul of a statute with unsettled case law and potentially devastating liquidated damages liability.

This book does not attempt to provide answers to questions on which the courts have divided. After nine years as a legal editor, I have learned that the most effective way to indicate what the courts decided is to "let the cases do the talking." Interpolation and speculation are the province of law review articles. This book simply represents the latest, most comprehensive source of information available on case law and regulations issued under the Age Discrimination in Employment Act of 1967, as amended, through November 1985.

The author owes a debt of gratitude to many individuals, but I must first acknowledge Senator Jacob K. Javits for his kind assistance. I wish to thank certain of my law instructors at the George Washington University-National Law Center in Washington, D.C.: Professors Leroy Merrifield, Don Rothschild, and Ben Schieber (visiting professor from Louisiana State University Law School) for their dedication to labor law, and for all their contributions to my legal education. A special thanks to Ms. Audrey Free, GWU-NLC.

Practitioners who contributed, directly or indirectly to my labor law education include Robert Deso (Deso, Greenberg & Thomas), Washington, D.C., and Douglas McDowell (McGuiness & Williams), Washington, D.C. Within the arbitration profession, I must acknowledge Richard I. Bloch and Mollie H. Bowers for their generosity and patience in allowing me to work with and learn from them.

Stanley E. Degler, Vice President and Executive Editor of The Bureau of National Affairs, Inc., Washington, D.C., and Mary Green Miner, Director of BNA Books, both created an environment in which the author could write such a manuscript.

FEP Cases Senior Legal Editor Stephen S. Rappoport was generous with his comments and suggestions throughout this project. Attorney Don Farwell provided useful advice on the structure of the first draft, leading to a superior final manuscript. And Books Editors Anne Scott and Ken Allread expended innumerable hours and inexhaustible patience dealing with a much-revised manuscript.

Last, and certainly not least, Long Patience should be rewarded. The author wishes to thank his wife, Margaret, and son, Jude, for their patience during my many absences on evenings and weekends in researching and writing the manuscript, and during my presence when all I talked about was age discrimination, *ad nauseum*.

Joseph E. Kalet

Washington, D.C.
November, 1985

1

Introduction to the ADEA

Legislative History

On January 23, 1967, President Lyndon B. Johnson recommended the Age Discrimination in Employment Act in his Older Americans Message:

> "Hundreds of thousands, not yet old, not yet voluntarily retired, find themselves jobless because of arbitrary age discrimination. Despite our present low rate of unemployment, there has been a persistent average of 850,000 people age 45 and over who are unemployed . . . . In economic terms, this is a serious—and sense-less—loss to a nation on the move. But the greater loss is the cruel sacrifice in happiness and well-being, which joblessness imposes on these citizens and their families. Opportunity must be opened to the many Americans over 45 who are qualified and willing to work. We must end arbitrary age limits on hiring."[1]

The Age Discrimination in Employment Act (ADEA) of 1967 was an outgrowth of the civil rights legislation that started with the Equal Pay Act of 1963, followed by Title VII of the Civil Rights Act of 1964, the Voting Rights Act, and so forth.

However, efforts to prohibit arbitrary age discrimination through legislation occurred as early as the 1950s.[2] Early efforts to include age as a protected class within those classes protected under Title VII of the Civil Rights Act of 1964 were unsuccessful, at least in part due to the perception that there was insufficient information available to make a considered judgment about the nature of age discrimination.[3] As a compromise, Title VII contained a provision directing the Secretary of Labor to make a "full and complete study of the factors which might tend to result in discrimination in employment because of age and of the consequences of such discrimination on the economy and individuals affected."[4] The report was transmitted to Congress by the Labor Secretary approximately one year later.[5]

In 1966, Congress directed the Labor Secretary to submit specific legislative proposals for prohibiting age discrimination,[6] which was followed by a draft

---

[1]113 CONG. REC. 34743–44 (1967).

[2]*See* Age Discrimination Hearings Before the Subcommittee on Labor of the Senate Committee on Labor and Public Welfare, 90th Congress, 1st. Session 23 (1967); statement of Senator Javits.

[3]110 CONG. REC. 2596–99, 9911–13, 13490–92 (1964).

[4]Section 715, 78 Stat. 265 (since superseded by §10 of the EEO Act of 1972, 86 Stat. 111).

[5]Report of the Secretary of Labor, *The Older American Worker: Age Discrimination in Employment* (1965).

[6]FLSA Amendments of 1966, §606, 80 Stat. 845.

bill in 1967.[7] Subsequently, President Johnson issued his recommendation for the ADEA in his Older Americans Message.[8]

Congress undertook studies of its own and both Houses conducted hearings on the proposed legislation.[9]

The Secretary of Labor's report made findings which were confirmed by the Executive Branch and Congress that:

(1) Many employers adopted specific age limits in those states that did not have age discrimination prohibitions even though many other employers were able to operate successfully in the absence of these limits;

(2) In the aggregate, the age limits had a marked effect on the employment of older workers;

(3) Although age discrimination rarely was based on the sort of animus motivating other forms of discrimination (e.g., racial, religious, union), age discrimination was based on stereotypes unsupported by objective fact and was often defended on grounds different from its actual causes;

(4) The available empirical evidence demonstrated that arbitrary age limits were in fact generally unfounded and that, overall, the performance of older workers was at least as good as that of younger workers;

(5) Arbitrary age discrimination was profoundly harmful in at least two ways: It deprived the national economy of the productive labor of millions of individuals and imposed on the U.S. Treasury substantially increased costs in unemployment insurance and Social Security benefits and, it inflicted economic and psychological injury to those workers who were deprived of employment because of age discrimination.

The Report led directly to the enactment of the ADEA in 1967. The Act's Preamble emphasizes both the individual and social costs of age discrimination.[10]

The original intent of the drafters of what was to become the ADEA was merely to accord age the same protected status as that extended to race and sex under Title VII. However, it became clear early on that age was a different "animal," and that mere inclusion of the term "age" into Title VII would not be an adequate way to address age discrimination. Since all workers would eventually be within this protected class and that class knows no bounds as to other immutable characteristics, the drafters of the early proposals decided instead that a separate statute would be necessary.

Because Title VII had already established a framework within which the ban on employment discrimination could be enforced, the Title VII enforcement scheme and proof considerations were followed extensively in the drafting of the ADEA. But the absence of a full remedial scheme in Title VII, apparently for political reasons, required the drafters to look elsewhere. They found what

---

[7]113 CONG. REC. 1377 (1967).

[8]*Supra* note 1.

[9]*See* Age Discrimination in Employment: Hearings Before the Subcommt. on Labor of the Senate Commt. on Labor and Public Welfare, 90th Cong., 1st Sess. (1967); Age Discrimination in Employment: Hearings Before the General Subcommt. on Labor of the House Commt. on Education and Labor, 90th Cong., 1st Sess. (1967); *see also* Hearings on Retirement and the Individual before the Senate Select Commt. on Aging, 90th Cong., 1st Sess. (1967).

[10]Section 2, 29 U.S.C. §621.

they were looking for in the Fair Labor Standards Act of 1938 (FLSA), with its long and extensive record of remedial devices, both legal and equitable, and with the juxtaposition of liquidated damages and the good-faith defense via the Portal-to-Portal Act of 1947, amending the FLSA.

The ultimate legislation that Congress passed as the ADEA is in fact a hybrid: part Title VII, part FLSA. (See Chapter 4 at "FLSA/Title VII Hybrid.") As originally enacted, the ADEA prohibited discrimination on the basis of age against individuals within the protected age group of 40 to 65 years, inclusive, for private sector employees.[11]

The Act was amended in 1974 to extend its coverage to federal and state government employees. The Supreme Court upheld that extension of the Act's coverage, rejecting a claim that state sovereignty under the Tenth Amendment to the Constitution prohibited it. The extension did not "directly impair" a state's ability to "structure integral operations in areas of traditional governmental functions," the Court ruled.[12] Subsequent amendments to the Act have extended its coverage to federal employees, raised the ceiling to age 70 for private sector employees, and removed entirely the upper age limit for federal employees' protection under the Act.

EEOC Role

Following the 1978 amendments, the Equal Employment Opportunity Commission (EEOC) was given the responsibility for conciliation, investigation, and recordkeeping under the ADEA, and enforcement of the Act in both the federal and private sectors, administratively as well as in the courts. Prior to the 1978 amendments, the Secretary of Labor was responsible for these functions. This transfer of functions was accomplished under Reorganization Plan No. 1, authorized by the Reorganization Act of 1977.[13] The Reorganization Act authorized the President to rearrange executive departments and agencies. However, either house of Congress could veto this change, known as the so-called "one-house veto" provision. Procedurally, the Act required the President to transmit any proposed reorganization plan to both houses, and such a plan would become effective if neither house passed a resolution of disapproval within 60 days.[14]

As authorized by the Act, President Carter prepared and submitted to Congress Reorganization Plan No. 1 of 1978,[15] which was designed to reorganize and expand the functions of the EEOC, including *inter alia*, enforcement responsibility for the ADEA. Since neither house passed a resolution of disapproval, the entire Plan, including the transfer of enforcement authority for the ADEA from the Labor Secretary to the EEOC, and the "one-house veto" provision, became effective.[16]

---

[11]Pub. L. No. 90–202, effective June 12, 1968, 29 U.S.C. §621–634.

[12]EEOC v. Wyoming, 460 U.S. 226, 31 FEP 74 (1983).

[13]Pub. L. No. 95–17, 91 Stat. 29, 5 U.S.C. §§901–912.

[14]5 U.S.C. §§903, 906(a).

[15]43 FED. REG. 19807, 92 Stat. 3871, 1978 U.S. CODE CONG. & AD. NEWS 9795–9800.

[16]*See generally* EEOC v. Allstate Insurance Co., 467 U.S. 1232, 34 FEP 1785 (1984); Burger, Chief J., dissenting from dismissal of appeal for lack of jurisdiction.

In 1983, the Supreme Court decided *Immigration & Naturalization Service v. Chadha*,[17] which involved a "veto" provision in the enabling legislation that was essentially identical to that in the Reorganization Act of 1978. The Court determined that the one-house veto provision was unconstitutional. In one broad stroke, the Court invalidated every use of the legislative veto provision, despite its presence in over 200 federal laws since the mid-1930s. The Court declared that the veto clause violated constitutional mandates of separation of powers, bicameralism, and presentment.[18] In effect, the Court held that the convenience, flexibility, and efficiency of the device could not overcome the fact that it was clearly inconsistent with our constitutional structure.

Following *Chadha*, the EEOC was faced with a similar challenge to its enforcement authority because of the presence of the unconstitutional legislative veto provision in the Reorganization Act of 1978. In *EEOC v. CBS, Inc*,[19] the Second Circuit answered several questions raised by the Commission to justify its continued ability to enforce the Act, despite the defective provision. The Commission argued that the legislative veto provision was "severable" from the rest of the Reorganization Act, and that this reading of the Act would not subvert the congressional intent that the Commission have enforcement authority. Excision of an offending or defective clause is often used to preserve an otherwise valid statutory enactment, but the Second Circuit rejected the claim of severability. It observed that the consequences of exercising the veto provision, the comments on the floor of Congress, and materials contained in the committee reports demonstrated that the veto provision was a "key provision," an "integral and necessary" part of the Act, and that Congress would not have passed the Act without this provision.[20]

The Commission argued that Congress approved and ratified by acquiescence Reorganization Plan No. 1 when it appropriated funds for EEOC enforcement of the ADEA. However, the Second Circuit regarded appropriations bills as "particularly unsuitable" vehicles for implying ratification of unauthorized actions, especially actions that are unconstitutional as opposed to merely technically improper, inasmuch as the substantive aspect of such bills are subject to much less scrutiny than the substantive programs themselves.[21]

Finally, the appeals court observed that Section 905 of the Civil Service Reform Act of 1978 (CSRA) Pub. L. No. 95–454, 92 Stat. 1111, 1224, 5 U.S.C. 1101 (note), states that any provision of Reorganization Plan No. 1 or 2 that is inconsistent with the CSRA is superseded, and that this language tends to invalidate Plan No. 1, since Section 905 makes no reference to the specific transfer of enforcement authority at issue, and is not the type of "deliberate" action by Congress that would serve to ratify an otherwise unauthorized transfer.

The appeals court granted the EEOC's motion for a stay until December 31, 1984, reasoning that automatic dismissal would be an unnecessarily drastic

---

[17]462 U.S. 919, 51 U.S.L.W. 4903 (1983).
[18]*Id.*
[19]743 F.2d 969, 35 FEP 1127 (CA 2, 1984).
[20]*Id.*, 35 FEP at 1131.
[21]*Id.*, 35 FEP at 1132.

remedy. This provided Congress with an opportunity to affect a change in the legislation, to determine whether and how the EEOC would continue enforcing the ADEA.[22] By October 1984, Congress had passed and the President had signed H.R. 6225, sponsored by Rep. Jack Brooks (D., Tex.), chairman of the House Government Operations Committee. The bill was enacted into law on October 19, 1984 as Pub. L. No. 98–532, and amends Title 5, Chapter 9 of the Reorganization Act, to read:

> "Section 1. The Congress hereby ratifies and affirms as law each reorganization plan that has, prior to the date of enactment of this Act, been implemented pursuant to the provisions of chapter 9 of title 5, United States code, or any predecessor Federal reorganization statute.
> "Section 2. Any actions taken prior to the date of enactment of this Act pursuant to a reorganization plan that is ratified and affirmed by section 1 shall be considered to have been taken pursuant to a reorganization expressly approved by Act of Congress."

This amendment to Title 5 constituted a retroactive severance of the legislative veto provision. The EEOC's authority to enforce the ADEA and other statutes under the aegis of the Reorganization Act of 1977 was thus affirmed.

---

[22]*Id.*

2

What the Act Provides

Section by Section Analysis

The ADEA prohibits job discrimination against workers between the ages of 40 and 70 years, with no age ceiling for federal workers. The Act is intended to "promote the employment of older persons based on their ability rather than age; to prohibit arbitrary age discrimination in employment; to help employers and workers find ways of meeting problems arising from the impact of age on employment."[1]

Section 3 of the Act authorizes the Secretary of Labor, now the EEOC, to undertake studies and provide information to labor unions, management, and the general public about the needs and abilities of older workers, as well as their potential for continued employment and contribution to the economy. To that end, the EEOC is encouraged to undertake research with a view to reducing barriers to employment of older persons and the promotion of measures for utilizing their skills; to publish the findings of studies and other materials and otherwise make them available to employers, professional societies, the various media, and other interested persons for the promotion of employment; to foster, through the public employment service system and cooperative effort, the development of facilities of public and private agencies for expanding the opportunities and potentials of older workers; and to sponsor and assist state and community informational and educational programs.

Section 4 of the Act makes it an unlawful employment practice for an employer to treat employees or make employment decisions on the basis of age concerning hiring, discharging, training, and classifying. Section 4 also prohibits employment agencies from classifying, failing or refusing to refer for employment, or discriminating against an individual in any other way, because of such individual's age. Labor organizations are barred from excluding or expelling from membership or otherwise discriminating against individuals because of age. They are also barred from limiting, segregating, or classifying individuals, or failing or refusing to refer for employment individuals in any way that would deprive or tend to deprive any individual of employment opportunities, or otherwise adversely affect an individual's status as an employee or job applicant because of age. Labor organizations are also precluded from causing or attempting to cause an employer to discriminate against an individual based on age.

---

[1] 29 U.S.C. §621(b) (1984).

7

Section 4 also makes it unlawful for an employer, employment agency, or labor organization to discriminate against any individual because that individual has opposed any practice prohibited by the Act or has made a charge, testified, assisted, or participated in any manner in an investigation, proceeding, or litigation under the Act. The printing or publication of notices or advertisements indicating a preference, limitation, specification, or discrimination based on age is prohibited.

Age can be a bona fide occupational qualification (BFOQ) under certain conditions, and Section 4 makes age as a BFOQ a valid basis for making an employment decision. Other exceptions to the general prohibitions on making age a basis for an employment decision include "other reasonable factors," employee benefit plans, and good cause.

The 1978 amendments to the Act changed the treatment of involuntary retirement. Previously, an employer could impose involuntary retirement if it were done in observance of a bona fide seniority system. Under the amendments, however, it is forbidden to retire employees involuntarily pursuant to a seniority system or employee benefit plan and thus, it is no longer permissible as a valid defense to a charge of unlawful forced retirement that the employer acted under the terms of a seniority system or benefit plan. Finally, Section 4 requires any covered employer to provide the same group health plan to employees over age 65 as is provided to employees under age 65.

Section 5 directs the Secretary of Labor, now the EEOC, to make an appropriate study of institutional and other arrangements giving rise to involuntary retirement and to report findings and any appropriate legislative recommendations to the President and Congress.

Section 6 provides for the delegation of functions, and the appointment of personnel and technical assistance in the administration of the Act. It also authorizes the Secretary to cooperate with other regional, state, and local agencies in furnishing technical assistance to employers, labor organizations, and employment agencies to aid in effectuating the purposes of the Act.

Section 7 authorizes the EEOC to investigate and to require the keeping of records "necessary or appropriate" for the administration of the Act. It establishes enforcement procedures and remedies as are provided under the Fair Labor Standards Act of 1938, as amended. Section 7 also requires the EEOC to attempt to eliminate discriminatory practices and to effect voluntary compliance with the Act through "informal methods of conciliation, conference and persuasion." Any "person aggrieved" may bring a civil action for "legal or equitable relief," but the right of such a person to bring an action terminates upon the commencement of an action by the EEOC to enforce the person's right. A jury trial is authorized for any issue of fact for recovery of amounts owing as a result of a violation of the Act. Section 7 also establishes timeliness requirements for filing a charge with the EEOC, including statute of limitations, tolling during conciliation period, and reliance on administrative rulings.

Section 8 requires the posting in conspicuous places of a notice prepared or approved by the EEOC setting forth information deemed appropriate by the Commission for administering the Act.

Section 9 authorizes the EEOC to issue rules and regulations it deems necessary or appropriate for enforcing the Act and allows the Commission to establish "reasonable exemptions" to and from any or all provisions of the Act as the Commission finds "necessary and proper in the public interest."

Section 10 establishes criminal penalties, including fines, imprisonment, or both for violating the Act.

Section 11 is the definitional section; it defines the meaning, for the purposes of the ADEA, of such words as "person"; "employer"; "employment agency"; "labor organization"; "employee"; "commerce"; and "industry affecting commerce."

Section 12 establishes age limits of covered individuals, 40 years to 70 years of age, and 40 years of age to unlimited for federal government employees and job applicants. This section also exempts "bona fide executives or high policymakers" from the prohibition against compulsory retirement and establishes a "retirement benefit test" that equals $44,000.[2]

Section 13 requires the EEOC to submit a report to Congress annually covering its activities for the preceding year and including such information, data, and recommendations for further legislation in connection with the matters covered under the Act as it finds advisable.

Section 14 explains the effect of a federal action under the Act as it supersedes any state action and the effect of a state action that was commenced before the federal action was filed.

Section 15 governs nondiscrimination on account of age in the federal government employment sector, including EEOC authority to enforce the Act against listed federal entities, and other aspects of enforcement, investigation, and bringing of actions against the federal government. This section also requires the EEOC to report to the President and Congress on the effects of ADEA coverage over federal government employment practices.

Section 16 governs the authorization of appropriation of sums necessary to carry out the purposes of the Act.

1978 Amendments

In 1978, Congress amended the ADEA in significant ways. (Pub. L. No. 95–256) The 1978 Amendments affected Sections 4, 5, 7, 12, 15, and 16 and sections in Title 5 of the U.S. Code concerning Government Organization and Employees. The amendments made substantive changes in the Act as well as causing a transfer of functions from the Secretary of Labor to the Equal Employment Opportunity Commission.[3] (See Chapter 1, "EEOC Role" for detailed discussion.)

One important change in the substantive provisions of the Act concerned the aspect of involuntary retirement. Section 4(f)(2) was amended effective April 6, 1978 for employees under age 65, and effective January 1, 1979 for employees age 65 through 69. The substance of the change was a proviso that no employee benefit plan "shall excuse the failure to hire any individual, and

---

[2]As amended by Pub. L. No. 98–459, eff. 10-9-84.

[3]Reorganization Plan No. 1 of 1978, §2, 43 FED. REG. 19807, 92 Stat. 3781, set out in Appendix to Title 5, Government Organization and Employees, eff. 1-1-79, as provided by §1–101 of Executive Order No. 12106, December 28, 1978, 44 FED. REG. 1053.

no such seniority system or employee benefit plan shall require or permit the involuntary retirement of any individual . . . because of the age of such individual.'' An exception to the effective date was made in the case of employees covered by a collective bargaining agreement in effect on September 1, 1977, which was entered into by a labor organization as defined by Section 6(d)(4) of the Fair Labor Standards Act of 1938,[4] and which would otherwise be prohibited by the 1978 amendments. For those employees, the exception was effective until the termination of the agreement or on January 1, 1980, whichever occurred first.

Section 5 of the Act was redesignated Section 5(a)(1) and Subsections (A), (B), (C), (D), (2), and (b) were added, all of which affect the Secretary of Labor's responsibility in conducting a study and reporting findings to the President and Congress. The amendments provide greater specificity to the areas to be studied and to the effects of other aspects of the 1978 amendments on employment practices within and without the federal government.

One of the changes made in Section 7 provides for a jury trial (Section 7(c)(2)) to a person seeking recovery of amounts owing as a result of a violation of the Act ''regardless of whether equitable relief is sought'' by any party in any such action. This amendment resolved the question whether a request for equitable relief precluded the plaintiff from obtaining a jury trial.

Section 7(d) of the Act was amended to substitute the filing of a charge, rather than notice of intent to sue, with the Secretary.

Section 7(e) was redesignated Section 7(e)(1) and was amended to include Section 7(e)(2) which applies to conciliation efforts commenced by the Secretary of Labor after the date of enactment of the 1978 Amendments. This subsection also allows for the tolling of the statute of limitations, as provided in Section 6 of the Portal-to-Portal Act of 1947, during the conciliation period, but for no longer than one year.

Section 12 was amended to raise the age of coverage of the Act from 65 to 70 and to provide for exemptions from coverage for certain executive employees and tenured teaching personnel. Sections 12(a), (c), and (d) took effect on January 1, 1979. Section 12(b) took effect on September 30, 1978. Section 12(d), permitting compulsory retirement of tenured employees in higher education, was repealed, effective July 1, 1982.

Section 15 of the Act was amended to add the phrase ''who are at least 40 years of age'' in Subsection (a) after the phrase ''All personnel actions affecting employees or applicants for employment.'' Subsection (a) was also changed to reflect the term ''personnel actions'' after ''except.'' Subsection (f) was added, which limits the reach of the Act to Subsection (b), under the authority of the Civil Service Commission; Subsection (g) requires the Commission to undertake a study of the effects of Subsection (b)'s coverage of federal government employment practices, and to report to the President and Congress its findings. The EEOC was substituted for the Civil Service Commission in Subsections (b) and (g) pursuant to Reorganization Plan No. 1 of 1978 (see this chapter, note 3).

Finally, the 1978 Amendments changed Section 16 to remove the language

---

[4]29 U.S.C. §206(d)(4) (1984).

concerning a limit on appropriations: "not in excess of $5,000,000 for any fiscal year," was removed; currently there is no dollar limit on Congressional appropriations for the administration of the Act.

Subsequent Amendments

Though the 1978 amendments consolidated administration and enforcement in one agency in an unprecedented manner, Congress has still found it necessary to "fine tune" the Act, to reflect new policy, new circumstances, and new data.

For example, Congress amended the language on overseas employees in Section 4(f)(1), "in a foreign country . . ."[5] and added Section 4(g)(1)–(3), concerning employers with overseas establishments.[6] (See also Section 11(f).)

Congress provided for health care coverage of employees' spouses aged 65–69 by further amending the Act.[7] Congress also repealed certain limits contained in Section 12 of the Act effective in 1982.

The Act's legislative history indicates that compromises were made in the course of including federal employees within the Act's coverage. In view of the pressures put upon our Social Security system and our unemployment benefits programs, it is not unlikely that Congress will eventually remove the upper age limit and provide unlimited protection for private and nonfederal sector employees, as it has done for federal employees. Further tinkering with the Act is to be expected.

---

[5]Pub. L. No. 98–459, eff. 10-9-84.

[6]*Id.*

[7]Pub. L. No. 98–369, §2301(b), eff. 1-1-85.

3

Coverage of the ADEA

The ADEA prohibits "employers," "labor organizations," "employment agencies," and state and political subdivisions from engaging in certain forms of conduct. The Act ostensibly protects "employees" without ever defining what is a statutory employee for purposes of coverage of the ADEA. The Act also does not address the issue of multinational corporations whose extraterritorial enterprises may engage in prohibited activity, and whether the Act can, or was intended to, reach such conduct. The courts have attempted to provide insight, answers, and an environment of consistent enforcement and reasonable interpretation of the Act on these issues. Needless to say, the results have been mixed.

Jurisdiction

The ADEA, as federal legislation, was designed to reach most employers in the private sector within the geographical limits of the United States, since there was no language limiting the Act's coverage to certain geographical areas.

The Seventh Circuit Court of Appeals provided a definitive answer to the reach of the ADEA in extraterritorial matters, and the right of U.S. citizens working for U.S. corporations abroad to make use of the ADEA via the Older Americans Act Amendments of 1984,[1] which extended protection of the ADEA to such citizens. The court considered the legislative history of the Act, its remedial intent, and its Title VII and Fair Labor Standards Act roots, in determining that the ADEA does not have extraterritorial effect.

PFEIFFER v. WRIGLEY CO.

755 F.2d 554, 37 FEP 85 (CA 7, 1985)

. . .

But even if the approach taken by the other circuits is not completely compelling on its own terms, we can find nothing in the Age Discrimination in Employment Act or its background that suggests the Act was intended to have an extraterritorial reach beyond what might be necessary to prevent transparent evasions of the sort suggested in our last paragraph. The federal agencies responsible for enforcing the Act have assumed, apparently from the beginning, that it was intended to be limited to domestic

---

[1]Pub. L. No. 98-459, 98 Stat. 1767, §802.

13

employment. *See, e.g.,* 29 C.F.R. §860.20 (1970). And to apply the Act extraterritorially could be more than a little awkward. The normal basis of national sovereignty is territorial. So if Germany has a law requiring employees to retire at the age of 65 (presumably to spread work in order to reduce unemployment), no one can doubt the authority of Germany to apply the law to Pfeiffer; and if it did so, and if the Age Discrimination in Employment Act were also applicable, Wrigley would find itself having to comply with inconsistent laws, which it could do only by moving Pfeiffer to another country. Incidentally, this particular problem would not arise under the Fair Labor Standards Act itself if that Act were applied abroad. There can be few if any nations that fix a maximum wage, or minimum hours of work, so there would be no conflict between the Act and local law—although having to pay American wages to foreign workers might of course impose a crushing competitive disadvantage on American firms abroad.

Pfeiffer's lawyer stated at oral argument that Germany does have a law, applicable to Pfeiffer, requiring retirement at age 65. Our own perhaps halting efforts to research the German law of retirement leave us unclear whether this is so, *see* Schaub, Arbeitsrechts Handbuch 280, no. 7; 505, no.13; 1013, §8.I (1972); and although questions of foreign law are treated as questions of fact (precisely because of the limited capabilities of domestic courts to research foreign law), and we could therefore treat counsel's statement as an admission (and a very damaging one to his cause), we hesitate to place heavy weight on an unguarded and possibly inaccurate statement made in the heat of oral argument. We shall therefore treat the hypothetical German law merely as an illustration of the problems that could arise in applying the Age Discrimination in Employment Act abroad.

The fear of outright collisions between domestic and foreign law—collisions both hard on the people caught in the cross-fire and a potential source of friction between the United States and foreign countries—lies behind the presumption against the extraterritorial application of federal statutes, on which *see, e.g., Foley Bros., Inc v. Filardo,* 336 U.S. 281, 285, 8 WH Cases 576 (1949); *Commodity Futures Trading Comm'n v. Nahas,* 738 F.2d 487, 493 (D.C. Cir. 1984). Although the presumption is not absolute, *see, e.g., Tamari v. Bache & Co.* (Lebanon) S.A.L., 730 F.2d 1103, 1107–08 and n.11 (7th Cir. 1984), we can think of no good reason for departing from it here. Indeed, its wisdom is confirmed by imagining the complications that could result from applying the Age Discrimination in Employment Act in a case where the employer was foreign and the employee American, or the employer American and the employee foreign, or both foreign. Pfeiffer would like us to limit our consideration to a case—his case—where both employer and employee are American (since for purposes of this appeal we must assume, as Pfeiffer alleges, that Deutsche Wrigley is just the alter ego of its American parent). But we cannot do that unless there is some principled basis for confining the extraterritorial reach of the statute (if it has any such reach) to his case. Nothing in the language of the statute suggests a basis for doing this but it can be argued that conflict of laws principles would automatically confine the Act's extraterritorial reach. This would certainly have been true in the old days, when the substantive law applicable to a tort suit was the law of the jurisdiction where the last act necessary to make the defendant's conduct tortious had occurred, which here was the discharge of Pfeiffer from his place of work in Germany. There is no tort without an injury, *see, e.g., Cenco Inc. v. Seidman & Seidman,* 686 F.2d 449, 453 (7th Cir. 1982), and there was no injury to Pfeiffer until he was actually let go, which happened in Germany. But modern conflicts principles are altogether more complex than this. Without having to go deeply into the question (which would require us first to decide where a court should look to find the conflict of laws principles applicable to a federal-question case, a question on which, as noted in Currie, Federal Courts 447 (3d ed. 1982), there is surprisingly little authority), we note that if either the plaintiff or the defendant were American and the contract of employment had been signed in America, an American court might well decide to apply American rather than foreign substantive law to decide the parties' tort rights and duties arising from the employment relationship—and maybe would do so wherever the contract had been signed. *See, e.g., Griffith v. United Air Lines, Inc.,* 416 Pa. 1, 13–25, 203 A.2d 796, 802–07 (1964); *Belanger v. Keydril Co.,* 596 F. Supp. 823, 826–27, 36 FEP Cases 132 (E.D. La. 1984); Restatement, Second, Conflict of Laws §145, comment f, at p. 424 (1971); Sedler, *Rules of Choice of Law Versus Choice-of-Law Rules: Judicial Method in Conflicts Tort Cases,* 44 TENN. L. REV. 975, 1036–37 (1977). Thus, conflict of law principles cannot be assumed to confine the operation of the Act to the situation presented in this case, where both parties are American although the employee did all his work abroad—unless Germany really does require retirement at age 65; for then it would be quite clear that the Age Discrimination in Employment Act must yield. See Restatement, Foreign Relations Law of the United States (Revised), tent. draft no. 3, §419(1)(a)(1982).

So conflict of law principles cannot be counted on to avoid entangling the Age Discrimination in Employment Act in disputes having less of a domestic focus than this case, if the Act is given extraterritorial effect; and this gives point to the observation that "federal statutes designed to be applied to conduct taking place outside the United States usually so provide," Restatement, Second, Foreign Relations Law of the United States, §38, note 1, at p. 108 (1965) (giving examples). . . .

. . .

But the Fair Labor Standards Act *explicitly* does not apply abroad (see section 213(f)); and it can be argued that if there really were a strong presumption against extraterritorial application of laws regulating employment, Congress would not have bothered to negative such application explicitly. Whatever force this argument might have in other contexts (perhaps little, because it may impute too much knowledge of background law to Congress and because it ignores a draftsman's prudent as well as natural inclination to make explicit even what may fairly be assumed to be implicit) is blunted here by the history of section 213(f). That section was added to the Fair Labor Standards Act by the Overseas Labor Standards Amendments of 1957 in order to overrule a Supreme Court decision that had given the Act a very modest extraterritorial reach by applying it to workers at an American military base overseas. *Vermilya-Brown Co. v. Connell,* 335 U.S. 377, 8 WH Cases 389 (1948); *see* S.Rep. No. 987, 85th Cong., 1st Sess. (1957). The hostility that Congress displayed to the courts' giving the Fair Labor Standards Act any extraterritorial application at all cannot be used to argue that Congress would have wanted the courts to give the Age Discrimination in Employment Act a general extraterritorial application.

Although there have been some attempts in recent years to give extraterritorial application to Title VII of the Civil Rights Act of 1964, which forbids racial, sexual, and related discrimination in employment, *see Bryant v. International Schools Services, Inc.,* 502 F. Supp. 472, 481–83, 24 FEP Cases 747 (D.N.J. 1980), *rev'd on other grounds,* 675 F.2d 562, 565, 28 FEP Cases 726 (3d Cir. 1982); 1 Larson Employment Discrimination §5.60 (1984 and Supp. 1984); *cf.* Note, *Civil Rights in Employment and the Multinational Corporations,* 10 CORNELL INT'L L.J. 87 (1976), these attempts are based on statutory language that has no counterpart in the Age Discrimination in Employment Act, and also long post-date the enactment of that Act in 1968. A lively debate would probably have ensued in Congress if anyone had thought the new law might be applied to employees living and working in foreign countries. There was no such debate, and while we do not read into silence a deliberate rejection of extraterritorial effect—it is not like Congress to negate every conjectural possibility; it has limited capacity for surveying the future, and encounters difficulty enough in resolving points actually in dispute—we are left with no basis for thinking that Congress in 1968 would have wanted us to apply the Act to workers living and working abroad.

The court concluded this portion of its analysis with an admonition that if the evidence indicated that the employer transferred the employee abroad in the last days or weeks of his employment ("we need not sketch the outer bounds of the limiting principle"), and then discharged him, the court would not be willing to say that the employer was immune from liability under the

Act.[2] It reasoned that in that hypothetical, the employee's "relevant work station" would be within the U.S. But since the employee in *Pfeiffer v. Wrigley Co.* had lived and worked continuously overseas during his entire period of employment by the employer, the court concluded that this made his "relevant work station" foreign, rather than domestic, and thereby deprived him of the protections of the Act.[3]

After argument in this case, but before the court had issued its decision, Congress passed the Older Americans Act Amendments of 1984 which extends the protection of the ADEA to U.S. citizens employed abroad by American corporations or their subsidiaries, except for situations where applying the Act would violate the law of the country where the citizen is employed. However, since the Amendments were not intended to be applied retroactively, and since the plaintiff in this case resided in a country having a law that conflicted with the ADEA, the court was not compelled to interpret the Act, as amended, to this situation.

Following *Pfeiffer*, an involuntarily retired employee attempted to apply retroactively the 1984 amendment extending the Act's coverage to American citizens employed by American employers outside the U.S. The District of Columbia Court of Appeals ruled that the amendment does not apply retroactively because the employer's 1981 conduct was entirely legal at the time.[4]

Another aspect of jurisdiction involves application of the ADEA to citizens of the District of Columbia, an area within the U.S. that is not a state. The District Court of the District of Columbia determined that a federal employee within the District should be treated the same as any federal employee within the confines of territorial U.S., within the meaning of Section 15 of the Act.[5]

Federal government employees are covered under the Act as a result of the 1974 amendments "prohibiting age discrimination in federal employment."[6] All state and local government employees are now covered under the Act as a result of the Supreme Court's decision in *EEOC v. Wyoming.*[7] (For a further discussion of ADEA application to the states, see this chapter, "Application to States.")

Protected Groups

As noted earlier, the Act does not define "employees" other than to create classes of protected individuals: those employees over age 40 and under age 70 for private sector and nonfederal public sector employers; and those employees over age 40 with no age limit for federal sector employment. Since

---

[2] 37 FEP 85, 89 (CA 7, 1985).

[3] *Id.*

[4] Ralis v. Radio Free Europe/Radio Liberty, Inc., 54 U.S.L.W. 2116 (1985).

[5] Kennedy v. Whitehurst, 509 F. Supp. 226, 25 FEP 362 (D DC, 1981), *aff'd*, 690 F.2d 951, 29 FEP 1373 (CA DC, 1982).

[6] 29 U.S.C. §633a. *See also* Lehman v. Nakshian, 453 U.S. 156, 26 FEP 65 (1981), for an explanation of the differences between federal and nonfederal ADEA rights.

[7] 460 U.S. 226, 31 FEP 74 (1983).

raising the ceiling from age 65 to age 70 in the 1978 amendments was regarded as a compromise between retaining the age 65 limit and removing any upper limits,[8] and in view of changes in demographics concerning older people and proposed changes in Social Security funding, it is not inconceivable that eventually Congress will give serious consideration to removing all upper age limits on protection from age discrimination in employment.

In any event, there has been much litigation concerning who is an "employee" under the Act, since this is the universal characteristic of the protected group that Congress specifically intended to protect from age discrimination. In *Hickey v. Arkla Industries, Inc.,*[9] the Fifth Circuit provided a well-reasoned look into what is necessary to find "employee" status, not only in the context of the particular employment relationship at issue, but also in light of what Congress intended by selective incorporation of the Fair Labor Standards Act, and its remedial purpose and provisions. The court determined that a manufacturer's sales representative whose relationship with the manufacturer was cancelled when he was 49 years old was not an "employee" within the meaning of the ADEA, even under the liberal "economic realities" test of the FLSA. The court observed that the sales representative was largely independent of the manufacturer's control, he had significant opportunities for profit and a continuing investment in his business, and he was entitled to cancel the relationship with the manufacturer on 30 days' notice. The fact that his business was dependent on the manufacturer as his major supplier does not establish "economic dependence" so as to create an "employer-employee" relationship, the court concluded.[10]

An important addition to the court's opinion was its rejection of the plaintiff's claim that the ADEA covers all individuals having an "economic relationship" with a business entity; the court stated that "employee status" is required for coverage under the Act.[11]

In *Dake v. Mutual of Omaha Insurance Co.,*[12] an insurance saleswoman was held to be an independent contractor, rather than an employee under the ADEA, since the employer exercised virtually no control over the saleswoman and she was not financially dependent on the employer. The district court formulated a "hybrid test" that involved the traditional FLSA-type "economic realities" test and a standard that it deemed more controlling: the employer's right to control the individual.[13] Under this bifurcated analysis, the court observed that the saleswoman was paid on a commission basis, did not have taxes withheld by other companies for whom she worked, used Form 1099 to file her taxes, received no additional compensation or fringe benefits from those companies, covered her own business expenses, was free to solicit whomever she chose, and was permitted to and did sell insurance for other insurance

---

[8]Nelson & Wilson, *The Age Discrimination in Employment Act*, ALI-ABA Course Materials J., Dec. 1979, at 32. *See also* H.R. Rep. No. 805, 90th Cong., 1st Sess. 13–15, *reprinted in* 1967 U.S. CODE CONG. & AD. NEWS 2225–27. *See also* 29 U.S.C. §624(a)(1)(A)-(c) (1979).

[9]688 F.2d 1009, 29 FEP 1719 (CA 5, 1982).

[10]*Id.*

[11]*Id.*, 29 FEP at 1722.

[12]600 F. Supp. 63, 36 FEP 1106 (D Ohio, 1984).

[13]*Id.*, 36 FEP at 1108.

companies. The court concluded that the saleswoman's earnings were based on how hard she worked and on her own sales ability, rather than on the companies' productivity or success, and her contract with one of these companies explicitly stated that she was to be considered an independent contractor, rather than an employee.[14]

The "protected class" under the ADEA is that group of individuals between the ages of 40 and 70 years (or all such individuals over age 40 years for the federal sector) who qualify as "employees" within the meaning of the Act and who do not fall within any of the exemptions that the Act provides.

Respondents Subject to Prohibitions

The ADEA reaches employers, labor organizations, employment agencies, and state and local governments. The federal government is also covered, but there are certain procedural and substantive differences that will be discussed in subsequent chapters.

Section 11(b) of the Act defines an "employer" as one engaged in an industry affecting commerce with 20 or more employees for each working day in each of 20 or more calendar weeks in the current or preceding year.[15] The usual corporate structures and relationships that arise in the context of litigation involving the Fair Labor Standards Act and the National Labor Relations Act also can be seen in ADEA litigation, such as parent-subsidiary relationships, holding companies and shell corporations, integration of operations and/or centralized control of labor relations, and so forth. The Second Circuit has provided a clear and comprehensive standard for determining whether a parent corporation and its subsidiary are sufficiently related to warrant ADEA coverage. It set down a four-factor test:

(1) Interrelation of operations;
(2) Common management;
(3) Centralized control of labor relations; and
(4) Common ownership or financial control.[16]

Conversely, a holding company was found not to be an "employer" under the ADEA where it was a wholly separate and legally recognizable entity and the relationship between it and the employer was not a sham.[17] Along these lines, a trade association employee failed to prove jurisdiction when she was unsuccessful in establishing an "agency" relationship or an integrated enterprise between the employer-association and its separate corporate members.[18] Whether religious organizations fall within the definition of "employer" that Congress intended under the ADEA is unresolved. One district court has relied on the absence of any clear, affirmative intent by Congress to include religious organizations,[19] and another district court reasoned that the Commerce Clause

---

[14]*Id.*

[15]29 U.S.C. §630(b) (1984).

[16]Marshall v. Arlene Knitwear, Inc., 608 F.2d 1369, 24 FEP 1356 (CA 2, 1979).

[17]Sobelman v. Commerce Bancshares, Inc., 444 F. Supp. 84, 16 FEP 974 (ED Mo, 1977).

[18]York v. Tennessee Crushed Stone Ass'n, 684 F.2d 360, 29 FEP 735 (CA 6, 1982).

[19]Ritter v. Mount St. Mary's College, 495 F. Supp. 724, 23 FEP 734 (D Md, 1980).

operates to extend the ADEA's "person engaged in an industry affecting commerce" to reach the religious school in that case.[20] The obvious conflicting policies here involve the remedial nature of the ADEA which encourages a broad reading of "employer" and the reluctance of courts to get embroiled in church-state disputes because of constitutional restraints.

Two other entities are covered by the ADEA proscriptions: "labor organization," which is broadly construed by the courts; and "employment agency" which encompasses any entity *regularly* involved in procuring employees for an employer.[21] A "triggering" mechanism for ADEA coverage of employment agencies involves engaging in a covered activity. For example, a district court relied on Section 860.35(b) of the Code of Federal Regulations to find that an employment agency that procures employees for some employers that are covered by the ADEA is therefore covered by the Act with respect to all of its activities; the court rejected the agency's claim that its actions were not covered unless the client for whom the employee is procured is in fact an "employer" under the ADEA.[22]

Union Liability.   An aspect of liability important to both employers and unions involves the issue of union liability: Once it has been determined that the union is at least partially liable for unlawful age discrimination, what effect does this have on the employer's liability? Is there a right to contribution from the union at the remedial stage of the proceeding? There appears to be a split among the circuits concerning the extent of the union's liability; however, this "appearance" of a split may be illusory since it is possible that the courts are actually basing their decisions on different issues.

In *Marshall v. Eastern Airlines, Inc.*,[23] a district court ruled that if an employer is found to have violated the ADEA by its involuntary retirement of employees it may not receive contribution from the union. In contrast, the Second Circuit pointed out that the remedial scheme of the ADEA does not allow recovery of monetary damages against a labor organization, because the Fair Labor Standards Act—the source of the ADEA's remedial scheme— expressly excludes labor organizations from the definition of "employer."[24] But this does not bar imposition of an *equitable* remedy on the union, and this remedy includes back pay, the court ruled, since "one of the purposes of a back pay award is to spur unions . . . to eliminate unlawful discrimination."[25]

Application to States

In a landmark decision, *EEOC v. Wyoming*,[26] the Supreme Court settled an important question involving a clash between state sovereignty under the Tenth

[20]Usery v. Manchester E. Catholic Regional School Bd., 430 F. Supp. 188, 15 FEP 1096 (D NH, 1977).

[21]Cannon v. University of Chicago, 648 F.2d 1104 (CA 7, 1981).

[22]Brennan v. Aldert Root, 16 FEP 1643 (ED NC, 1974).

[23]Marshall v. Eastern Airlines, Inc., 474 F. Supp. 364, 20 FEP 908 (SD Fla, 1979), *aff'd*, 645 F.2d 69, 27 FEP 1686 (CA 5, 1981), *cert. denied sub nom.* EEOC v. Eastern Airlines, Inc., 454 U.S. 818, 26 FEP 1687 (1981).

[24]Air Line Pilots Ass'n v. TWA, 713 F.2d 940, 32 FEP 1185 (CA 2, 1983).

[25]*Id.*, 32 FEP at 1198.

[26]460 U.S. 226, 31 FEP 74 (1983).

Amendment to the Constitution and the Commerce Clause. The Court ruled that the Tenth Amendment does not preclude Congress, pursuant to its powers under the Commerce Clause, from extending the ADEA to cover state and local government employees, where such extension does not "directly impair" a state's ability to "structure integral operations in areas of traditional governmental functions."[27]

This case, which was an important and lengthy decision, relied to a significant degree on an earlier Supreme Court decision involving extension of the Fair Labor Standards Act to state and local governments. In *National League of Cities v. Usery*,[28] the Court first adopted the language of "traditional governmental functions"[29] to delineate which functions would fall under the FLSA and which would not.

However, the Supreme Court rejected this standard of "traditional governmental functions" as unworkable and impractical in *Garcia v. San Antonio Metropolitan Area Transit Authority*.[30] What remains of the original basis for *EEOC v. Wyoming* is that Congress may have validly employed the Commerce Clause to fashion legislation such as the ADEA to cover state and local governments without running afoul of the Tenth Amendment's protection of state sovereignty; the standard for asserting such coverage over the states is unclear, and what remains of the Tenth Amendment's protection for states is unclear.

Prohibitions

The Act prohibits discriminatory treatment in employment decisions where the employment decision is based on age, unless age is a bona fide occupational qualification (BFOQ),[31] or some exemption applies. But the forms which this treatment can take are myriad. The most obvious situation would involve a decision by the employer to terminate or involuntarily retire a member of the protected class who was performing adequately and replace him with someone under age 40. It is conceivable that an employer could replace a protected individual with someone outside the protected age group for nonfederal sector employees by selecting the replacement from the other end of the protected age group. That is, replace a protected employee with someone over age 70, and this arguably would not constitute age discrimination. But for practical purposes, case law revolves around replacements who are younger than the aggrieved individuals who bring the charges or file the complaints.

The prohibited conduct includes, but is not limited to, refusal to hire, discharge, involuntary retirement, refusal to train or transfer, and unfair treatment in other areas of employment conditions.[32] Following Congress' experience with such remedial legislation as the Fair Labor Standards Act and Title VII

---

[27]*Id.*, 31 FEP at 80.
[28]426 U.S. 833, 22 WH Cases 1064 (1976).
[29]*Id.*, 22 WH Cases at 1069.
[30]27 WH Cases 65 (1985).
[31]29 U.S.C. §§623(f)(1) (1984).
[32]29 U.S.C. §623(a) (1984).

of the Civil Rights Act of 1964 the legislators included a bar against lowering the wages of employees outside the protected class to remove any wage disparity with protected employees.[33] Similar proscriptions apply to labor organizations and employment agencies.[34]

An important question involves whether an employee who has been the victim of age discrimination must show that he was replaced by someone outside the protected age group, or merely that his replacement was younger. The courts have taken a relativistic approach to this issue: the answer depends on the age of the discriminatee and the age of the replacement. The First Circuit has observed that replacing a 60-year old with a 35-year old employee or even a 45-year old employee within the protected group, is more indicative of discrimination than replacing a 45-year old employee with a 42-year old employee.[35] By the same token, replacement by "someone older would suggest no age discrimination, but would not disprove it conclusively. The older replacement could have been hired, for example, to ward off a threatened discrimination suit."[36] (For a further discussion of this aspect of an ADEA case, see Chapter 5, "ADEA Proof Considerations.")

Borrowing from other remedial legislation and experience, Congress also included a protection against retaliation because an employee opposed a prohibited practice, or resorted to ADEA processes.[37] For example, a 64-year old male comptroller was replaced by a 49-year old female who allegedly was unqualified for the job. The male employee filed charges with the EEOC, and subsequently suffered retaliatory treatment *after* his discharge. The Eleventh Circuit ruled that the individual may be covered by the ADEA's ban on retaliation since the retaliatory act came close on the heels of the employee's termination and may be of such a nature as to be fairly includable as a cause of action here.[38]

Finally, employment agencies are prohibited from engaging in advertising with language that indicates a preference for younger workers, or a prejudice against individuals within the protected age group.[39] The elimination from "help wanted" ads such references as "girl" or "boy," "recent high school or college graduate," and other terms indicating a youthful candidate for employment are due directly to regulations promulgated under the ADEA.[40]

Limitations

As with most legislation, there are exceptions and limitations. The ADEA follows this pattern and excepts such things as employee benefit plans and apprenticeship programs, and exempts such individuals as "executives" and

---

[33]*Id.*

[34]*Id.*

[35]Loeb v. Textron, Inc., 600 F.2d 1003, 1013 n.9, 20 FEP 29 (CA 1, 1979).

[36]*Id.*

[37]29 U.S.C. §623(d) (1984).

[38]Helwig v. Suburban Chevrolet, 33 FEP 1261 (D Md, 1983).

[39]29 U.S.C. §623(e).

[40]29 CFR §§1625–1628 (1984). For a more complete discussion of the type of language approved or prohibited by the EEOC, consult the regulations.

employees with unlimited tenure. The reasons for these exceptions and exemptions are as much based on policy as administrative convenience since it would be difficult, if not impossible, for an agency to reach every conceivable employment relationship that can be envisioned. These limitations reflect a legislative determination that the absence of ADEA coverage in these instances will not greatly impede ADEA compliance and enforcement as a whole.

Exceptions

The ADEA specifically provides at Section 4(f)(1) that any employment decision based on age is not unlawful if a "bona fide occupational qualification" is reasonably necessary to the normal operation of the particular business, or if "reasonable factors other than age"[41] justify that employment decision. Section 4(f)(2) allows an employer to "observe the terms of a bona fide seniority system or any bona fide employee benefit plan such as retirement, pension, or insurance plan, which is not a subterfuge to evade the purpose of the Act,"[42] except that no such plan will excuse the failure to hire any individual and no seniority system or benefit plan will require or permit an involuntary retirement based on age. (Because of the importance and the volume of litigation concerning BFOQ exemptions, this subject is covered in greater detail in Chapter 5.)

The EEOC has also promulgated regulations exempting apprenticeship programs from coverage. And the Act exempts "bona fide" executives between the ages of 65 and 70 at a certain income level from the protection against involuntary retirement. (Such a protection was also available until July 1, 1982, for teachers between 65 and 70 who had unlimited tenure at the postsecondary level.)

Employee Benefit Plans.   An early decision on the employee benefit plan exemption established the criteria for falling within the exemption. In *Marshall v. Eastern Airlines, Inc.,*[43] a district court observed that the exemption "is an affirmative defense and must be plead and proven by the defendant. The defendant must show that it (1) observes the terms of the plan; (2) the plan was a bona fide employee benefit plan; and (3) it is not a subterfuge to evade the purposes of the ADEA."[44] There was no claim that the employer had failed to observe the terms of the plan or that the plan was not bona fide in the sense that it failed to pay substantial benefits; the court was required to examine whether the employer's actions in lowering the normal retirement age, after enactment of the Act, from 65 years to 62 years, constituted a "subterfuge to evade the purposes" of the Act. It answered in the affirmative, in view of the Secretary of Labor's enforcement position at the time of the employer's amendment to its plan that Section 4(f)(2) would not allow involuntary retirement, and the employer presented no evidence that the early re-

---

[41]29 U.S.C. §623(f)(1).

[42]29 U.S.C. §623(f)(2).

[43]Marshall v. Eastern Airlines, Inc., 474 F. Supp. 364, 20 FEP 908 (SD Fla, 1979).

[44]*Id.*, 20 FEP at 910.

tirement amendment had any business purpose other than arbitrary age discrimination.[45]

A fertile ground for ADEA cases involves the airline industry, wherein flight attendants and pilots have been involved in much litigation concerning age-based employment decisions. One such case concerned the employee benefit plan that was changed by an airline in its collective bargaining agreement with the union, to the effect that pilots retiring at the mandatory age of 60 were prevented from obtaining a lump-sum payment for all accrued vacation time at their retirement date even though younger pilots who decided to retire early could receive such payments.

In *EEOC v. Airline Pilots Association*,[46] a district court initially ruled that the ADEA does not require that older employees receive preferential treatment over younger employees, and therefore, it is irrelevant whether older employees receive lower benefits than they did in the past.[47] The appropriate inquiry is whether older employees receive lower benefits than younger employees, and if so, why. The court proceeded to an examination of the employer's claim that the "total package" of vacation benefits contained in the collective bargaining contract provides older pilots with greater benefits than younger pilots, and determined that this does not preclude a challenge to the provision that requires the pilots retiring at age 60 to use up some of their accrued vacation time before retirement, while allowing pilots retiring before age 60 to receive a lump-sum payment for their accrued vacation time at their retirement.[48] Ultimately, the court ruled that the airline had not provided a sufficient justification for the offending provision; it observed that the union had proposed the provision, and the airline had been neutral on that issue.

In 1978, Congress amended the ADEA to raise the minimum mandatory retirement age from 65 years to 70 years for nonfederal workers.[49] The amendment also provided that "in case of employees covered by a collective bargaining agreement which is in effect on September 1, 1977, . . . and which would otherwise be prohibited by the amendment, the amendment shall take effect upon the termination of such agreement or on January 1, 1980, whichever occurs first."[50] The deferral of the second clause of the amendment until January 1, 1980 continued the right granted an employer in the original act "to observe the terms of a bona fide employee benefit plan."[51] The effect of the deferral was that if a collective bargaining agreement did not entitle the workers covered by it to continue working to age 70, the employer could continue to observe the terms of his retirement plan until the collective bargaining agreement terminated or until January 1, 1980, whichever came first.

This was the setting when in 1979, following a strike, the employer put into effect a new provision in a new collective bargaining agreement raising the prior "normal" retirement age from 65 years to 70 years. Employees who

---

[45]*Id.*
[46]489 F. Supp. 1003, 22 FEP 1609 (D Minn, 1980).
[47]*Id.*, 22 FEP at 1611.
[48]*Id.*
[49]29 U.S.C. §623(f)(2) (1984), as amended by §3(a), Pub L. No. 95–256, 92 Stat. 189.
[50]*Id.*
[51]*Id.*

were required to retire under the old agreement at age 65 brought an action under ADEA, seeking to impose liability on the employer for their involuntary retirement which occurred *after* the effective date of the 1978 amendment raising the protected age group from 65 to 70. The Seventh Circuit was faced with the question as to when the 1978 amendment became effective for purposes of the employer's involuntary retirement of these individuals who were retired in compliance with the collective bargaining agreement then in existence.

In *EEOC v. United Air Lines, Inc.*,[52] the appeals court ruled that the airline's bargaining agreement making 65 the "normal" age of retirement remained in effect until replaced by the new agreement in 1979, and the employees who were forced to retire before the new agreement went into effect were not entitled to relief under the ADEA, despite the 1978 amendment raising the minimum mandatory retirement age to 70. It reasoned that the section of the amendment delaying applicability of the amendment until expiration of any existing bargaining agreement applies to the airline's contract, notwithstanding its designation of 65 as the "normal" rather than "mandatory" retirement age; the prior bargaining agreement did not expire when the employees struck, but expired when the new agreement replaced it.[53] Therefore, the court concluded, none of the employees forced to retire were forced to retire in violation of the Act.[54]

Bona Fide Seniority Systems. The Act as amended provides that it is lawful for an employer to "observe the terms of a bona fide seniority system" which is not a subterfuge to evade the Act, except that no such system will require or permit involuntary retirement of any employee under age 70 based on age.[55] However, seniority systems generally favor the older employee. Nevertheless, the Sixth Circuit had an opportunity to expound on this provision of the ADEA in *Morelock v. NCR Corp.*[56] The employer's facially neutral seniority system created senior and junior technician classifications out of a former single classification and subsequently prohibited bumping of junior technicians by senior technicians. The court ruled that this system was "bona fide" within the meaning of the Act since the motive for creating the two classifications was economic, the classifications were based on skill and ability, not on age, and there is no evidence to support an argument that the provision eliminating bumping rights was adopted in anticipation of any need for decentralization and resulting reductions in force.[57] Further, according to the appeals court, the adjectives "senior" and "junior" connote job duties and responsibilities, rather than age; employees both over and under age 40 occupied each classification at all times.[58]

In examining the *bona fides* of the seniority system, the court drew upon a decision of the Supreme Court that provided the impetus for the 1978 amend-

---

[52]37 FEP 36 (CA 7, 1985).
[53]*Id.*
[54]*Id.* at 39.
[55]29 U.S.C. §623(f).
[56]586 F.2d 1096, 18 FEP 225 (CA 6, 1978), *cert. denied*, 441 U.S. 906, 21 FEP 1139 (1979).
[57]*Id.*, 18 FEP at 231.
[58]*Id.* at 232.

ments to Section 4(f)(2): *United Airlines, Inc. v. McMann*.[59] Though Congress expressly rejected the holding of this decision when it amended the Act, the Supreme Court's definition of what constitutes "subterfuge" for purposes of evading the mandates of the Act still stands, and it is this language which the Sixth Circuit relied upon:

> "In ordinary parlance, and in dictionary definitions as well, a subterfuge is a scheme, plan, stratagem, or artifice of evasion. In the context of this statute, "subterfuge" must be given its ordinary meaning and we must assume Congress intended it in that sense.[60]

In light of the *McMann* definition of "subterfuge," the Sixth Circuit ruled that the seniority system at issue in *Morelock v. NCR Corp.* was not a subterfuge to evade the purposes of the Act. The laid-off employees who brought the action had alleged that their layoffs were the result of age-based discrimination, the court observed, but the employees had stipulated to the fact that the layoffs were due to a lack of work within their senior technician classifications. This precluded any claim that the employer had created the senior and junior technician classifications out of a former single classification—and then eliminated the rights of senior techs to bump junior techs—as a subterfuge to evade the purpose of the Act, the court reasoned.[61] Even if the stipulation was not binding, the court concluded, the number of senior technicians laid off is not so excessive in comparison with the number of junior techs laid off as to warrant the conclusion that the employer was discriminating on the basis of age.[62]

The EEOC regulations establish guidelines for determining the *bona fides* of a seniority system:

> "(a) Though a seniority system may be qualified by such factors as merit, capacity, or ability, any bona fide seniority system must be based on length of service as the primary criterion for the equitable allocation of available employment opportunities and prerogatives among younger and older workers.
>
> "(b) Adoption of a purported seniority system which gives those with longer service lesser rights, and results in discharge or less favored treatment to those within the protection of the Act, may, depending upon the circumstances, be a 'subterfuge to evade the purposes' of the Act.
>
> "(c) Unless the essential terms and conditions of an alleged seniority system have been communicated to the affected employees and can be shown to be applied uniformly to all of those affected, regardless of age, it will not be considered a bona fide seniority system within the meaning of the Act.
>
> "(d) It should be noted that seniority systems which segregate, classify, or otherwise discriminate against individuals on the basis of race, color, religion, sex, or national origin, are prohibited under Title VII of the Civil Rights Act of 1964, where that Act otherwise applies. The 'bona fides' of such a system will be closely scrutinized to ensure that such a system is, in fact, bona fide under the ADEA."[63]

Bona Fide Executives.   An important exclusion from the general pro-

---

[59]434 U.S. 192, 16 FEP 146 (1977).

[60]*Id.* at 203, 16 FEP at 151. *See also* EEOC v. Home Ins. Co., 553 F. Supp. 704, 30 FEP 841, 850–51 (SD NY, 1982).

[61]Morelock v. NCR Corp., *supra* note 56, 18 FEP at 232.

[62]*Id.*

[63]29 CFR §1625.8 (1984).

scription against involuntary retirement of nonfederal employees between the ages of 65 and 70 is that for a "bona fide executive" or an individual in a "high policy making position" as provided in Section 12(c)(1) of the Act.[64] One of the earliest cases to examine Section 12(c)(1) in detail was *Whittlesey v. Union Carbide Corp.*[65] The employer's chief labor counsel was forced to retire at age 65, and the employer raised his status as a "bona fide executive" as a defense to a charge of unlawful age discrimination. The court initially ruled that the position of Chief Labor Counsel was not, in the context of the particular employer, a "bona fide executive" position or one that involved "high policy making" within the meaning of the ADEA. The plaintiff was not looked to for significant contributions to formulation of employer policy, the court observed, even though his advice extended beyond mere interpretation of legal requirements.[66] The court added that "high pay" is not determinative as to whether a position comes within the exemption; the test is one of function, not of pay, it concluded.[67]

However, the EEOC has promulgated regulations stating that this exemption will not bar involuntary retirement if the retiree is within two years of retirement and is entitled to a pension of at least $44,000 per year.[68]

In addition, the regulations also exempt bona fide apprenticeship programs by authorizing age limits for entry into such programs.[69]

The ADEA's limitations from coverage for employee benefit plans, bona fide seniority systems, bona fide executives and individuals in "high policy making positions," and for apprentices in bona fide programs have been used frequently by employers as defenses to claims of unlawful age discrimination. These statutory defenses far exceed the number of cases litigated that involved such traditional defenses as *res judicata* and collateral estoppel. (A complete discussion of employer defenses to such age claims appears in Chapter 5, "Defenses.")

---

[64]29 U.S.C. §631(c)(1) (1984).
[65]567 F. Supp. 1320, 32 FEP 473 (SD NY, 1983), *aff'd*, 742 F.2d 724, 35 FEP 1089 (CA 2, 1984).
[66]*Id.*, 32 FEP at 474.
[67]*Id.* at 478.
[68]29 CFR §1627.12, pursuant to Pub. L. No. 98–459, eff. 10-9-84.
[69]*See* 29 CFR Part 1625 (1984).

4

ADEA Enforcement Procedures

Background

The Age Discrimination in Employment Act has three enforcement schemes:

(1) Private;
(2) Government agency (Equal Employment Opportunity Commission); and
(3) Intergovernmental deferral scheme to ensure that the ADEA will complement, rather than thwart, state enforcement in those jurisdictions with similar state statutes.

The ADEA plaintiff must pursue an administrative determination from the EEOC and can seek a judicial determination or a review of the EEOC decision.

Section 7(b) of the Act incorporates provisions of the Fair Labor Standards Act, authorizing a private suit for unpaid wages, and authorizing the EEOC to bring an action for unpaid wages and injunctive relief.[1] The Act was subsequently amended to provide the private plaintiff with the right to pursue "legal or equitable" relief under the Act.[2]

Under Section 7(c), any "aggrieved person" has the right to bring a private action, but that right terminates upon commencement of an action by the EEOC to enforce the right of the individual under the Act.[3]

Section 15 of the Act provides federal employees and applicants for federal employment with an intergovernmental administrative route, through the procedures of the particular federal agency involved to the EEOC for final resolution.[4] If the Commission's efforts at conciliation or an administrative determination are unsatisfactory, the individual may pursue his claim in federal court.

The 1978 Reorganization Plan, adopted pursuant to the Reorganization Act of 1977,[5] transferred from the Secretary of Labor to the EEOC authority for enforcing the ADEA in both the federal and nonfederal sectors, with the requirement that federal employees must exhaust the administrative process before going to the courts. However, agency procedures are not uniform or uniformly applied.

Section 7(d) of the Act provides that no civil action may be commenced by

---

[1] 29 U.S.C. §626(b) (1984).
[2] 29 U.S.C. §626(c) (1984).
[3] *Id.*
[4] 29 U.S.C. §633a.
[5] 5 U.S.C. §901 (1977). *See also* Chapter 1, at "EEOC Role."

an individual until 60 days after a charge alleging unlawful discrimination has been filed with the Commission. The charge must be filed within 180 days after the alleged unlawful practice occurred. Section 14(b) provides that where a state has a law prohibiting discrimination in employment because of age and establishing or authorizing a state authority to grant or seek relief from such discriminatory practice, no suit may be brought under Section 7 before the expiration of 60 days after proceedings have been commenced under state law, unless such proceedings have been earlier terminated.

In any action to which Section 14(b) applies, a charge must be filed with the EEOC within 300 days after the alleged unlawful practice occurred, or within 30 days after receipt by the individual of a notice of termination of the proceedings under the state law, whichever is earlier.[6] Upon receiving such a charge, the Commission must notify all persons named in the charge as prospective defendants in the action and must attempt to eliminate any alleged unlawful practice by "informal methods of conciliation, conference, and persuasion."[7] Because of the explicit charge filing requirements, Congress provided that during the Commission's attempts to effect voluntary compliance, the statute of limitations shall be tolled, but not for longer than one year. The statute of limitations under the ADEA is the statute provided for in the Portal-to-Portal Act: two years; three years for "willful" violations.

The ADEA also requires every employer, employment agency, and labor organization to post a notice prepared or approved by the EEOC setting forth such information as the Commission deems appropriate to effectuate the purposes of the Act.[8]

A very important grant of authority is the ADEA's provision in Section 9 that the EEOC may issue such rules and regulations as it may consider necessary or appropriate for carrying out the Act; and may establish such reasonable exceptions to and exemptions from any or all provisions of the Act as the Commission finds necessary and proper in the public interest.[9] (See Appendix B, "Text of EEOC Regulations on Enforcement of ADEA," 29 CFR Parts 1625–1627.)

Accrual of Cause of Action

Because the charging party is required to file within a set time frame from the occurrence of the alleged discrimination, it is important to determine when the discriminatory conduct "occurred." In some instances, there will be no dispute as to the date of the occurrence, where an employment decision is immediately effective, such as a denial of promotion or a termination. However, there are instances where the employee is notified that a decision has been made, but that decision will not be implemented for a period of time. In such a situation, the employee may reasonably believe that no discrimination has "occurred," for purposes of filing a charge with the EEOC or an action in federal court.

---

[6]Section 7(d)(2), 29 U.S.C. §626(d)(2).

[7]*Id.*

[8]Section 8, 29 U.S.C. §627 (1984).

[9]Section 9, 29 U.S.C. §628 (1984).

The Sixth Circuit has ruled that an action filed by present and former employees for age discrimination caused by the seniority system accrued when the plaintiffs' employment opportunities were adversely affected.[10] The facially neutral seniority system had been implemented more than six years before the filing of the action, the court observed, but this did not mean that that was the date of the "occurrence" of the discriminatory action. The plaintiffs had filed their action within two years of the start of a RIF under the seniority system, and the court concluded that an employee's cause of action does not accrue until his employment opportunities are adversely affected "by application to him of the provisions of that seniority system."[11] To hold otherwise, the court reasoned, would permit perpetual age discrimination through a seniority system by an employer whose violation had already continued without attack for several years.

This decision involves an important "door" for plaintiffs; the "continuing violation" theory. When an employer maintains an unlawful discriminatory policy, courts have regarded the continuation of that policy as a recurring, or "continuing," violation. Such a theory has its roots in the case law developed by the National Labor Relations Board under the Taft-Hartley Act, and the courts have applied this theory in the context of an ADEA action without difficulty. For example, in *EEOC v. Home Insurance Co.*,[12] the district court ruled that the employer's adoption and maintenance of an unlawful mandatory retirement policy was a continuing violation under the ADEA, and the timeliness of the claim asserting unlawful termination under the policy should be determined with reference to the earlier of (1) the last day of employment, or, if applicable, (2) the date on which the unlawful policy was eliminated.

The court was faced with a claim that the cause of action available to the 143 plaintiffs accrued on the date of notification of the plan's amendment and the new retirement date. The employer proffered two Supreme Court decisions to buttress its claim that notification, rather than implementation, was the date on which a cause of action accrues. In *Delaware State College v. Ricks*,[13] the Supreme Court ruled that a Liberian academician's right to bring an action on racial grounds for his denial of tenure accrued on the date he was officially notified that he was being denied tenure. In *Chardon v. Fernandez*,[14] the Court affirmed its decision in *Ricks,* and reversed an appellate court opinion holding *Ricks* to be limited to a denial-of-tenure case, and thus, inapplicable where the unlawful employment practice alleged was termination.

The *Home Insurance* court first noted that *Ricks* and *Chardon* are applicable to ADEA cases.[15] It is well established, the court observed, that an unlawful discriminatory policy maintained by the employer constitutes a continuing

---

[10]Morelock v. NCR Corp., 586 F.2d 1096, 18 FEP 225 (CA 6, 1978), *cert. denied,* 441 U.S. 906, 21 FEP 1139 (1979). *See also* Miller v. ITT, 37 FEP 8 (CA 2, 1985).

[11]Morelock v. NCR Corp., 18 FEP at 229.

[12]553 F. Supp. 704, 30 FEP 841 (SD NY, 1982).

[13]449 U.S. 250, 24 FEP 827 (1980).

[14]454 U.S. 6, 27 FEP 57 (1981) (*per curiam*).

[15]Pfister v. Allied Corp., 539 F. Supp, 224, 30 FEP 846 (SD NY, 1982); Aaronsen v. Crown Zellerbach, 662 F.2d 584, 27 FEP 518 (CA 9, 1981).

violation.[16] However, the court reasoned, the finding that the retirement system was a continuing violation of the ADEA leads to a "vexatious question":

"Where a continuing violation of the ADEA in the form of an unlawful retirement-plan provision calling for mandatory retirement results in the termination of an employee, did Congress intend that the applicable statute of limitations for a termination claim begin to run on the date the employee is terminated or the date on which he is made aware when he will be terminated?

"In resolving this issue, we begin with the recognition that *Ricks* and *Chardon* strike a balance between the remedial purposes of civil rights legislation such as the ADEA and the employer's entitlement to obtain repose as recognized in the applicable statutes of limitations. *See Ricks, supra,* 449 U.S. at 256–57, citing *Johnson v. Railway Express Agency, Inc.,* 421 U.S. 454, 463–64, 10 FEP Cases 817 (1975).

"Where no continuing violation can be alleged, as in both *Ricks* and *Chardon, see Ricks, supra,* 444 U.S. at 258, the considerations in favor of beginning the limitations periods from the time of notification are strong. First, the employer is no longer engaged in conduct violative of statutorily protected civil rights; defendant's entitlement to repose in such instances has strong appeal. Second, the employer is protected against having to produce, many years subsequent to the occurrence of an unlawful employment practice, witnesses and documents that may well no longer be available. This concern for avoiding stale claims is especially pronounced in the context of civil rights-employment actions, where the intent with which an allegedly discriminatory action was taken is often of paramount significance to a determination of liability.

"By contrast, where a continuing violation can be alleged, as here, these concerns as to a defendant's prejudice are absent or diminished: an employer maintaining a company-wide unlawful employment practice is in a less sympathetic position when seeking repose; more significantly, the continued nature of the policy represents its "affirmative perpetuation", *Kennan v. Pan Am. World Airways, Inc.,* 424 F. Supp. 721, 726, 13 FEP Cases 1530 (N.D.Cal. 1976), and is susceptible to characterization as a conscious waiver of limitations period protection. *See generally* Note, *Continuing Violations of Title VII: A Suggested Approach,* 63 MINN. L. REV. 119, 143–44 (1978). Moreover, since the employer remains subject to suit by a current employee or by the EEOC, the concern respecting production of evidence as to past acts is considerably diminished. Simply put, an employer that maintains a continuing violation neither deserves nor obtains repose."[17]

The district court examined the reasons underlying Congress' enunciation of a particular limitations period within a statute, and reasoned that the need to protect unsuspecting defendants from "surprise" suits was lacking in the context of an employer maintaining a companywide *policy*. Whether one accepts the reasoning that the continuation of the policy constitutes "affirmative perpetuation" to the extent that the court will read a waiver of limitations period protection, it is clear that the existence of the functioning system will obviate any concerns against stale claims and production of documents by the employer.

The continuing violation doctrine does not make timely ADEA charges filed more than 300 days after layoffs of individuals who contended that the layoffs were one part of an integrated and continuing policy of discrimination, ac-

---

[16]*Supra* note 12, citing Guardians Ass'n v. Civil Serv. Comm'n, 633 F.2d 232, 23 FEP 677 (CA 2, 1980).

[17]*Supra* note 12, 30 FEP at 847–48.

cording to a district court, since the prohibited conduct with respect to the layoffs occurred at the time that the decisions were made and communicated to them.[18]

Another district court has ruled that an ADEA charge an employee filed in August 1980 is untimely, even though he had remained on the payroll in a sinecure position until May 1980, because he had been notified in May 1979 that he would be terminated one year later.[19] The court, applying *Ricks* to the effect that notification is the date on which a cause accrues, ruled that the employee's charge was untimely, even though he had filed it within 300 days of his termination, since he had filed it more than one year after receiving notification of the decision to terminate.[20]

The Seventh Circuit affirmed a grant of summary judgment to an employer, despite claims that the employer's actions constituted a continuing violation, where no post-termination decision or act was made the basis of a charge, and the suit was commenced more than two years after the employees received their dismissal notices.[21] And finally, the Fourth Circuit has ruled that an ADEA charge that an individual filed in August 1979 cannot relate forward to cover his discharge in October 1979, where the charge did not allege a continuous course of discriminatory conduct.[22]

The determination of when a plaintiff's cause of action accrued is vital to maintaining that action. Whether the plaintiff filed a charge with the EEOC or a lawsuit in federal court, the action can only go forward if it is determined that the plaintiff filed within the applicable limitations period. The "continuing violation" theory or doctrine provides the plaintiff with a door to filing that is opened as long as the employment policy or practice is still in effect at the time of filing or if the filing is made within the appropriate time limits, as measured against the last application of the employment practice or policy to the complaining party. The utility of the "continuing violation" theory has asserted itself repeatedly, as evidenced by the courts' frequency in finding such a violation where an employment policy or practice is clearly in existence. Absence of such a finding not only would preclude certain classes of plaintiffs from asserting their rights, but would also allow the practice to perpetuate. However, the absence of such a policy or practice makes the charging party's obligation to show timely filing more difficult.

Private Action

An aggrieved person must file a charge with the EEOC within 180 days of the unlawful practice.[23] The Act recognizes "deferral states"—states having their own EEOC-type agencies and age discrimination statutes.[24] Section 7(d)(2)

---

[18]Yokum v. St. Johnsbury Trucking Co., 595 F. Supp. 1532, 36 FEP 529 (D Conn, 1984).

[19]Sprott v. Avon Prods., Inc., 596 F. Supp. 178, 36 FEP 539 (SD NY, 1984).

[20]*Id.*, 36 FEP at 540.

[21]Herman v. National Broadcasting Co., 744 F.2d 604, 35 FEP 1653 (CA 7, 1984).

[22]Thomas v. Brown & Root, Inc., 35 FEP 1649 (CA 4, 1984).

[23]Section 7(d)(1), 29 U.S.C. §626(d)(1) (1984).

[24]Section 14, 29 U.S.C. §633 (1984).

extends the filing period in these "deferral states" to 300 days after the violation occurred or within 30 days after the individual receives notice of the termination of the state proceedings, whichever is earlier. Therefore, at the administrative level there is the "180/300" day filing limit, reflecting the charge filing practices directly with the EEOC (180 days) or following state agency filing (300 days).

The charging party who has filed a complaint with the EEOC within the proper filing period must wait 60 days before bringing a civil action in court.[25] This waiting time allows the EEOC to attempt "voluntary compliance with the requirements of this Act through informal methods of conciliation, conference, and persuasion."[26]

In *Oscar Mayer v. Evans*,[27] the Supreme Court established that an ADEA claimant must resort to an appropriate state administrative proceeding, where one exists, before bringing an ADEA action. The Court relied on Title VII precedent. It reasoned that Section 14(b) of the Act, like Section 706(b) of the Civil Rights Act of 1964,[28] requires a complainant to resort to appropriate state administrative proceedings before bringing a federal ADEA action, since both statutes share a common purpose—elimination of discrimination in the workplace—and because the language and legislative history of the statutes support this interpretation.

Section 14(a) of the ADEA provides that all state proceedings are superseded upon "commencement" of an ADEA action.[29] The *Oscar Mayer* decision holds that despite this provision, complaining parties are not excused from the Section 14(b) requirement of filing a state administrative complaint at least 60 days before "commencing" the federal ADEA action; state agencies must be given at least some opportunity to solve problems of discrimination, the Court held.[30]

Because of the importance of the meaning of "commence" in terms of ADEA filing, the Court determined that Section 14(b) did not require an age discrimination claimant to "commence" state proceedings within the time limits set forth in state law, since even time-barred actions may be "commenced" under the Federal Rules of Civil Procedure merely by filing a complaint. It concluded that a complainant could comply with Section 14(b) by filing a signed complaint with a state FEP agency, and that the federal court action should be held in abeyance until either the state complaint is dismissed as untimely or 60 days pass without settlement; suspending the federal court action is preferable to dismissal of the action with no leave to refile.[31]

Based on this language, a district court has ruled that failure to file a timely charge in a deferral state will not be fatal to an action under the ADEA.[32]

---

[25]Section 7(d)(2), 29 U.S.C. §626(d)(2) (1984).

[26]*Id.*

[27]441 U.S. 750, 19 FEP 1167 (1979).

[28]42 U.S.C. §2000e-5(c) (1984).

[29]29 U.S.C. § 633(a) (1984).

[30]*Supra* note 27.

[31]*Id.*

[32]Clark v. American Home Prods. Corp., 34 FEP 813 (D Mass, 1982).

Filing of a Charge and Notice

In the course of administrative practice, the EEOC's receipt of a charge initiates its investigative machinery under Section 7 of the ADEA. Although receipt of a charge is not a *sine qua non* for EEOC investigative efforts, the Commission usually follows the receipt of a charge with notice to the charged party of the filing of the charge. If the Commission's efforts at conciliation are unsuccessful, the agency can be expected to issue a subpoena to assist in its investigation. The subpoena duces tecum ("bring the documents with you") is the most common form of subpoena used in such investigations.

In 1984, the Supreme Court had an opportunity to answer the question: What is necessary for the EEOC to gain a court order enforcing a subpoena duces tecum against an intransigent employer in the course of an investigation of a charge of unlawful employment practices? The Court ruled in *EEOC v. Shell Oil Co.*[33] that a proper charge is a jurisdictional prerequisite for judicial enforcement of such a subpoena. Although the decision was unanimous, the Court divided on the degree of specificity needed in the notice to make the charge *adequate* for purposes of judicial enforcement. Five Justices held that the notice was to include all the information that must be included in the charge itself, and four Justices opted for a notice that was more informative than the charge.

The dispute involved a "pattern or practice" claim under Title VII, and the EEOC charged that the employer "has violated and continues to violate" the statute by discriminating against blacks and females, "on a continuing basis from at least July 2, 1965, until the present."[34] Title VII became effective on July 2, 1965.

The employer sought to have the subpoena quashed on the ground that the EEOC had failed to disclose facts sufficient to satisfy the notice requirement in Section 706(b) of the Act, but the district court enforced the subpoena, declaring that the purpose of the charge "is only to initiate the EEOC investigation, not to state sufficient facts to make out a prima facie case."[35] A panel of the Eighth Circuit reversed, holding that the EEOC had failed to comply with either the Section 706(b) regulation requiring a charge to state the "date, place and circumstances of the alleged unlawful employment practice," or with its own regulations, requiring a charge to contain a "statement of facts, including pertinent dates, constituting the alleged unlawful employment practice."[36] The appeals court concluded that a charge and notice "should at least inform the employer of the approximate dates of the unlawful practices," including enough information to show that these dates "have some basis in fact," and contain a "statement of the circumstances" of the claimed violations, "supported by some factual or statistical basis."[37]

The Supreme Court noted that three considerations controlled review of the Eighth Circuit's decision:

---

[33]466 U.S. 54, 34 FEP 709 (1984).

[34]*Id.*, 34 FEP at 721.

[35]Shell Oil Co. v. EEOC, 523 F. Supp. 79, 27 FEP 230 (ED Mo, 1981).

[36]Shell Oil Co. v. EEOC, 676 F.2d 322, 29 FEP 1519 (CA 8, 1982).

[37]*Id.*

(1) A charge is not the equivalent of a complaint initiating a lawsuit but only places the Commission on notice that a third party believes the employer has engaged in an unlawful employment practice;

(2) A charge does have a function in the enforcement procedure, to the extent that the EEOC is entitled to gain access only to evidence that is "relevant" to the charge; and

(3) The Commission's ability to investigate charges of systemic discrimination should not be impaired.[38]

The regulation involved in *EEOC v. Shell* requires that a Commissioner, when filing a "pattern-or-practice" charge, must state "the facts . . . constituting the alleged unlawful employment practices." The extent of this factual disclosure is what was at issue, since the charged party wanted as much disclosure and specificity as possible, the Commission preferred to "play its cards close to the vest," thereby leaving flexibility for additional charges and plaintiffs, and the courts had a need to determine the bona fides of the charge.

The Supreme Court rejected the Court of Appeals view that the Commission must disclose some portion of the statistical data on which the allegations of systemic discrimination are founded since the court's interpretation is sustained by none of the three pertinent legislative purposes:

(1) This construction would in effect oblige the Commissioner to substantiate his allegations *before* the EEOC initiates an investigation, the purpose of which is to determine whether there is reason to believe those allegations are true. Such an obligation is plainly inconsistent with the structure of the enforcement procedure;

(2) Disclosure of the data on which the Commissioner's allegations are based would not limit the range of materials to which the EEOC could demand access, because the Commissioner may insist that the employer disclose any evidence "relevant" to the allegations in the charge, regardless of the strength of the evidentiary foundation for those allegations; and

(3) Imposing such a duty on the EEOC to reveal the information that precipitated the charge would enable a recalcitrant employer to challenge the adequacy of the Commission's disclosures and to appeal an adverse ruling by the trial court on that issue, ultimately causing a significant impediment to the EEOC's ability expeditiously to investigate claims of systemic discrimination.[39]

The Court ultimately concluded that a charge should identify, "insofar as the Commission is able," the group of persons that may have been discriminated against, the categories of positions from which they have been excluded, the method by which discrimination may have been affected, and the period of time in which discrimination is suspected to have occurred.[40]

The same information should be included in the notice given under Section 706(b), the Court added, since this would provide the employer with fair notice

---

[38]*Supra* note 33.

[39]*Id.*, 34 FEP at 717.

[40]*Id.*, 34 FEP at 718.

of the allegations against it; would enable the employer to undertake his own inquiry into employment practices and to comply voluntarily with the Act; and would alert the employer to the range of personnel records that might be relevant to the pending investigation, thus ensuring against inadvertent destruction of such records.[41]

In requiring the EEOC to provide in the notice all the information that was provided in the charge, the Court was attempting to balance the charged party's need to receive fair and adequate notice of the charge, and the agency's need to prevent disclosure of the information it needed for enforcement purposes.

A *sine qua non* of the notice aspect of the EEOC proceeding is that the charged party actually receive notice of the charge. A district court evaluated a letter that a former employee sent to the Labor Department stating that the employer had hired a younger and less qualified person to replace him because of his age and high salary. The court found that the letter was not adequate as a notice of right to sue or as a charge, since the former employee had requested the Department not to notify the employer of his age claim, and the employer did not receive notice until almost two years after the discharge.[42]

Timely Filing and 180/300-Day Rule. Compliance with the terms of the Act may be deemed to have occurred where the employer has actual notice within the statutory time limits. For example, another district court has ruled that the employer had notice within the 300-day filing period, even though the former employee did not file an ADEA charge until 536 days after her termination on age discrimination grounds. However the employee did write a letter to the employer four days after her discharge indicating that the proffered reasons for the discharge were not true and that she had been replaced by a much younger woman.[43] The court observed that the employer had been notified of the charge through a state FEP agency complaint within five months of the termination, and that it had subsequently participated in unsuccessful conciliation negotiations with the agency's representatives. Further, the court concluded, the employer was unable to demonstrate any prejudice arising from the employee's untimely ADEA charge.

But when is a charge "filed"? The Fifth Circuit had an opportunity to answer that question, and did so definitively. It ruled that the aggrieved employee "filed" her ADEA charge with the EEOC when the Commission received it, and not when she deposited the charge in the mail, since this rule governs charge-filing under Title VII, and the employee was unable to show why her Age Act claim should be treated differently.[44]

A large number of disputes arising under the charge-filing requirements concern equitable tolling, that is, suspension of the running of the time period within which a charge must be filed because of some intervening event or mitigating circumstance. Failure to allow the tolling in some circumstances, the theory declares, would cause an unfair or unjust result. However, the party

---

[41]*Id.* at 720.

[42]Frasco v. Joseph Schlitz Brewing Co., 532 F. Supp. 1020, 29 FEP 1337 (MD NC, 1982). *See also* Nelson v. Massey-Ferguson, 36 FEP 365 (ED Wis, 1984).

[43]James v. Miller-Wohl Co., 35 FEP 1846 (WD NY, 1984).

[44]Taylor v. General Tel. Co. of the SW., 37 FEP 1228 (CA 5, 1985).

seeking the tolling must clearly demonstrate both that such an extenuating circumstance exists and that failure to consider that circumstance in the employee's situation results in a degree of prejudice to the employee's case.

A district court has ruled that the period within which the former employee was required to file the EEOC charge would be equitably tolled, notwithstanding that she should have realized that her state FEP agency complaint, which failed to mention the ADEA, did not encompass a filing of a charge and that she should have been aware of EEOC requirements through her responsibilities as a store manager.[45] The court relied on the facts that the state complaint made it clear that she was challenging her termination on age discrimination grounds and that this gave the employer notice; the former employee should not be prevented from asserting her claim as a result of the agency's negligence, in the absence of any prejudice accruing to the employer.

The Second Circuit has ruled that no equitable grounds would justify tolling the 300-day period within which a former employee was required to file his ADEA charge after his termination since he was a well-educated attorney familiar with the law, there was no evidence that he was misled or prevented from filing the charge, and he testified to his awareness, as early as three years before he filed the charge of the employer's age discrimination.[46]

In the absence of any basis for tolling the filing period, the courts have followed Title VII case law, as enunciated by the Supreme Court in *Mohasco Corp. v. Silver*,[47] to the effect that a charging party in a deferral state has the extended 300-day period in which to file a charge with the EEOC, even if he failed to file a timely charge with the state FEP agency.[48] However, this gives rise to the so-called "240-day rule," whereby a charging party in a deferral state has the 300-day limit, minus 60 days' deferral to the respective state FEP agency. The effects of a blanket extension of the 300-day filing limit to charging parties in deferral states have not been measured on the deferral states' FEP agencies.

Termination of Proceedings.   The issue of when a state FEP agency "terminates" its "proceedings" for the purpose of allowing the EEOC to start processing a charge within the 300-day extended charge-filing period was recently examined by the First Circuit. In *Isaac v. Harvard Univ.*,[49] the appeals court ruled that a charge initially submitted to the EEOC 241 days after the alleged act of discrimination, referred to the state agency on day 251, and sent back to the EEOC pursuant to a state agency-EEOC worksharing agreement on day 263, was timely filed, notwithstanding the employer's claim that the state agency could not "terminate" its processing of the charge without completely relinquishing the case, since Title VII permits the EEOC to process a charge after 60 days no matter what a state agency has done. The interpretation

---

[45]*Supra* note 43.

[46]Miller v. ITT Corp., 37 FEP 8 (CA 2, 1985).

[47]Mohasco Corp. v. Silver, 447 U.S. 806, 23 FEP 1 (1980).

[48]Goodman v. Heublein, Inc., 645 F.2d 127, 25 FEP 645 (CA 2, 1981); Aaronsen v. Crown Zellerbach, 662 F.2d 584, 27 FEP 518 (CA 9, 1981); Clark v. American Home Prods. Corp., 34 FEP 813 (D Mass, 1982).

[49]Isaac v. Harvard Univ., 38 FEP 764 (CA 1, 1985).

of such statutory terms as "termination" and "proceeding" will continue to be a fertile area of ADEA litigation.

Posting of ADEA Notice.   Employees and job applicants cannot be expected to meet the charge-filing requirements of the Act if they are unaware of their rights. Section 8 of the ADEA requires every employer, employment agency, and labor organization to post and keep posted in conspicuous places at the work site a notice to be prepared or approved by the Secretary setting forth information as the Secretary deems appropriate to effectuate the purposes of the Act.[50] The regulation promulgated by the EEOC provides:

> "Every employer, employment agency, and labor organization which has an obligation under the Age Discrimination in Employment Act of 1967 shall post and keep posted in conspicuous places upon its premises the notice pertaining to the applicability of the Act prescribed by the Secretary of Labor or his authorized representative. Such a notice must be posted in prominent and accessible places where it can readily be observed by employees, applicants for employment and union members."[51]

The Fifth Circuit has ruled that the poster notifying employees of their rights under the ADEA must provide them with a meaningful opportunity of becoming aware of their ADEA rights so that it may reasonably be concluded that they either knew or should have known of their rights.[52] Notice adequate for one group of employees does not necessarily suffice for another group working primarily in a different location, it observed. To that end, the appeals court held, the employer's placing of a poster on the bulletin board at its regional office was inadequate to notify an area salesman, who maintained an in-home office, reported directly to the district sales manager, and visited the regional office only three times in his nearly 20-year employment history.

Subsequently, the Fifth Circuit declined to toll the filing limit for an employee who alleged that the employer had failed to comply with the posting requirement at the time of his retirement in 1974; the appeals court observed that the employee had seen the 1968 poster prepared by the Secretary of Labor and was therefore aware of his rights under the Act.[53]

Exhaustion of Administrative Remedies

Following an aggrieved person's filing of an age discrimination charge with the EEOC, the Commission is required to investigate and to attempt to effect voluntary compliance through informal methods of conciliation, and so forth. At this point, the charging party may also file an age discrimination complaint with the local agency responsible for handling such complaints under the local statute.[54] The ADEA contemplates a choice of forum for aggrieved individuals.[55]

---

[50]29 U.S.C. §627 (1984).

[51]29 CFR §850.10 (1984).

[52]Charlier v. S.C. Johnson & Son, Inc., 556 F.2d 751, 15 FEP 421 (CA 5, 1977).

[53]Templeton v. Western Union Tel. Co., 607 F.2d 89, 21 FEP 598 (CA 5, 1979).

[54]Kennedy v. Whitehurst, 690 F.2d 951, 29 FEP 1373, 1381 n.22 (CA DC, 1982).

[55]Holliday v. Ketchum, MacLeod & Grove, 584 F.2d 1281, 17 FEP 1175 (CA 3, 1978).

But before a federal charging party can actually proceed to court and initiate a lawsuit, he/she must exhaust the procedures and remedies set out in the Act, pursuant to Section 15.[56] Section 15 requires the federal charging party to provide the EEOC with notice of an intent to sue within 180 days of the unlawful practice, or actually filing a discrimination charge with the Commission. Failure to exhaust administrative remedies—a tenet of administrative law—will defeat an aggrieved person's attempt to bring an ADEA action in court.

The District of Columbia Circuit has determined that the government waived any objection to an allegedly untimely institution of an administrative proceeding and to the employee's failure, before bringing her ADEA action, to exhaust her administrative remedies, since the timeliness and exhaustion requirements are not jurisdictional in nature; they are statutory conditions precedent to instituting the litigation, and therefore, are subject to waiver, estoppel, and equitable tolling.[57] The court reasoned:

"As a preliminary matter, we must rule on the government appellee's claim that the district court lacked jurisdiction to hear appellant's prayer for attorneys' fees. Appellee argues that, because Mrs. Kennedy's discrimination complaints were allegedly filed in an untimely fashion with the relevant administrative agencies and because she failed to pursue to fruition her claims in those agencies, the district court was precluded as a matter of jurisdiction from hearing the instant case. With regard to the allegation of untimely filing, appellant responds that the timeliness requirement is not jurisdictional but rather is akin to a statute of limitations; accordingly, appellant argues, charges of untimeliness, however valid, are subject to waiver and estoppel and were here waived by appellee's failure to press the arguments in the district court. Similarly, appellant contends both that the ADEA exhaustion requirement is not a jurisdictional matter and that, at any event, she in fact met the requirement.

"We agree with appellant's position on both the timeliness and the exhaustion issues. To be sure, the requirements that a federal age discrimination complainant file a notice of complaint and exhaust available administrative remedies may be prerequisites for the institution of a lawsuit in federal court based on the discrimination allegation. *See, e.g., Milton v. Weinberger,* 645 F.2d 1070, 1074–77, 25 FEP Cases 134 (D.C. Cir. 1981); *Siegel v. Kreps,* 654 F2d 773, 783, 25 FEP Cases 672 (D.C. Cir. 1981) (Robinson, J., concurring in part and dissenting in part). We are convinced, however, that the timeliness and exhaustion requirements are *not* jurisdictional in nature but rather are statutory conditions precedent to the instigation of litigation and are therefore subject to waiver, estoppel, and equitable tolling. The failure to raise these issues in the district court thus precludes reliance on them here.

"As for the timeliness dispute, our ruling that the ADEA's timing requirements are not jurisdictional prerequisites is fortified by the Supreme Court's recent decision in *Zipes v. Trans World Airlines,* 455 U.S. ____, 28 FEP Cases 1 (1982). In *Zipes* the Court held that the timely filing with the EEOC of a charge of discrimination in violation of Title VII is not 'jurisdictional' in nature but rather is a mere statutory precondition subject to equitable defenses. *Accord Bethel v. Jefferson,* 589 F.2d 631, 641 n.64, 18 FEP Cases 789 (D.C. Cir. 1978). The analogy to the ADEA is strong in this regard, and we think it clear that Congress did not intend the statutory deadlines it inserted in the ADEA to be jurisdictional in character. Thus, we need not determine whether, in fact, appellant failed to

---

[56]29 U.S.C. §633a(d) (1984).
[57]*Supra* note 54.

comply with administrative regulations regarding timeliness or, indeed, whether those regulations bind appellant at all. Appellee's failure to raise the issue in the district court precludes its consideration here.

"With regard to the claim that appellant's prayer for fees should be dismissed for her failure to exhaust administrative remedies, it would again appear that this requirement is not jurisdictional in character for the reasons stated above. *See Bethel*, 589 F.2d at 640–46. At any event, appellant satisfied the only exhaustion requirement mandated by section 15 of the ADEA, that of either providing the EEOC with notice of an intent to sue within 180 days of the unlawful practice, or actually filing a discrimination complaint with the EEOC. *See* 29 U.S.C. §633a(d) (1976); *Siegel v. Kreps,* 654 F.2d at 778 n.16.''[58]

A district court that was hearing the employer's motion to dismiss his former employee's claim of forced early retirement on the ground that he failed to timely file his ADEA charge, ruled that it would consider, as though it were incorporated into the complaint, a certain charge that the employee filed concerning his layoff and the notice of right to sue that he received regarding that earlier charge.[59] The court held that the former employee may not litigate the claim of forced early retirement unless he can supply competent evidence that he timely filed the charge regarding his retirement claim and that the charge was fully exhausted.[60]

The court relied on a ruling of the Fourth Circuit that a plaintiff cannot expand his discrimination action to include matters not fully exhausted at the administrative level.[61]

Once the EEOC has pursued the administrative route, it will either bring an action in court on behalf of the aggrieved individual, or it will issue that person a statement that it did not find cause for bringing such an action, and it will provide the person with a notice of right to sue. A private action will follow rules established in the Federal Rules of Civil Procedure, with a few exceptions provided for in the ADEA. An agency action will involve other issues.

Agency vs. Private Actions

The ADEA provides that any "person aggrieved" may bring a suit for legal or equitable relief that will effectuate the purposes of the Act.[62] The EEOC may also bring an action, and if it does, the aggrieved person loses his right to bring his individual action.[63] Therefore, there are two avenues that can be pursued in maintaining an action under the federal ADEA: the agency action and the private action. Each action has distinct procedural and substantive differences and the courts have attempted to delineate which results would most clearly effectuate the purposes of the Act.

A district court hearing an action filed by the EEOC on behalf of an individual plaintiff has determined that the Secretary of Labor's failure to provide notice

---

[58]*Id.,* 29 FEP at 1381.

[59]Nelson v. Massey-Ferguson, 36 FEP 365 (ED Wis, 1984).

[60]*Id.* at 366.

[61]Lawson v. Burlington Indus., 683 F.2d 862, 29 FEP 1224 (CA 4, 1982), *cert. denied,* 459 U.S. 944, 29 FEP 1752 (1982).

[62]29 U.S.C. §626(c) (1984).

[63]*Id.*

of the action that is required of individuals does not bar the agency from
proceeding, since the only condition imposed by the Act on a public enforcement action is the requirement in 29 U.S.C. Section 626(d) that the agency
attempt to effect voluntary compliance.[64] The court observed:

> "The interests which the Secretary is enforcing are broader and have to do with
> protection of the public and deterrence of age discrimination as well as compen-
> sation of the individual."[65]

It is this distinction that underlies the different treatment accorded to the
agency. In this case, the individual employee would have been time barred by
the 29 U.S.C. Section 255(a) two-year limitations period for filing the action
against the employer, but the court acknowledged the EEOC's efforts at conciliation and tolled the limitations period, thus allowing the action on behalf
of the employee to proceed. In this sense, the agency may do for the employee
what he cannot do for himself, and the distinguishing characteristic is the
public interest overtones of the agency action that are absent in the private
action.

Another example of the differences between an EEOC action and an individual action can be seen in *EEOC v. Home Insurance Co.*[66] The district court
was faced with an agency action and a challenge by the employer that the
action was barred because the employees had failed to file timely charges. The
employer further alleged that the agency was not entitled to obtain back pay
on behalf of terminated employees who did not file written consents to be
represented by the EEOC and who were not named as party plaintiffs in the
complaint. In rejecting these claims, the court declared:

> "We are of the view that there is a significant difference between a suit brought
> by the agency charged with the primary enforcement of the statute and one
> commenced by an individual or group of individuals, especially since the Secretary
> must, as a prerequisite to the initiation of suit, attempt to obtain the employer's
> compliance through conciliation efforts. ADEA §17(b), 29 U.S.C. §626(b). Con-
> cerning the EEOC's authority to proceed under §17 without obtaining written
> consents or naming the claimants as party plaintiffs, which it is required to do
> under FLSA §16(c), this distinction may be attributable to the availability of
> liquidated, or double, damages under the latter provision, which is absent in a
> proceeding under FLSA §17. In light of these factors, we are of the opinion that
> reading into §17 the complex and somewhat cumbersome requirements contained
> in §16(b) and (c) would be unwarranted and that, accordingly, such requirements
> are inapplicable to suits, such as this, brought under §17."[67]

The Act's imposition of an obligation on the EEOC to attempt compliance
also entitles the Commission to exercise a greater freedom to proceed on behalf
of the public interest. However, a pending ADEA action filed by an individual
plaintiff may not be extinguished by an EEOC action, according to the Second
Circuit Court of Appeals.[68] The court examined the language of Section 7(c)(1)
of the Act, which provides that the right to "bring" a private action terminates

---

[64]EEOC v. Kansas, 28 FEP 1036, 1038 (D Kan, 1982).
[65]*Id.*
[66]553 F. Supp. 704, 30 FEP 841 (SD NY, 1982).
[67]*Id.*, 30 FEP at 849.
[68]Burns v. Equitable Life Assurance Soc'y of the U.S., 696 F.2d 21, 30 FEP 873 (CA 2, 1982).

on the commencement of an EEOC action and which incorporates language of the Fair Labor Standards Act.[69] The court reasoned that the narrow question to be resolved was whether the Act's grant to an aggrieved party of the right "to bring" an action meant "to commence or maintain," or only "to commence." The district court had ruled that the latter phrase was what Congress intended, and it had denied the employer's motion to dismiss.[70]

The appeals court observed that the ADEA expressly incorporates the procedures originally fashioned by the 87th Congress to govern enforcement of the FLSA.[71] The House-Senate Conference Report accompanying the 1961 amendments to the FLSA makes it clear, the court observed, that a pending private suit is not preempted by an action brought by the Secretary of Labor.[72] Thus, it reasoned, if the ADEA is understood to incorporate not only the procedural provisions of the FLSA, but also Congressional understanding of the broad scope of private enforcement of the FLSA under those provisions, independent of public enforcement, then a pending private suit under the ADEA is not preempted by an EEOC action.[73]

This allocation of enforcement authority between public and private plaintiffs also furthers two important policy considerations: It avoids pressure on private counsel to delay filing in hopes of learning whether EEOC litigation will preempt private efforts; and encourages private parties to proceed with cases requiring urgent remedial action with the knowledge that preemptive public litigation will not frustrate their efforts to press their claims diligently.

The private/public enforcement scheme also points up the dichotomy between the ADEA's Title VII roots and its FLSA roots; in this sense, the ADEA is truly a "hybrid" with latent potential for assertion of rights, and hidden obstacles to the exercise of those rights.

FLSA/Title VII Hybrid

LORILLARD v. PONS

434 U.S. 575, 16 FEP Cases 885 (1978)

. . .

The enforcement scheme for the statute is complex—the product of considerable attention during the legislative debates preceding passage of the Act. Several alternative proposals were considered by Congress. The Administration submitted a bill, modeled after §10(c), (e) of the National Labor Relations Act, 29 U.S.C. §160(c), (e), which would have granted power to the Secretary of Labor to issue cease and desist orders enforceable in the courts of appeals, but would not have granted a private right of action to aggrieved individuals, S. 830, H. R. 4221, 90th Cong., 1st Sess. Senator Javits introduced an alternative proposal to make discrimination based on age unlawful under the Fair Labor Standards Act (FLSA), 29 U.S.C. §201 et seq.; the normal

[69]29 U.S.C. §626(c)(1) (1984).

[70]Burns v. Equitable Life Assurance Soc'y, 530 F. Supp. 768, 28 FEP 951 (SD NY, 1981).

[71]*Supra* note 68, 30 FEP at 874, citing 29 U.S.C. §626(b).

[72]*Supra* note 66, 30 FEP at 874, citing Conf. Rep. No. 327, 87th Cong., 1st Sess. 20, *reprinted* in 1961 U.S. CODE CONG. & AD. NEWS 1706, 1714.

[73]*Id.,* 30 FEP at 874.

enforcement provisions of the FLSA, 29 U.S.C. §216 et seq., then would have been applicable, permitting suits by either the Secretary of Labor or the injured individual, S. 788, 90th Cong., 1st Sess. A third alternative that was considered would have adopted the statutory pattern of Title VII of the Civil Rights Act of 1964 and utilized the Equal Employment Opportunity Commission. 42 U.S.C. §§2000e–4, 2000e–5.

The bill that was ultimately enacted is something of a hybrid, reflecting, on the one hand, Congress' desire to use an existing statutory scheme and a bureaucracy with which employers and employees would be familiar and, on the other hand, its dissatisfaction with some elements of each of the preexisting schemes.[4] Pursuant to §7(b) of the Act, 29 U.S.C. §626(b), violations of the ADEA generally are to be treated as violations of the FLSA. "Amounts owing . . . as a result of a violation" of the ADEA are to be treated as "unpaid minimum wages or overtime compensation" under the FLSA and the rights created by the ADEA are to be "enforced in accordance with the powers, remedies and procedures" of specified sections of the FLSA. 29 U.S.C. §626(b).[5]

Following the model of the FLSA, the ADEA establishes two primary enforcement mechanisms. Under the FLSA provisions incorporated in §7(b) of the ADEA, 29 U.S.C. §626(b), the Secretary of Labor may bring suit on behalf of an aggrieved individual for injunctive and monetary relief. 29 U.S.C. §§216(c), 217. The incorporated FLSA provisions together with §7(c) of the ADEA, 29 U.S.C. §626(c), in addition, authorize private civil actions for "such legal or equitable relief as will effectuate the purposes of" the Act.[6] Although not required by the FLSA, prior to the initiation of any ADEA action, an individual must give notice to the Secretary of Labor of his intention to sue in order that the Secretary can attempt to eliminate the alleged unlawful practice through informal methods. §7(d), 29 U.S.C. §626(d). After allowing the Secretary 60 days to conciliate the alleged unlawful practice, the individual may file suit. The right of the individual to sue on his own terminates, however, if the Secretary commences an action on his behalf. §7(c), 29 U.S.C. §626(c).

II

Looking first to the procedural provisions of the statute, we find a significant indication of Congress' intent in its directive that the ADEA be enforced in accordance with the "powers, remedies and *procedures*," of the FLSA. §7(b), 29 U.S.C. §626(b) (emphasis added). Long before Congress enacted the ADEA, it was well established that there was a right to a jury trial in private actions pursuant to the FLSA. Indeed, every court to consider the issue had so held.[7] Congress is presumed to be aware of an administrative or judicial interpretation of a statute and to adopt that interpretation when it re-enacts a statute without change, see *Albermarle Paper Co. v. Moody*, 422 U.S. 405, 414 n.8, 10 FEP Cases 1181, 1186 (1975); *NLRB v. Gullett Gin Co.*, 340 U.S. 361, 366, 27 LRRM 2230 (1951); *National Lead Co. v. United States*, 252 U.S. 140, 147 (1920); 2A C. Sands, Sutherland's Statutes and Statutory Construction §49.09 and cases cited (1973). So too, where, as here, Congress adopts a new law incorporating sections of a prior law, Congress normally can be presumed to have had knowledge of the interpretation given to the incorporated law, at least insofar as it affects the new statute.

That presumption is particularly appropriate here since, in enacting the ADEA, Congress exhibited both a detailed knowledge of the FLSA provisions and their judicial interpretation and a willingness to depart from those provisions regarded as undesirable or inappropriate for incorporation. For example, in construing the enforcement sections of the FLSA, the courts had consistently declared that injunctive relief was not available in suits by private individuals but only in suits by the Secretary, *Powell v. Washington Post Co.*, ___ U.S. App. D.C. ___ , 267 F.2d 651, 14 WH Cases 140 (1959); *Roberg v. Henry Phipps Estate*, 156 F.2d 958, 963, 6 WH Cases 177 (CA2 1946); *Bowe v. Judson C. Burns*, 137 F.2d 37, 3 WH Cases 253 (CA3 1943). Congress made plain its decision to follow a different course in the ADEA by expressly permitting "such . . . equitable relief as may be appropriate to effectuate the purposes of [the ADEA] including without limitation judgments compelling employment, reinstatement or promotion in *any* action brought to enforce'' the Act. §7(b), 29 U.S.C. §626(b) (emphasis added). Similarly, while incorporating into the ADEA the FLSA provisions authorizing awards of liquidated damages, Congress altered the circumstances under which such awards would be available in ADEA actions by mandating that such damages be awarded only where the violation of the ADEA is willful.[8] Finally, Congress expressly declined to incorporate into the ADEA the criminal penalties established for violations of the FLSA.[9]

[4-9][Footnotes omitted.]

The ''selectivity'' that Congress exhibited in incorporating provisions and in modifying certain FLSA practices led the Supreme Court to believe that Congress intended to incorporate fully the remedies and procedures of the FLSA, except where it specifically provided otherwise. Senator Jacob Javits, one of the floor managers of the bill, described the enforcement section which became part of the Act as: ''The enforcement techniques provided by (the ADEA) are directly analogous to those available under the Fair Labor Standards Act; in fact (the ADEA) incorporates by reference, to the greatest extent possible, the provisions of the (FLSA).''[74]

This legislative engrafting in the ADEA has become known as the doctrine of ''selective incorporation,'' and following *Lorillard v. Pons* it is used by adversaries and the courts to discern the Congressional intent behind a statute that is silent or ambiguous on the point in contention.

Conversely, some aspects of the ADEA are necessarily different from the FLSA or Title VII. Under the FLSA, Congress restricted the right to discover information from employers charged with violations so as to avoid ''surprise'' liability and its associated discovery costs on the employer. But a district court in Pennsylvania has ruled that individuals bringing an action under the ADEA may discover information partly to aid their own case and partly to facilitate the flow of information to individuals who might want to join their actions.[75] Though the FLSA—the source of ADEA remedies and procedures—limits discovery only to individuals seeking relief in their own right, the court noted, the ADEA allows discovery for broader purposes.[76] The FLSA concerns for ''surprise'' liability and its associated discovery costs have little relevance in an ADEA action, the court concluded, since the employers's potential liability should come as no surprise and because the information requested—in this case names, addresses, and other information—is relatively simple and straightforward.[77]

The *Vivone* case illustrates the point that the ADEA may have been drafted with FLSA language, but FLSA policy may make inapplicable FLSA procedure on ADEA plaintiffs. *Lorillard v. Pons* clearly shows that certain underlying public policies that motivated procedures in the FLSA are still compelling for ADEA purposes; but *Vivone* shows the other side of the coin. Advocates should keep in mind that neither ADEA language nor FLSA procedural practice may

---

[74]113 CONG. REC. 31254, 31255.
[75]Vivone v. Acme Mkts., Inc., 37 FEP 561 (ED Pa, 1985).
[76]*Id.*
[77]*Id.*

preclude a court from determining that the policies of the ADEA would be furthered by a particular interpretation of the ADEA's procedural language.

Effect of EEOC Filing on Private Action

Section 7(c)(1) of the ADEA provides that an aggrieved individual may "bring" a civil action in any court of competent jurisdiction.[78] However, Section 7(c)(1) also conditions this right on the EEOC's commencement of an action to enforce the right of such employee under the Act. Two former employees filed age discrimination charges against their former employer; two years later, the EEOC filed an action against the employer alleging the same ADEA violations and seeking relief on behalf of some 434 former employees, some of whom were already participating in the earlier employee-sponsored action. The employer argued that the conditional right of a private person to bring an action was preempted by the EEOC's subsequent filing of its action.

The employees argued that the Act should be interpreted to permit pending actions to continue and to bar only the initiation of new lawsuits after the filing of a complaint with the EEOC. The narrow issue posed was whether the statutory phrase "to bring" meant "to commence or maintain," or only "to commence." The Second Circuit ruled that private ADEA actions are not preempted by later-filed EEOC complaints, because Section 7(c)(1) incorporates language of the Fair Labor Standards Act, and the FLSA legislative history makes it clear that pending private actions are not preempted.[79]

Because of the policy considerations underlying an agency action vis-à-vis a private action, the EEOC has a right that could be considered superior to that of the private plaintiff. This superior right can be asserted on behalf of an employee who is precluded from asserting his own rights. In an action by the EEOC, the employer pointed to the fact that the employees in question had failed to file timely charges and written consents to be represented by the Commission; it claimed that this precluded the Commission from acting in a manner that was not available to the individual plaintiffs under the Act. The district court rejected these deficiencies as bases for depriving the EEOC of the authority to act. It reasoned:

> "Defendant contends that, in addition to the statute of limitations bar, two other procedural bars are present in this suit: first, the terminated employees on whose behalf plaintiff seeks monetary relief failed to file timely charges pursuant to ADEA §7(d);[9] and second, plaintiff cannot obtain backpay under FLSA §17, on behalf of those from whom it has neither secured timely consents nor whom it has identified in the complaint or other paper filed with the Court.
>
> "Defendant's first contention is directly contrary to *Reich v. Dow Badische Co.*, 575 F.2d 363, 367, 17 FEP Cases 363 (2d Cir.), *cert. denied*, 439 U.S. 1006, 18 FEP Cases 966 (1978), in which the Second Circuit stated:
>
>> 'Failure to meet the sixty day notice requirements of Sections 626(d) and 633(b) . . . does not extinguish the employee's substantive right; it does terminate the individual's right to commence an action in his own name, but the Secretary retains the right to sue to enforce the grievant's rights wholly without reference to the notice requirements. *Dunlop v. Crown Cork*

---

[78]29 U.S.C. §626(c)(1) (1984).
[79]*Supra* note 68.

& *Seal Co.* (D.Md. 1976), 405 F. Supp. 774, 11 FEP Cases 1446 . . . . The Secretary's right to sue continues until the expiration of the statute of limitations.'

575 F.2d at 367–68. *See also Marshall v. Chamberlain Mfg Co.,* 601 F.2d 100, 104–05, 20 FEP Cases 147 (3d Cir. 1979).

"Defendant's second contention is likewise unsupportable. Section 17 of the FLSA, unlike FLSA §16(b) and (c), 29 U.S.C. §216(b), (c), contains no indication that written consents and the naming of claimants in the complaint as party plaintiffs are required thereunder, and courts have refused to read into this section such requirements. *See EEOC v. Gilbarco, Inc.,* 615 F.2d 985, 21 FEP Cases 1045 (4th Cir. 1980); *Wirtz v. Novinger's Inc.,* 261 F. Supp. 698, 17 WH Cases 560 (M.D.Pa. 1966); *Wirtz v. W.G. Lockhart Const. Co.,* 230 F. Supp. 823, 16 WH Cases 514 (N.D. Ohio 1964). Defendant's citation of the opinion of Judge Murnaghan in *Gilbarco, supra,* 615 F.2d at 991–1018 (concurring in part and dissenting in part), is unpersuasive, especially insofar as that opinion relies upon the lack of any colorable rationale for Congress 'to give the Secretary, under §17, a substantial advantage denied the Secretary himself under §16(c) and denied individual and class or collective action plaintiffs under §16(b).' *Id.* at 992. We are of the view that there is a significant difference between a suit brought by the agency charged with the primary enforcement of the statute and one commenced by an individual or group of individuals, especially since the Secretary must, as a prerequisite to the initiation of suit, attempt to obtain the employer's compliance through conciliation efforts. ADEA §17(b), 29 U.S.C. §626(b). Concerning the EEOC's authority to proceed under §17 without obtaining written consents or naming the claimants as party plaintiffs, which it is required to do under FLSA §16(c), this distinction may be attributable to the availability of liquidated, or double, damages under the latter provision, which is absent in a proceeding under FLSA §17. In light of these factors, we are of the opinion that reading into §17 the complex and somewhat cumbersome requirements contained in §16(b) and (c) would be unwarranted and that, accordingly, such requirements are inapplicable to suits, such as this, brought under §17."[80]

---

[9][Footnote omitted.]

It is clear that once a plaintiff has commenced a private action, the conditional right to "bring" that action has been exercised and the EEOC's right to bring an action may not preclude the further maintenance of the private action. Further, the EEOC can do on behalf of plaintiffs what they may be precluded from doing on their own because of the strong public policy considerations underlying the establishment of the agency action.

However, the Eleventh Circuit was faced with a job applicant's motion to intervene in an EEOC action under the ADEA against the prospective employer, where the EEOC had named her as a charging party in its action. The appeals court observed that Rule 24(a) of the Federal Rules of Civil Procedure provided for an "intervention as of right," whereas Rule 24(b) provided for only "permissive intervention." Although the district court treated the private plaintiff's request as a request for intervention as of right under Rule 24(a), the appeals court said that denial of the request under either subsection of Rule 24 would not have been an abuse of discretion. The plaintiff had earlier brought her own ADEA action, and the appeals court concluded that this action was still viable,

---

[80]*Supra* note 66, 30 FEP at 849.

since Congress did not intend that an EEOC action enforcing the ADEA would cut off a previously instituted private ADEA action.[81]

Class Action

Rule 23 of the Federal Rules of Civil Procedure governs most class action suits in federal courts except where the governing statute provides otherwise. The ADEA is such a statute. As we saw earlier, the ADEA borrows heavily from the Fair Labor Standards Act for its procedural scheme. Section 7(b) of the Act explicitly states that the Act is to be enforced in accordance with the "powers, remedies and procedures" provided under selected provisions of the FLSA.[82] Section 16(b) of the FLSA—selectively incorporated into the ADEA under Section 7(b)—provides that no employee "shall be a party plaintiff to any such action unless he gives his consent in writing to become such a party and such consent is filed in the court in which such action is brought."[83] This distinction from the Rule 23 "opt-out" requirement is called the "opt-in" provision, as it is used both in FLSA and in ADEA litigation. (See this chapter at "Opt-In Procedures.")

Initially, the ADEA requires the charging parties in a class action to seek classwide relief. The absence of the class action, though, is not necessarily fatal to a request for classwide relief. The Ninth Circuit has granted classwide relief to plaintiffs who were not proceeding in a class action under Section 16(b) of the Act, on the basis of the employer's age-based policy that was applicable to all similarly situated employees.[84] The court observed that the standards for classwide relief under Title VII should be applied to the ADEA, and the trial court's determination that the policy was clear and constituted a willful violation of the ADEA justified the systemwide injunctive relief.[85] However, the court did note that under Section 16(b), the plaintiffs would not be able to pursue systemwide monetary relief.

Class Certification

A former employee who filed a timely notice of intent to sue was entitled to bring an ADEA action against the employer on behalf of all similarly situated employees who had consented to the action, the Ninth Circuit ruled, even though the other employees may not have individually filed their notices of intent to sue since their inclusion as members of the class neither compromises the purpose of the notice nor prejudices the employer.[86] The court relied on

[81]EEOC v. Eastern Airlines, 35 FEP 503, 508 (CA 11, 1984). *See also* Castle v. Sangamo Weston, Inc., 36 FEP 113 (CA 11, 1984).

[82]29 U.S.C. §626(b) (1984).

[83]29 U.S.C. §216(b) (1984).

[84]Criswell v. Western Air Lines, 709 F.2d 544, 32 FEP 1204 (CA 9, 1983), *aff'd on other grounds*, 472 U.S. ____, 37 FEP 1829 (1985).

[85]*Id.*

[86]Bean v. Crocker Nat'l Bank, 600 F.2d 754, 20 FEP 533 (CA 9, 1979).

the remedial purpose of the ADEA, as the Supreme Court construed it in *Oscar Mayer v. Evans*.[87]

Conversely, the Fifth Circuit refused to certify a putative class in a former employee's ADEA action where no other members filed an intent to sue and the former employee's notice and subsequent negotiations did not purport to include others similarly situated.[88] The plaintiff had argued that his notice satisfied the members' obligation to provide notice because his notice encompassed their claims, but the appeals court observed that the district court determined otherwise on this factual notice.

The Fifth Circuit had previously ruled that class actions are opt-in actions, i.e., "affirmatively consensual,"[89] and that providing a notice of intent to sue is a prerequisite to maintaining a class action under the ADEA.[90]

Class Notification

An important aspect of the class action is that of providing notice to putative class members. Because class members under the "opt-in" provision of the ADEA, via FLSA procedure, are not bound by a judgment unless they have affirmatively consented to or opted in to the action, a difficulty arises as to how these potential plaintiffs may be notified of their right to opt in. There is substantial support in FLSA case law that a district court may not authorize a class-based notice;[91] these cases are persuasive and could be controlling on this issue in an ADEA action. On the other hand, there is substantial support under the FLSA for the proposition that a district court may authorize notice to a conditional class.[92] The Third Circuit heard an appeal from a district court that had conditionally certified a class for purposes of a class action under the ADEA, had ordered the employer to provide a mailing list, and had authorized the sending of a notice of the pending ADEA action to all potential opt-in claimants. The appeals court refused to overturn the district court order; it did not affirm the basis for the order, but merely observed that the order was interlocutory in nature, and that any harm in its enforcement was slight and could be corrected.[93]

The Eighth Circuit has ruled that the district court which originally heard the dispute lacked authority to direct that notice be sent to potential class members for purposes of encouraging them to join the pending or any proposed lawsuit; it also ruled that counsel for the employees who were bringing the ADEA action also could not send notice to these potential members, in light of the ethical issues concerning solicitation and the absence of any intent to

---

[87]441 U.S. 750, 19 FEP 1167 (1979).

[88]McCorstin v. U.S. Steel Corp., 621 F.2d 749, 23 FEP 320 (CA 5, 1980).

[89]Price v. Maryland Casualty Co., 561 F.2d 609, 16 FEP 84 (CA 4, 1977).

[90]LaChappelle v. Owens-Illinois, 513 F.2d 286, 10 FEP 1010 (CA 5, 1975).

[91]Dolan v. Project Constr., 725 F.2d 1263, 26 WH Cases 984 (CA 10, 1984); Kinney Shoe Corp. v. Vorhes, 564 F.2d 859, 23 WH Cases 593 (CA 9, 1977).

[92]Braunstein v. Eastern Photographic Labs, Inc., 600 F.2d 335, 23 WH Cases 1299 (CA 2, 1979), *cert. denied*, 441 U.S. 944, 24 WH Cases 107 (1979).

[93]Lusardi v. Xerox Corp., 747 F.2d 174, 36 FEP 258 (CA 3, 1984).

further the political or associational freedoms either of counsel or of the class member individually.[94]

The Supreme Court will inevitably resolve this serious question, in view of the clear split among the circuits.

Opt-In Procedures

Because the ADEA follows the procedural structure of the Fair Labor Standards Act,[95] FLSA class action procedures control in an ADEA class action. As we saw earlier this chapter, Section 16(b) of the FLSA requires an aggrieved person to affirmatively "opt in" to such a class action by filing a consent in the court in which the action has been brought.[96] The Fifth Circuit, in a per curiam decision, addressed the difference between this "opt-in" requirement and the traditional "opt-out" provision of Rule 23(b) of the Federal Rules of Civil Procedure. It observed:

> "There is a fundamental, irreconcilable difference between the class action described by Rule 23 and that provided for by FLSA § 16(b). In a Rule 23 proceeding a class is described; if the action is maintainable as a class action, each person within the description is considered to be a class member and, as such, is bound by judgment, whether favorable or unfavorable, unless he has 'opted out' of the suit.[7] Under § 16(b) of FLSA, on the other hand, no person can become a party plaintiff and no person will be bound by or may benefit from judgment unless he has affirmatively 'opted into' the class; that is, given his written, filed consent."[97]

---

[7][Footnote omitted.]

This distinction between the FLSA "opt-in" requirement and the Rule 23(b) "opt-out" provision is well recognized both in FLSA and in ADEA litigation.[98] Additionally, the Ninth Circuit has ruled that unnamed parties in a class action under the ADEA may join in the litigation without personally having complied with the notice requirements of Section 7(d).[99]

Section 15 of the ADEA, which regulates nondiscrimination in the federal government, essentially exempts from these procedural provisions class action plaintiffs proceeding against the government.[100] Class certification, according to one court, is not available under the FLSA/ADEA "opt-in" provision; the plaintiff, a formerly reemployed disability annuitant seeking to maintain a class action challenging the federal government's treatment of reemployed disability annuitants who are over age 60, was nevertheless entitled to certification of the proffered class, under Rule 23(b).[101]

The "opt-in" procedure for nonfederal employees generally follows case law established under the Fair Labor Standards Act.

---

[94]McKenna v. Champion Int'l Corp., 36 FEP 326 (CA 8, 1984).

[95]29 U.S.C. §626(b) (1984).

[96]29 U.S.C. §216(b) (1984).

[97]*Supra* note 90, 10 FEP at 1011–12.

[98]*Supra* note 89.

[99]*Supra* note 86, 20 FEP at 536–37, citing Albermarle v. Moody, 422 U.S. 405, 414 n.18, 10 FEP 1181, 1186 (1975).

[100]29 U.S.C. §633a(f) (1984).

[101]Moysey v. Andrus, 481 F. Supp. 850, 21 FEP 836 (D DC, 1979).

Statute of Limitations

The limitations period for the ADEA, as with most of its procedural make-up, is borrowed. However, instead of borrowing directly from the Fair Labor Standards Act, the ADEA under Section 7(e) takes the limitations provision of the Portal-to-Portal Act.[102] Under the Portal-to-Portal Act, the period within which a plaintiff must initiate suit is two years from the time the cause of action accrues. However, "willful" violation of the FLSA extends the limitations period to three years.

The issue of whether a particular employment decision or practice is "willful" determines whether the charging party will have a two-year or three-year window for complaint filing, and whether that party will have an opportunity to pursue liquidated damages. Under the FLSA, liquidated damages are available where a court determines that a violation of the Act was done willfully. The same holds true for the ADEA charging party. (See Chapter 6, "Liquidated Damages.")

An unresolved question was whether the standard for "willfulness" under the FLSA would apply to ADEA cases. The Supreme Court resolved that issue in *TWA v. Thurston*.[103] The Court observed that under the FLSA, willfullness is essentially cognitive (the employer knew that the FLSA was "in the picture"). However, it refused to adapt *in toto* the FLSA standard, reasoning instead:

(1) The employer could be assessed punitive damages even if it did not intend to violate the ADEA;

(2) The Second Circuit's statement that violation of the ADEA is "willful" if the employer knew or showed reckless disregard for the matter of whether its conduct was prohibited by the Act is reasonable in view of the legislative history of the Act's liquidated damages provision;

(3) Violation of the Act cannot be considered "willful" if the employer simply knew of the potential applicability of the Act even if the FLSA "in the picture" standard is appropriate for statute-of-limitations purposes, since the same standard should not govern a provision dealing with liquidated damages;

(4) Applying the "in the picture" standard would frustrate congressional intent by allowing recovery of liquidated damages even if the employer acted reasonably and in good faith; and

(5) The "in the picture" standard would lead to liquidated damages in every case, since employers are obligated under the Act to post the ADEA notice. The legislative history and the structure of the ADEA indicate a two-tiered liability scheme, the Court concluded.[104]

It is unclear whether the TWA standard for liquidated damages also applies to limitations period issues, or whether the FLSA "in the picture" standard should govern statute of limitations disputes and whether the TWA "willful" violations standard controls only liquidated damages liability.

---

[102]Section 7(e)(1), 29 U.S.C. §626(e)(1), incorporating 29 U.S.C. §255 (1984).
[103]469 U.S. ____, 36 FEP 977 (1985).
[104]*Id.*

Discovery

Although the Federal Rules of Civil Procedure favor broad discovery, an employer was successful in compelling the former employee who sued him under the ADEA to return internal reports prepared by another former worker, summarizing the worker's evaluation of the employer's compliance with various EEO guidelines.[105] The district court issued a protective order compelling the plaintiff to return the documents in his possession, reasoning that "to allow the plaintiffs access to the written opinions and conclusions of the members of (defendant's) own research team would discourage companies . . . from making investigations which are calculated to have a positive effect on equalizing employment opportunities."[106] The plaintiff's need for the documents was substantially undercut, the court concluded, by the fact that most of the material contained therein was available through normal discovery channels, without jeopardizing the employer's attempts at candid self-evaluation.

In a subsequent proceeding between these parties, the court ruled that the employee was entitled to have the employer answer interrogatories seeking information relating to jobs for which he was not qualified even though the employer contended that discovery should be limited to only those positions for which the plaintiff was qualified because this was an individual employee's action.[107] The court reasoned that the plaintiff was entitled to discover whether his division or facility as a whole was plagued by age discrimination because such a finding might support an inference that his discharge was motivated by similar animus. The court also ordered the employer to answer an interrogatory requesting it to identify all documents that support its contention that the plaintiff's discharge was not attributable to age discrimination. The employer had argued that this interrogatory required it to "prove a negative" but the court regarded the interrogatory as merely requiring the employer to identify any documents that purport to show a nondiscriminatory reason for the discharge.[108]

Courts recognize the importance of the discovery allowed to the charging party and the need to avoid the "fishing expedition" discovery orders that can harass a defendant. The battle lines are drawn based on the evidence obtained, and a "battle royale" was fought between an airline and the pilots who charged it with age discrimination. In *Monroe v. United Air Lines*,[109] the district court initially ordered the airline to disclose the names of pilots about whom medical information was furnished in response to earlier interrogatories. In a subsequent proceeding, the district court observed that the litigation resembled "trench warfare of World War I, ranging across the entire field of Discovery rather than the Somme."[110] The dispute in this proceeding involved a conflict between the "barbed wire" of the attorney-client privilege and the work-product rule.[111]

---

[105]Wehr v. Burroughs Corp., 20 FEP 526 (ED Pa, 1977).
[106]*Id.* at 527, *citing* Banks v. Lockheed-Georgia Co., 4 FEP 117, 118 (ND Ga, 1971).
[107]*Id.* at 531 n.5.
[108]*Id.* at 532.
[109]32 FEP 1126 (ND Ill, 1981).
[110]Monroe v. United Air Lines, Inc., 32 FEP 1127 (ND Ill, 1981).
[111]*Id.*

The pilots wanted and the airline resisted disclosure of some 49 documents. The court weighed the various claims and decided that the attorney-client privilege did not apply to documents concerning corporate policy on mandatory retirement that do not also provide input for obtaining legal advice, that do not supply actual legal advice, or that do not transmit among the airline's executives such legal advice as has been obtained.[112] The disputed documents for the most part dealt with corporate *policy,* the court emphasized, and this fact allowed for the disclosure of such material. The presence of legal advice within the policy documents would presumably have altered the court's determinations, but the absence of such advice enabled it to rule in favor of disclosure.

The court also ruled that the attorney-client privilege did not extend to protect information concerning input to lawyers for legal advice and input to nonlawyer management officials for policy decision making. Federal Rules of Civil Procedure Rule 26(b)(3) protects "mental impressions, conclusions, opinions, or legal theories," the court concluded, and documents which do not reflect these characteristics are discoverable.[113]

The pilots who originally brought the action had also charged their union with violating the Act via the mandatory retirement system that was the basis for the suit. The union, as codefendant, sought discovery of a document entitled "Action Memorandum to Pilots," that earlier had been protected from disclosure based on the attorney-client privilege. The memorandum was a letter from the law firm representing the plaintiff-pilots to certain clients. The memo would clearly have been protected, but for the fact that copies were inexplicably found in the union's files. The union contended that the presence of the memo in its files reflected a waiver of the attorney-client privilege, but the federal magistrate had ruled that the memo was privileged because "there is no evidence of voluntary waiver."[114] The union failed timely to object to this determination, but the district court declared that it was precluded from overruling the Magistrate's decision in the absence of clear error or a ruling contrary to law.[115] The memo—privileged under normal circumstances—would be allowed, at least partially because the union's counsel failed timely to object to the Magistrate's ruling on the waiver issue.

The airline's continued intransigence resulted in the imposition of sanctions against it for failure to disclose medical files responsive to the interrogatory on pilot medical records; for failure to supply a complete list of names pursuant to another interrogatory; and for its failure to provide all documents concerning or relating to in-flight accidents.[116] In a rare ruling, the district court also assessed attorney's fees against the airline for its refusal to comply with the court's determination on the interrogatories; the court set the fees at one-fifth of expenses incurred in preparing the original memorandum and in related work in support of the motion to compel disclosure, one-half of the expenses

---

[112]*Id.* at 1128, citing Upjohn Co. v. United States, 449 U.S. 383, 49 U.S.L.W. 4093 (1981).

[113]*Id.* at 1132 n.110.

[114]*Id.* at 1133.

[115]*Id.* at 1134.

[116]*Id.*

incurred in preparation of all other memoranda and in related work in connection with the motion to compel responses to certain interrogatories, one-half of the expenses incurred in connection with the motion for sanctions, and all expenses incurred in determining that the airline's several responses to one interrogatory contained significant changes.[117] The court's patience appeared to have run out.

The airline won the next round when the court ruled it did not have to divulge information about any administrative or judical action taken against it for violation of certain safety statutes and regulations, where the requested discovery sought information dealing with safety problems unrelated to the pilots' physical or mental capacities. The pilots' request for medical records of flight deck crew members who applied for special medical certification from the Federal Aviation Administration was limited to only those medical files that are deemed by the airline's medical staff to be covered by the discovery requests.[118]

The plaintiffs sought to obtain a document that the airline had prepared in conjunction with an effort to induce the FAA to extend the age-60 retirement rule to second officers. The district court held that the document was discoverable, since it cannot be said to have been prepared in anticipation of litigation or for trial, within the meaning of Rule 26(b)(3) of the Federal Rules of Civil Procedure.[119] Although the court acknowledged that the document could assist the airline in future litigation, it ruled that Rule 26(b)(3) requires a "closer nexus" than existed between the document and litigation: "part of what the lawyer does to gird himself for the specific battle."[120] This literal reading of Rule 26(b)(3) may have unforeseen ramifications. Attorneys need only provide language in such work products that clearly indicates an intention to use the document in litigation arising from the subject matter of the document; conversely, courts using this restrictive interpretation of the rule may open themselves to a flood of documents that are poorly drafted work products.

The plaintiffs subsequently sought records concerning the airline's treatment of employees' physical problems to compare this with its treatment of employees' age-related problems and with its treatment of employees' alcohol-related problems. The court authorized production of documents, but it also issued a protective order covering the disclosure of personnel and training files of the plaintiffs, and excluding from its coverage those documents whose data already have been made public and files from which the person's name has been deleted.[121]

The last skirmish in the battle involved disclosure of documents prepared by the union's aeromedical adviser. The union argued that the adviser, as a medical doctor, was an independent professional. Because he was not a party to the action and not an employee of the union, it reasoned, the doctor could not be ordered to comply with the discovery request pursuant to Rule 34 of

---

[117]*Id.* at 1137.
[118]*Id.* at 1137, 1139.
[119]Monroe v. United Airlines, Inc., 32 FEP 1245, 1246 (ND Ill, 1981).
[120]*Id.* at 1246.
[121]*Id.* at 1248.

the Federal Rules. However, the court said that the doctor's relationship with the union, including his full-time union-related medical work, had all the classic indicia of an employer-employee relationship. It ruled that the doctor was an employee of the union and that the documents were discoverable.[122]

A former hospital unit administrative director who alleged that her discharge was age-based was allowed to depose employees regarding her participation in a meeting that concerned the implementation of a wellness program, a district court ruled. The state had a "peer review privilege" statute that the hospital argued precluded such depositions, but the court observed that the questioning might aid the plaintiff in establishing a prima facie case or in showing pretextuality of the purported reasons for the discharge; and the depositions would not concern the adequacy or inadequacy of care, in contravention of the state law.[123]

The Eleventh Circuit reversed a decision of a district court concerning EEOC documents that a charged party sought to discover. The district court ordered the Commission to disclose the documents, but the appeals court ruled that the district court had abused its discretion.[124] The appeals court initially observed that the district court's order, unaccompanied by a contempt holding, was nevertheless appealable because the attorneys involved were in the position of being outside third parties claiming a work product privilege over material that had been ordered to be produced for a third party.[125]

The discovery material consisted of witness statements and notes from interviews with witnesses that had been prepared by attorneys for private individuals in anticipation of their own ADEA action. The documents were turned over to the EEOC prior to the dismissal of their private action and the information had been consolidated with the Commission's action. This situation provided the court with a basis for discerning a third-party status for the attorneys who originally had represented the private plaintiffs. That status, in turn, overcame the procedural defect of the missing contempt holding.

As to the merits of the district court's disclosure order, the appeals court noted that the original private plaintiffs had not waived the work product privilege when they turned the materials over to the EEOC and the employer failed to show that it could not obtain the information it sought from the normal discovery process. The court found it significant that the employer had failed even to request the names and addresses of the witnesses who had already been interviewed.[126]

Finally, a district court ruling on discovery in a class action points up the critical differences between the burdens and liabilities Congress considered in enacting the Fair Labor Standards Act, and in engrafting the FLSA procedures onto the ADEA. The court allowed private plaintiffs who brought the age action to discover the names, addresses, and certain other information concerning potential class members, based on its interpretation of the policy differences between the two statutes. It reasoned:

---

[122]Monroe v. United Airlines, 32 FEP 1253, 1254 (ND Ill, 1981).

[123]Schafer v. Parkview Memorial Hosp., 35 FEP 1489, 1492–93 (ND Ind, 1984).

[124]Castle v. Sangamo Weston, Inc., 36 FEP 113 (CA 11, 1984).

[125]*Id*. at 114. *But see* Lusardi v. Xerox Corp., 747 F.2d 174, 36 FEP 258 (CA 3, 1984).

[126]*Id*.

"An appropriate first step toward a satisfactory resolution of this controversy is to analyze the nature of the discovery requested. With respect to each of the following positions, vice-president, district manager, store supervisor and associate store supervisor, plaintiffs seek the following information: (1) name; (2) job title; (3) home address; (4) date of birth; (5) date of hire; (6) date of entry into current position; and (7) 'forced ratings'. These inquiries cover the period 1970–82, and are to include all persons holding any such position during that period. The total number of employees and former employees involved in the requests is estimated not to exceed 280.

"The contrast between this kind of discovery and the burdensome, potentially overwhelming, discovery Congress visualized, and sought to prevent, when it enacted the Portal-to-Portal Act, is noteworthy. As the legislative history of that statute makes clear, Congress was concerned that employers throughout the nation would be forced to comb through payroll records of their entire work force, trying to determine whether, with the newly mandated travel-time included, additional overtime compensation should have been paid. In effect, Congress concluded that such 'surprise' liability, and the attendant discovery burdens, could be imposed upon employers, but only on behalf of persons actively seeking such relief in their own right. Such considerations have little relevance in ADEA suits; the liability asserted should not come as a surprise, and the information sought is relatively simple and straightforward.

"Moreover, and more conclusively, there is nothing in the ADEA's invocation of the FLSA procedural remedies which can reasonably be regarded as curtailing the ordinary discovery rights of the litigants. In my view, all of the information now sought by plaintiffs would be discoverable in aid of their own individual claims of age discrimination. They are plainly entitled to bolster their individual claims by attempting to prove a pattern or practice. The persons whose identities are sought presumably have knowledge of the facts, and could be called as witnesses. Thus, the discovery sought should be precluded only upon a finding that it would be unduly burdensome, or is sought in bad faith, for some ulterior purpose. In my view, the burdens are relatively modest. The discovery is being sought for mixed reasons, partly (perhaps) to aid plaintiffs' individual cases, and partly to set the stage for a free flow of information to potential additional plaintiffs. I see no particular harm in that: the ADEA is, after all, a remedial statute, implementation of which should not be discouraged."[127]

Jury Trial

As is explained more fully in the beginning of Chapter 6 ("Legal Remedies"), our judicial system is divided essentially into two categories: legal issues and remedies, and equitable issues and remedies. The ADEA, being a hybrid of both Title VII ("equitable" issues, no right to trial by jury) and the Fair Labor Standards Act ("legal" issues, right to jury trial via the Seventh Amendment to the Constitution), developed a conflicting line of cases on the jury trial issue.

In 1978, the Supreme Court ruled in *Lorillard v. Pons*[128] that an ADEA plaintiff seeking lost wages was entitled to a jury trial. Because the ADEA specifically refers to FLSA "procedures" for enforcement purposes, the Court reasoned, FLSA provision for a jury trial should control, rather than the Title VII principle. It was clear that the determination of amounts due, monetary

---

[127]Vivone v. Acme Mkts., Inc., 37 FEP 561 (ED Pa, 1985).
[128]434 U.S. 575, 16 FEP 885 (1978).

amounts similar to FLSA back wages, was a legal determination, rather than an equitable one. Section 7(b) of the ADEA even states that amounts owing to an individual as a result of a violation of the Act ''shall be deemed to be unpaid minimum wages or unpaid overtime compensation'' for purposes of the FLSA.[129]

Section 7(c)(2) now states that a person is entitled to a trial by jury ''of any issue of fact in any such action for recovery of amounts owing as a result of a violation of this Act, regardless of whether equitable relief is sought by any party in any such action.'' Because Section 7(c)(1) provides for an individual's right to seek[130] ''legal or equitable'' relief, the *Lorillard v. Pons* decision failed to answer the scope of the right to a trial by jury, the issues which fell within the pursuit of ''lost wages,'' and what types of remedies would not be tried by a jury. Congress' amendment to the Act, specifically the Section 7(c)(2) language, essentially opens the doors to a jury trial for any private plaintiff who seeks recovery of amounts owing, ''regardless of whether equitable relief is sought.''[131] Since virtually all ADEA claimants will seek ''amounts owing,'' presumably all such plaintiffs are entitled to a jury trial.

However, a bifurcated process is involved in presenting issues to the trier: the jury will decide issues of law and the court will decide issues of equity. This practice reflects the hybrid nature of the ADEA: Title VII-type issues involving equitable considerations go to the court; FLSA-type issues of monetary liability (back pay and liquidated damages) go to the jury. The legislative history concerning the 1978 amendment to Section 7 which resulted in the Section 7(b) language at issue indicates that Congress intended this interpretation.[132]

Following *Lorillard v. Pons,* a district court determined that the plaintiff's delay in making his demand for a jury trial for over three years after filing the action precludes him from asserting a right to a jury trial.[133] Because at least one other court within that district had ruled that an individual plaintiff had a right to a jury trial under the ADEA, the district court held that *Lorillard* did not create a new right but merely settled a split among the circuits on this question. The absence of any showing that a denial of a jury trial will prejudice the plaintiff allowed the court to use its discretion in denying the jury trial demand.

The ADEA's provision in Section 7(b) authorizing a jury trial ''of any issue of fact in any such action for recovery of amounts owing,'' according to one district court, entitles the plaintiff to a jury trial on all issues of fact necessary to recovery or nonrecovery of damages.[134] The court reasoned that so long as the jury is first permitted to exercise its fact-finding powers, the court is required to make its factual determinations, at least to the extent that they are not

---

[129]29 U.S.C. §626(b).

[130]29 U.S.C. §626(c)(2).

[131]29 U.S.C. §626(b).

[132]H.R. Rep. No. 950, 95th Cong., 2d Sess. 13. *reprinted in* 1978 U.S. CODE CONG. & AD. NEWS 528, 535.

[133]Tonka v. AT&T Co., 20 FEP 539 (ND Ga, 1978), *aff'd,* 592 F.2d 1182, 20 FEP 544 (CA 5, 1979).

[134]Criswell v. Western Air Lines, 514 F. Supp. 384, 29 FEP 350 (CD Cal, 1981), *aff'd,* 709 F.2d 544, 32 FEP 1204 (CA 9, 1983), *aff'd on other grounds,* 472 U.S. ____, 37 FEP 1829 (1985).

inconsistent with the verdict. The court also determined that it had authority to decide the plaintiffs' equitable claims, notwithstanding the fact that special interrogatories were not submitted to the jury.

The Second Circuit has ruled that an employee who brought his ADEA action without the assistance of counsel waived his right to a jury trial by his failure timely to request a jury trial.[135] Rule 38(b) of the Federal Rules of Civil Procedure requires that a demand for jury trial be made "in writing at any time after the commencement of the action and not later than 10 days after the service of the last pleading directed to such issue." The employee argued that he could not have waived his right because there was no knowing and intelligent refusal to make the demand, in view of his ignorance of the dictates of Rule 38(b). The court was unpersuaded by the employee's argument that the application of Rule 38 to a pro se litigant was unfair since the Rule treated represented and unrepresented litigants equally.[136]

The Eighth Circuit heard an action brought by a female 43-year-old former elementary school teacher who alleged both age and sex discrimination. At the time she filed her Title VII and ADEA action, the court noted, the plaintiff was unrepresented by counsel and she failed to demand a jury trial. The court ruled that she had waived her right to have her age claim presented to a jury, since under Federal Rule 38(d), waiver "by failure to make a timely demand is complete even though it was inadvertent, unintended and regardless of the explanation or excuse."[137]

Prior to the transfer of functions for enforcing the ADEA from the Secretary of Labor to the EEOC a district court ruled that the Labor Secretary was entitled to a jury trial on all questions of fact, in an action brought on behalf of two individuals.[138] Acknowledging *Lorillard v. Pons* and Congress' subsequent amendment to Section 7 of the Act, the court ruled that the Act did not explicitly forbid a jury trial in an action brought by the Secretary. It declined to find that the Secretary was not a "person" who is entitled to a jury trial under the Act, and it found that there was no reason to deny a jury trial merely because equitable relief was being sought in addition to legal remedies.[139] Although the defendant's position had some merit, the court concluded that to rule otherwise would allow the individual plaintiffs' rights to a jury trial to be circumvented merely by the Secretary's commencement of an action.[140]

Jury Instructions

The issue of a right to jury trial in private sector ADEA cases is well settled after *Lorillard v. Pons,* including the retroactivity of that decision. Issues of

---

[135]Washington v. New York City Bd. of Estimate, 709 F.2d 792, 32 FEP 45 (CA 2, 1983), *cert. denied,* 464 U.S. 1013, 35 FEP 1893 (1983).

[136]*Id.,* 32 FEP at 50.

[137]Scharnhorst v. Independent School Dist. No. 710, 686 F.2d 637, 32 FEP 51, 54 (CA 8, 1982). *See also* Simon v. Wiremold Co., 35 FEP 1819 (WD Pa, 1984).

[138]EEOC v. Blue Star Foods, Inc., 22 FEP 504 (SD Iowa, 1980).

[139]*Id.* at 506.

[140]*Id.*

timely demand and/or waiver of the right are fact-specific and do not involve complex legal questions. The one fertile area of litigation involving ADEA jury trials concerns instructions to the jury.

The Eighth Circuit upheld instructions in an unsuccessful job applicant's ADEA action. The district court refused to instruct the jury that they had to find for the plaintiff if they found that the supervisor's statements about the age of the applicant proved that age was a determining factor in the applicant's failure to be hired. The appeals court found that the trial court's refusal was proper since the instructions were misleading because they presupposed that the supervisor made such statements, and the supervisor had in fact denied making such statements.[141] The supervisor's denial, according to the appeals court, created a factual dispute for the jury, and the instructions completely ignored the employer's defense that the plaintiff was not hired because he had no application on file.[142]

The Second Circuit remanded an ADEA action to the district court and ordered it to instruct the jury on the proper burden of proof that the plaintiff must bear in a case of circumstantial evidence.[143] The employer had argued that the trial court should have instructed the jury that the plaintiff must show that his replacement was substantially younger than he, in order to show that the discharge was motivated in whole or in part by the plaintiff's age. The court observed that one of the elements of a prima facie case based on circumstantial evidence is the replacement of the plaintiff "by a younger employee or keeping the post open to receive one."[144] It ruled that on retrial the court should instruct the jury accordingly.

A district court instructed the jury that unless the employer proffered "credible evidence" of legitimate, nondiscriminatory reasons for its actions, the plaintiff would be entitled to a favorable verdict upon the establishment of his prima facie case. The employer argued on appeal that this instruction misstated its evidentiary burden and that the trial court should have used the term "admissible evidence" in its instructions. The Sixth Circuit rejected the employer's argument reasoning that the concept of credibility is inherent in evidence that would allow the trier of fact rationally to conclude that the employment decision had not been motivated by discriminatory animus.[145] The appeals court observed that the trial court had also instructed the jury that the plaintiff had the burden of proving each issue by a preponderance of the evidence, and it affirmed that portion of the court's opinion.[146]

Because of the importance of the jury instructions, the American Bar Association has established a committee to propose model jury instructions to be used in private sector ADEA actions. These proposed jury instructions appear at Appendix D.

---

[141]DeHues v. Western Elec. Co., 710 F.2d 1344, 32 FEP 387 (CA 8, 1983).

[142]*Id.*, 32 FEP at 389.

[143]Haskell v. Kaman Corp., 35 FEP 941 (CA 2, 1984).

[144]*Id.* at 947, citing Stanojev v. Ebasco Servs., Inc., 643 F.2d 914, 924 n.7, 25 FEP 355 (CA 2, 1981).

[145]Davis v. Combustion Eng'g, 35 FEP 975 (CA 6, 1984).

[146]*Id.* at 977–78. *See also* Cancellier v. Federated Dep't Stores, 672 F.2d 1312, 28 FEP 1151 (CA 9), *cert. denied,* 459 U.S. 859 (1982).

Federal Employees' Jury Demand

In 1981, the Supreme Court ruled that federal employees do not have a right to a jury trial in an ADEA action against the federal government.[147] The Court observed that there is a strong presumption against waiver of sovereign immunity in the absence of any generally applicable right to jury trial when the federal government consents to be sued.[148] The *Lorillard v. Pons* decision authorizing a jury trial to private plaintiffs who seek "legal" relief does not apply to an action brought by individuals charging the federal government, the Court ruled, because the *Lorillard* right was based on the Seventh Amendment to the Constitution, which in turn applies to private lawsuits but not to those involving the United States.[149]

Although Congress selectively incorporated portions of the Fair Labor Standards Act into the ADEA, including procedures and a private right to a jury trial, the Court reasoned that the FLSA enforcement scheme was not sufficient to find such a right for parties suing the U.S. because Congress had not incorporated the FLSA procedures into Section 15 of the ADEA—the provision authorizing federal employees and applicants for federal jobs to maintain an ADEA action against the government.[150] The Court concluded that the legislative history of Section 15 did not support a holding that there is a right to a jury trial for parties suing the federal government under the ADEA because:

(1) There is not a single reference in that legislative history to the subject of jury trials in such actions;

(2) When Congress amended Section 7(c) of the Act to provide for jury trials in actions against private and state and local government employers it did not amend Section 15 to provide for jury trials in actions against the federal government; and

(3) Congress instead enacted a provision declaring that U.S. Government personnel actions covered by Section 15 of the ADEA are not covered by any other section of the Act.[151] It is clear that Congress intended separate and distinct enforcement mechanisms for private and nonfederal sector plaintiffs vis-à-vis federal sector plaintiffs.[152]

---

[147]Lehman v. Nakshian, 453 U.S. 156, 26 FEP 65 (1981).

[148]*Id.*, 26 FEP at 67–68.

[149]*Id.*

[150]*Id., relying on* 29 U.S.C. §633a(c) (1984).

[151]*Id.*, 26 FEP at 69.

[152]Kennedy v. Whitehurst, 690 F.2d 951, 29 FEP 1373, at 1375–76 (CA DC, 1982).

5

ADEA Proof Considerations

Proving Discrimination

The seminal case establishing the order, allocation of burdens, and standards of proof is *McDonnell Douglas Corp. v. Green.*[1] In order to withstand the employer's motion for dismissal or summary judgment, the aggrieved employee must establish a prima facie case of age discrimination. (The prima facie case and standards and burdens of proof are discussed later in this chapter.)

Disparate Treatment

In proving discrimination, there are two essential theories on which to found a claim: (1) disparate treatment, and (2) adverse impact. The Supreme Court has said that "disparate treatment" amounts to less favorable treatment because of an individual protected characteristic such as age.[2] Proof of discriminatory intent is "critical," the Court added, but it noted that in some situations such an intent can be inferred from the mere fact of differences in treatment.[3]

Disparate impact, however, involves employment practices that are facially neutral in their treatment of different groups, but that in fact fall more harshly on one group than another and the difference cannot be justified by a business necessity.[4] Proof of a discriminatory *motive* is not required in such cases.[5]

At least one authority has observed that the overwhelming number of cases brought under the ADEA are based on the disparate treatment theory.[6] Since seniority systems are typically skewed in favor of the more senior, hence "older" worker, it is a logical inference to discern age discrimination as occurring predominantly on an individualized basis.

Individual Selection

In *McDonnell Douglas*, the Supreme Court established the order of proof in a disparate treatment case:

(1) The employee had to establish a prima facie case;

---

[1]411 U.S. 792, 5 FEP 965 (1973).

[2]Teamsters v. United States, 431 U.S. 324, 14 FEP 1514 (1977).

[3]*Id.*

[4]*Id.*

[5]*Id.*

[6]B. Schlei & P. Grossman, EMPLOYMENT DISCRIMINATION LAW (2nd ed.; Washington, D.C.: The Bureau of National Affairs, 1983), p. 497 and note 119.

(2) The employer was then entitled to attempt to rebut it;
(3) The employee could then attempt to show that the employer's explanation for its conduct was pretextual.[7]

Subsequently, the Court refined the respective burdens in *Texas Department of Community Affairs v. Burdine*,[8] wherein the Court emphasized that the burden that shifted to the employer once a prima facie case was established was that of producing evidence in support of a legitimate, nondiscriminatory reason; the employer was not required to prove that it actually was motivated by the asserted reason.[9]

McDonnell Douglas and *Burdine* arose in the context of Title VII allegations. The different statutory frameworks and the different characteristics between race, sex, religion, and handicap on the one hand, and age on the other, have led courts to modify an individual plaintiff's burden in establishing his prima facie case. An early modification of the *McDonnell Douglas* factors concerned an employee who was terminated during a reduction in force. The Fifth Circuit ruled that the employee should not have been required to show that he was replaced by someone outside the protected age group.

McCORSTIN v. UNITED STATES STEEL CORP.

621 F.2d 749, 23 FEP 320 (CA 5, 1980)

. . .

The appellee argued and the district court held that the appellant failed to satisfy the fourth prong of the *McDonnell test* that he was replaced by a person outside the protected class, i.e., a person under forty years of age.[6] Indeed, McCorstin conceded below that he had not been so replaced. It is extremely questionable whether he had been replaced at all following the reduction in force. Foreclosed from claiming satisfaction of *McDonnell*'s fourth requirement, the appellant argues that the requirement should not and was not meant to apply in the instant case because age is not a discrete and immutable characteristic such as sex or race, but rather is a continuum. Additionally, McCorstin argues that a reduction in force is a business practice different in kind from routine discharge involving one-to-one substitutions.

To appraise the appellant's argument we must examine the statutory language, the elements of which any prima facie evidence test must reflect. Section 4(a)(1) of the ADEA, 29 U.S.C.A. §623(a)(1), provides:
(a) It shall be unlawful for an employer—
(1) to fail or refuse to hire or to discharge any individual or otherwise discriminate against any individual with respect to his compensation, terms, conditions, or privileges of employment, because of such individual's age.

Based upon the statutory language, it is possible to categorize the *McDonnell* factors in the age discrimination context. The first and third factors, that the employee be in the protected age group and has been discharged, are no more than standing requirements under the statute. That is, discharge constitutes the cognizable injury and being a member of the protected class satisfies the requirement of being within the zone of interests protected by the statute. *See United States v. SCRAP*, 412 U.S. 669 (1973); *Association of Data Processing v. Camp*, 397 U.S. 150 (1970). The third prong, that the employee is qualified for the job, is, at most, a negation of a possible rebuttal to

---

[7]*Supra* note 1.
[8]450 U.S. 248, 25 FEP 113 (1981).
[9]*Id.*

the claim of discrimination that has been deemed reasonable to place within the employee's burden of proof. It is clear, therefore, that the fourth factor only was intended to demonstrate discrimination, that is, unequal treatment, by the relatively objective evidence of replacement by a member of a nonprotected class.

Recognizing the methodology of the test impels the conclusion that the test in *McDonnell* was never intended to be the *only* prima facie evidence test for discrimination, age or otherwise. In *McDonnell* itself, the Supreme Court noted:

The facts necessarily will vary in Title VII cases, and the specification above of the prima facie proof required from respondent is not necessarily applicable in every respect to differing factual situations.

411 U.S. 802, 5 FEP Cases at 969. This circuit has also recognized that the *McDonnell* test is not the alpha and omega of possible tests in the age discrimination context. *See Marshall v. Goodyear Tire & Rubber Co.*, 554 F.2d 730, 14 FEP Cases 139 (5th Cir. 1977). *See also Peters v. Jefferson Chemical Co.*, 516 F.2d 447, 450, 11 FEP Cases 296, 298 (5th Cir. 1975). Because the *McDonnell* test reduces to the fourth factor as the basis for a claim of discrimination, its mechanical application would result in the proscription and prevention of one type of discrimination resulting in discharge only, the situation in which a person had been replaced by someone outside of the protected class. *See Ramirez v. Sloss*, 615 F.2d 163, 22 FEP Cases 768 (5th Cir. 1980).[7] This Procrustean limitation on the ADEA would be tantamount to holding that only price-fixing agreements are contracts in restraint of trade in violation of Section 1 of the Sherman Act. Discrimination, unfortunately, exists in forms as myriad as the creative perverseness of human beings can provide.

A mechanistic application of the *McDonnell* prima facie test is especially dangerous in the context of age discrimination. Seldom will a sixty-year-old be replaced by a person in the twenties. Rather the sixty-year-old will be replaced by a fifty-five-year-old, who, in turn, is succeeded by a person in the forties, who also will be replaced by a younger person. Eventually, a person outside the protected class will be elevated but rarely to the position of the one fired. This is especially true in management and technical fields where knowledge and experience, the product of years, are necessary prerequisites to appointment of persons on high rungs of the corporate ladder.

The above discussion is not to be construed as a denunciation of the *McDonnell* test. On the contrary, the test provides an amount of certainty to courts and litigants alike on the allocation of proof and the orderly presentation of evidence. In those cases, however, when it was not intended to apply and, factually, cannot apply, the plaintiff must enjoy more leeway in a presentation of a prima facie case. Consequently, a more onerous burden must fall on the court to determine when and whether the plaintiff has demonstrated facts sufficient for a reasonable jury to infer that discrimination has occurred. Should the court determine that evidence exists sufficient to raise a presumption that unlawful discrimination has occurred, the burden of proof will shift to the defendant to demonstrate that the discharge occurred for reasons other than discrimination. In those situations where *McDonnell* does not apply the line of demarcation denoting the existence of a prima facie case is not bright, but in the area of subtle discrimination more specificity on the court's part would lead inexorably to less protection for victims.

Based upon the facts adduced at trial, we conclude that the *McDonnell* test should not have been applied. First, because there was a reduction in force, that is, a shrinking of the work force, even the threshold requirement of McCorstin's being replaced is inappropriate. Second, because the discrimination involves age, rather than sex or race, a requirement that the replacement be from a nonprotected group fails to take the reality of the working place into account. Because of the value of experience rarely are sixty-year-olds replaced by those under forty. The replacement process is more subtle but just as injurious to the worker who has been discharged. That the person is replaced by a person ten years younger rather than twenty years does not diminish the discrimination; the subtlety only tends to disguise it.

[6-7][Footnotes omitted.]

A disparate treatment theory of age discrimination involves the prima facie case, the employer's articulation of a nondiscriminatory reason, if any, for the action, and the employee's proof of pretext of that proffered reason, or a showing that age was a "determining" factor in the employment decision. The only truism that exists in every age case is that the proof "will vary depending upon the specific factual situation."[10]

Classwide Analysis. The "high visibility" forms of age discrimination are involuntary retirement and reductions in force (RIFs), as contrasted with refusal to hire or transfer/train. The wholesale termination of long-time workers via a RIF is front-page news, and provides the bulk of class action suits under the ADEA. Such a case involved 15 employees who alleged that they were laid off in violation of the Act, and the employer's claim that an economically motivated RIF necessitated the employment decisions. In *Williams v. General Motors*,[11] the Fifth Circuit examined the employees' case and determined that they need not show that they were replaced by younger persons to establish a prima facie case, thus dispensing with the fourth prong of the *McDonnell Douglas* test. The illogic of a rigid adherence to the *McDonnell Douglas* factors was amply demonstrated in *Williams*, where the plaintiffs' inability to meet the fourth prong of the prima facie case would have precluded them from proceeding, and would have sent a message to employers everywhere that the RIF was an acceptable vehicle for disposing of unwanted employees.

The Fifth Circuit noted with satisfaction that the Supreme Court in *McDonnell Douglas* did not require fanatic adherence: "The facts necessarily will vary . . . , and the specification above of the prima facie proof required . . . is not necessarily applicable in every respect to differing factual situations."[12]

The appeals court provided the employees with an alternative test for establishing their prima facie case: they must show that they were qualified to assume another position at the time of discharge or demotion; and they must produce evidence—circumstantial or direct—from which it might reasonably be concluded that the employer intended to discriminate in reaching its decision.[13] With regard to the circumstantial evidence, the court observed, statistical evidence or evidence of employer subterfuge would suffice to establish the employer's intent to discriminate on the basis of age so long as such evidence served the general purpose of supporting the asserted proposition and excluding other propositions.[14]

The appeals court cautioned that statistical evidence "has no magic properties . . . the expert (witness)'s admission that as age increased so did likelihood of retention during the reduction supports a proposition diametrically opposed to plaintiffs' case."[15]

---

[10]Moses v. Falstaff Brewing Corp., 550 F.2d 1113, 1114, 14 FEP 813, 814 (CA 8, 1977).

[11]656 F.2d 120, 26 FEP 1381 (CA 5, 1981), citing McDonnell Douglas v. Green, 411 U.S. 792, 5 FEP 965 (1973).

[12]*Id.*, 26 FEP at 1388 n.12, citing McDonnell Douglas at 411 U.S. 802 n.13, 5 FEP at 969.

[13]*Id.*

[14]*Id.*, 26 FEP at 1388.

[15]*Id.* at n.14.

Although a classwide analytical approach infers that class certification has occurred or is imminent, the ADEA does not require plaintiffs seeking class certification to follow the requirements of Rule 23 of the Federal Rules of Civil Procedure. Instead, it adopts a provision of the Fair Labor Standards Act for monetary damages that requires an individual to "opt out" of the proffered class if he/she seeks to avoid being bound by the judgment of the court.[16] This also means that where the plaintiffs seek injunctive relief, failure to file a class action pursuant to 29 U.S.C. Section 626(b), as it incorporates 29 U.S.C. Section 216(b), *does not* preclude classwide relief. The rationale underlying this outcome, according to the Ninth Circuit, is that "the evil to be eliminated is discrimination on the basis of classwide characteristics, and for this reason the interests of other members of the class are vindicated by the actual plaintiffs."[17] The Ninth Circuit reasoned that a classwide injunction extending beyond the immediate plaintiffs to the action would effectuate the policies of the Act as well as provide individual relief.[18] The appeals court concluded that the employer's actions were taken pursuant to a classwide, age-based policy equally applicable to flight deck crew-members, and the "remedy must be co-extensive with the right."[19] Classwide analysis relies on extant employer practices and selection devices, but it also relies heavily on statistics to provide a factual basis for comparing the treatment of class members to that of those outside the class.

Use of Statistics.   Mark Twain once said: "There are three kinds of lies: lies; damn lies; and statistics." Regardless of one's perception of these numbers and their weight in age discrimination cases, statistics are a part of many such actions, and the advocate who works in this field will need to become familiar with the leading cases, as well as some of the more commonly used terms of art.

Statistical evidence has been used repeatedly in Title VII cases, and its acceptance into ADEA cases was not long in coming. In an early age case involving a single plaintiff, a district court observed that "statistics play a part when correlated with other factors in a case."[20] Subsequently, the Fifth Circuit ruled that, assuming Title VII standards are strictly applicable to ADEA claims, the employee failed to make out a prima facie case because his statistical evidence did not demonstrate that age was an impediment to the promotion for which he was denied.[21] The Ninth Circuit went further and described the context of statistical evidence in an age case, and what was necessary to establish a prima facie case via statistics:

> "proof sufficient to establish a prima facie case of age discrimination does not necessarily establish the same inference of improper motive as under a Title VII

---

[16]29 U.S.C. §626(b), as it incorporates 29 U.S.C. §216(b).

[17]Criswell v. Western Air Lines, 709 F.2d 544, 32 FEP 1204, 1215 (CA 9, 1983), *aff'd on other grounds,* 472 U.S. _____, 37 FEP 1829 (1985), citing Bowe v. Colgate-Palmolive Co., 416 F.2d 711, 719–20, 2 FEP 121 (CA 7, 1969).

[18]*Id.*, 32 FEP at 1216, citing Sprogis v. United Air Lines, Inc., 444 F.2d 1194, 1201, 3 FEP 621 (CA 7, 1971), *cert. denied,* 404 U.S. 991, 4 FEP 37 (1972).

[19]*Id.*, 32 FEP at 1216.

[20]Hodgson v. Ideal Corrugated Box Co., 10 FEP 744, 749 (ND WVa, 1974).

[21]Lindsey v. Southwestern Bell Tel. Co., 546 F.2d 1123, 15 FEP 138 (CA 5, 1977).

disparate treatment case. 'The aging process causes employees constantly to exit the labor market while younger ones enter, simply the replacement of an older employee by a younger worker does not raise the same inference of improper motive that attends replacement of a black by a white person in a Title VII case.'

"(Plaintiff) introduced sufficient statistical evidence to establish a prima facie case. This evidence consisted of three exhibits, prepared . . . in response to interrogatories, which listed each member of the sales force, their ages and dates of service, and those employees terminated as a result of the hydronics plant closure. A plaintiff can rely on statistical evidence alone to establish the discriminatory impact of an employer's selection criteria."[22]

The Ninth Circuit cited *Geller v. Markham*[23] as authority for the use of statistics in establishing a prima facie case of age discrimination, but that circuit was ruling in a case where a nationwide RIF resulted in the termination of some 40 employees; the plaintiff's statistical evidence was simply insufficient to prove his claim. In *Geller v. Markham*, however, the Second Circuit was presented with substantial statistical evidence indicating that 92.6 percent of all teachers over 40 years of age were within the class of individuals precluded by school board policy from hiring, a figure approximately "600 times the level generally required for statistical significance."[24]

But this presentation of *Geller*, under the disparate impact theory, is based on acceptance of statistical evidence in Title VII cases on that theory. The seminal case of statistics as evidence in Title VII disparate impact cases is *Teamsters v. United States*.[25] *Teamsters* involved a pattern-or-practice action under Title VII's ban on race discrimination. The Supreme Court ruled that the plaintiffs had the burden of proving a prima facie case that the employer's regular practice was to discriminate intentionally against the protected class.

Statistics showing racial imbalance in the composition of the employer's work force as compared with the composition of the population of the community from which the employees were hired was probative, the Court reasoned, since it was to be expected that nondiscriminatory hiring practices in time would result in a work force more or less representative of the racial composition of the community.[26] Considerations such as a small sample size and evidence showing that figures for the general population might not accurately reflect the pool of qualified job applicants would also be relevant, it concluded.[27]

Applying *Teamsters*, the Fifth Circuit ruled that the burden to show intentional discrimination could be met solely with statistics if the plaintiffs showed a sufficiently great disparity between the employer's treatment of members of a protected group versus nonmembers.[28] This echoes the Supreme Court's

---

[22]Kelly v. American Standard, Inc., 640 F.2d 974, 25 FEP 94, 98 (CA 9, 1981), citing Marshall v. Goodyear Tire & Rubber Co., 554 F.2d 730, 736, 15 FEP 139 (CA 5, 1977) and Geller v. Markham, 635 F.2d 1027, 24 FEP 920 (CA 2, 1980).

[23]Kelly v. American Standard, Inc., *supra* note 22.

[24]*Id.*, 24 FEP at 924.

[25]431 U.S. 324, 14 FEP 1514 (1977).

[26]*Id.*, 14 FEP at 1520–21.

[27]*Id.*

[28]Payne v. Travenol Laboratories, 673 F.2d 798, 28 FEP 1212 (CA 5, 1981), *cert. denied*, 459 U.S. 1038 (1982).

observation about "statistically significant" data in *Teamsters*. The Fifth Circuit also said that the statistical showing of disparate results might also be buttressed with evidence of a history of discrimination by the employer, individual instances of discrimination, and opportunities to discriminate that existed in the employer's decision-making processes.[29]

The field of statistics is divided into two groups: (1) descriptive statistics, which summarize informational data by using averages and measures of dispersion; and (2) statistical inference, which uses the informational data to arrive at statements of probability.[30] Following voluminous and complex statistical evidence, the Tenth Circuit determined that the employer violated the ADEA by selecting employees for a RIF who fell within the 52 to 64 age range; the statistics established a prima facie case, and the employer did not show that its actions were not discriminatory toward the protected age group, that its policies were necessary to a safe and efficient operation of its business, or that the performance rating system used in selecting employees for layoff was necessary throughout all of its employee classifications.[31]

The Fifth Circuit has furthered the acceptance of statistics in evidence when it observed that circumstantial evidence such as statistics would suffice to establish the employer's intent to discriminate, so long as such evidence serves the general purpose of supporting the asserted proposition and excluding other propositions.[32] Similarly, the Third Circuit upheld an award of liquidated damages against an employer based on evidence that younger and less qualified employees were retained, that the statistical significance of the employer's pattern of discharge fell more heavily on older employees, and that information retained in employees' files demonstrated the employer's preference for younger employees.[33]

There are several ways in which statistics can be used to prove a contention or to buttress a claim: pass/fail comparisons, population/work force comparisons, multiple regression analysis, and "cohort" analysis.[34] Equally important in making a statistical argument is the source of data used to construct the argument. These include: applicant flow data, general population data, and qualified labor market data.[35]

Statistics are readily accepted by most courts, and are vital to any pattern-or-practice action. Plaintiffs have the obligation of proving intent, either directly or indirectly via circumstantial evidence—statistics. Any advocate involved in employment discrimination law will eventually need the assistance of a reputable statistician to present or rebut a case.

---

[29]*Id.*

[30]EEOC v. Sandia Corp., 649 F.2d 1383, 23 FEP 799, 802 (CA 10, 1980).

[31]*Id.*

[32]Williams v. General Motors Corp., 656 F.2d 120, 26 FEP 1381, 1388 (CA 5, 1981). *See also* Goldstein v. Manhattan Indus., 37 FEP 1217 (CA 11, 1985).

[33]McDowell v. Avtex Fibers, 740 F.2d 214, 35 FEP 371, 375 (CA 3, 1984). *Contra*, Yartzoff v. Oregon, 36 FEP 16 (CA 9, 1984).

[34]B. Schlei & P. Grossman, eds., EMPLOYMENT DISCRIMINATION LAW (Washington, D.C.: The Bureau of National Affairs, Inc., 1983) pp. 1332–47.

[35]*Id.*

The Prima Facie Case

In *McDonnell Douglas v. Green*, the Supreme Court set down the requirements for establishing a prima facie case of employment discrimination:

(1) The employee/job applicant was in the protected group;
(2) The employee/job applicant applied and was qualified for the job;
(3) The employee/job applicant was adversely affected; and
(4) The employer continued to seek someone with qualifications similar to those that the employee/job applicant possessed.[36]

The Court ruled that after an employee/job applicant establishes a prima facie case, the employer is required to articulate some legitimate, nondiscriminatory reason for the decision to reject. If the employer can articulate some such reason, the Court concluded, the employee/job applicant must have an opportunity to show that that proffered reason is pretextual and that the employer was really motivated by unlawful discrimination.[37]

Soon after *McDonnell Douglas*, the Sixth Circuit observed the natural progression of older workers to leave and be replaced by younger workers, and that this "factor of progression and replacement is not necessarily involved in cases involving the immutable characteristics of race, sex and national origin . . . we do not believe that Congress intended automatic presumptions to apply whenever a worker is replaced by another of a different age."[38] The Ninth Circuit echoed this sentiment when it observed that "proof sufficient to establish a prima facie case of age discrimination does not necessarily establish the same inference of improper motive as under a Title VII disparate treatment case . . . the replacement of an older employee by a younger worker does not raise the same inference of improper motive that attends replacement of a black by a white person in a Title VII case."[39]

Because of the recognition that the *McDonnell Douglas* test was not sufficiently demanding and that plaintiffs would have a relatively easy time showing that they had been replaced by younger workers, the courts began adopting a more stringent approach to establishing a prima facie case. The First Circuit observed that the Supreme Court stated that *McDonnell Douglas* was not intended to be "rigid, mechanized, or ritualistic."[40] Courts essentially require a *nexus*—some showing that there is a connection between the plaintiff's age and the adverse action that would give rise to an inference of unlawful motive.[41] But the Supreme Court's caveat that *McDonnell Douglas* was not intended to be rigid is nowhere more true than in cases involving fact situations that do not allow for compliance with that test.

The Second Circuit has ruled that the elimination of a vice presidency in a

---

[36]411 U.S. 792, 5 FEP 965 (1973). *See also* Texas Dep't of Community Affairs v. Burdine, 450 U.S. 248, 25 FEP 113 (1981).

[37]*Id.*, 5 FEP at 970.

[38]Laugesen v. Anaconda Co., 510 F.2d 307, 313, 10 FEP 567, 571, n.4 (CA 6, 1975).

[39]Kelly v. American Standard, Inc., 640 F.2d 974, 980, 25 FEP 94, 98 (CA 9, 1981), citing Marshall v. Goodyear Tire & Rubber Co., 554 F.2d 730, 736, 15 FEP 139, 141 (CA 5, 1977).

[40]Loeb v. Textron, Inc., 600 F.2d 1003, 1016, 1017, 20 FEP 29 (CA 1, 1979), citing Furnco Constr. Corp. v. Waters, 438 U.S. 567, 577, 17 FEP 1062, 1066 (1978).

[41]Lovelace v. Sherwin-Williams Co., 681 F.2d 230, 29 FEP 172 (CA 4, 1982); Halsell v. Kimberly-Clark Corp., 683 F.2d 285, 29 FEP 1185 (CA 8, 1982), *cert. denied*, 459 U.S. 1205 (1983).

corporation following the discharge of the employee who had filled that position precluded the 63-year-old plaintiff from meeting the *McDonnell Douglas* requirement that he show he was replaced by a younger person or that the position was kept open.[42] Other employment actions such as promotion, demotion, or RIF involve factual situations that may preclude the plaintiff(s) from meeting *McDonnell Douglas*. The courts have attempted to apply that test flexibly— in a manner that requires showing some *nexus* between age and the adverse action that would give rise to an inference of unlawful motive, while simultaneously allowing for situations where the inability to meet the replacement requirement of the *McDonnell Douglas* test does not work an injustice.

The Fifth Circuit upheld a finding of a district court that a prima facie case was not established by a 47-year-old job applicant who was unsuccessful in obtaining the secretarial job she sought since no vacancy existed at the precise moment she applied for the job.[43] A former nursing home administrator who resigned upon being asked to start training her replacement one-and-one-half years before her projected retirement, rather than the six-month training period she thought was sufficient, failed to establish her prima facie case of constructive discharge, the Second Circuit has ruled.[44] According to the court, the nursing home's decision was reasonable, the administrator was not faced with a loss of pay or a change in title, and she had been asked to stay on as general supervisor to her successor with leeway to pursue her own interests in nursing home-state agency relations. Both these cases illustrate where plaintiffs failed to establish the all important *nexus* between their age and the alleged unlawful discrimination.

A complex situation involved the termination of a 57-year-old attorney who lost his job as a result of a reorganization. A district court observed that the plaintiff was not required, in establishing his prima facie case, to prove that he had applied for but failed to receive a specific position that he was qualified to assume.[45] The fact that two attorneys who were over 40 years old received offers to remain with the employer after it acquired their company did not make it unnecessary for the 57-year-old lawyer to establish his prima facie case, the court added.[46] It concluded that the plaintiff had to show that he sought to be placed somewhere in the organization but did not receive such placement, that younger individuals of similar qualifications received positions or offers of positions, and that, given his broad range of experience, he was qualified for at least some of the positions awarded to his younger counterparts or to attorneys hired from the outside.[47] An employee failed to provide any evidence from which it could be inferred that the employer more likely than not had terminated him based on age, according to a district court in Illinois, where he could not point to discriminatory statements, where statistics showed that the RIF which caused his layoff affected younger employees more severely

[42]Stanojev v. Ebasco Servs., Inc., 643 F.2d 914, 25 FEP 355 (CA 2, 1981).
[43]Marshall v. Airpax Elecs., 595 F.2d 1043, 19 FEP 1286 (CA 5, 1979).
[44]Pena v. Brattleboro Retreat, 702 F.2d 322, 31 FEP 198 (CA 2, 1983).
[45]Fugate v. Allied Corp., 582 F. Supp. 780, 34 FEP 1745 (ND Ill, 1984).
[46]*Id.*
[47]*Id.*, 34 FEP at 1748.

than older employees, and he did not show that he would have kept his job under the employer's own criteria.[48]

In *U.S. Postal Service Board of Governors v. Aikens*,[49] the Supreme Court ruled that a plaintiff seeking to establish a prima facie case under *McDonnell Douglas* need not establish his relative qualifications but only that he was qualified for the job. *Aikens* involved a black Postal Service employee and the Court observed that the plaintiff had clearly established a prima facie case in the trial court, that the case was fully tried on the merits, and that the district court erroneously focused on the question of prima facie case rather than directly on the question of discrimination.[50] The *Aikens* decision points up the confusion that exists concerning the plaintiff's ultimate burden—the burden of persuading the trier of fact that his explanation is more likely or that the employer's proffered explanation is unworthy of credence. Where both parties have met their burden, the court must decide which party's explanation of the employer's motivation is the more believable. This is the latest pronouncement on the *McDonnell Douglas-Burdine* line of reasoning concerning burden of proof. The lower courts will invariably discover new wrinkles in the course of applying *Aikens*.

Articulation of Nondiscriminatory Reason

Once the employee/job applicant has established his prima facie case, the employer must "articulate" some "legitimate, nondiscriminatory" reason for the employment decision under one of the Act's exemptions.[51] But there is some confusion as to whether the employer has a burden of merely going forward to produce some evidence while the plaintiff retains the ultimate burden, or whether the burden then shifts to the employer to prove that the proffered reason was the real reason for the employment decision. Some courts follow the Title VII analysis that the employer assumes only the *burden of production*,[52] while other courts regard the burden of persuasion as having shifted entirely to the employer.[53] The majority of courts appear to follow the Title VII approach.[54] (See also discussion, "Proof of Pretext," in this chapter.)

During a RIF, an employer terminated an older employee on a certain project and retained a younger employee; the older employee brought an ADEA action and established a prima facie case. The district court determined that the employer had in fact articulated a legitimate, nondiscriminatory reason when it relied on the older worker's performance of his job and his managerial

---

[48]Matthews v. Allis-Chalmers, 35 FEP 1404 (ND Ill, 1984).

[49]460 U.S. 711, 31 FEP 609 (1983).

[50]*Id.*

[51]Spagnuolo v. Whirlpool Corp., 641 F.2d 1109, 1112, 25 FEP 376, 378 (CA 4, 1981), *cert. denied*, 454 U.S. 860, 26 FEP 1688 (1981), citing Board of Trustees of Keene State College v. Sweeney, 439 U.S. 24, 18 FEP 520 (1978).

[52] Loeb v. Textron, Inc., *supra* note 40; Marshall v. Goodyear Tire & Rubber Co., 554 F.2d 730, 15 FEP 139 (CA 5, 1977); Laugesen v. Anaconda Co., 510 F.2d 307, 10 FEP 567 (CA 6, 1975).

[53]Moses v. Falstaff Brewing Co., 550 F.2d 1113, 14 FEP 813 (CA 8, 1977); Fellows v. Medford Corp., 16 FEP 764 (D Or, 1978).

[54]B. Schlei & P. Grossman, EMPLOYMENT DISCRIMINATION LAW (2nd ed.; Washington, D.C.: The Bureau of National Affairs, Inc., 1983), p. 500, note 134.

shortcomings.[55] This is a typical form of a legitimate, nondiscriminatory reason for an employment decision.

Most courts that follow the Title VII analysis of the employer's burden after the prima facie case is established require the employer to simply produce some tangible evidence of an objective nature that relates directly to the employee's/job applicant's inability to perform the job. Productivity standards, weight lifting requirements, and the like are typical legitimate, nondiscriminatory reasons that are often "articulated" by employers seeking to meet their burden of production. The airline industry has been engaged in a score of cases involving mandatory retirement of pilots and flight personnel, based on the perception and practice that the older worker (i.e., pilots over age 60) is more at risk, both to himself and to the passengers. However, this type of articulation is more in the nature of an affirmative defense, since the airline industry has not denied that the employment decision was based on age and that the individuals were within the protected age group and were replaced by younger individuals. (For further information on affirmative defenses, see this chapter at "Defenses.")

Defense of Business or Economic Necessity. In the employer's articulation of a legitimate, nondiscriminatory reason for the employment decision, there looms a difficult issue: the employer's economic or business need to implement that decision. The ADEA provides several statutory defenses to a finding of a violation of the Act, such as BFOQs and RFOAs (see "Defenses," this chapter), but it is silent on the claim of economic necessity.

An airline enforced a rule prohibiting downbidding that had a disparate impact on younger and older pilots. Although it forbade the movement of both to lower positions, it operated also to deprive the older pilots of an opportunity for continued employment, while having no such effect on the younger pilot. The airline claimed that this rule was based on business necessity to ensure the safety of its flight crew. The Ninth Circuit rejected this claim, since it was refuted by a jury determination at the trial court that the medical evidence at trial did not establish age as a bona fide occupational qualification, and therefore, there was no business necessity for the rule.[56] (This issue is often tied to the statutory defense of the "Bona Fide Occupational Qualification" or "BFOQ Defense," discussed later in this chapter.) An airline refused to hire older pilots because it alleged that the "burdensome effects" would threaten its economic health. The Sixth Circuit, however, applying Title VII case law, ruled that economic considerations cannot be the basis for the BFOQ defense under the Act.[57] The airline relied on two separate cost-related defenses: its pilot progression system and the "untraining" of pilots with significant experience. The Sixth Circuit emphasized that economic considerations cannot be the basis for a BFOQ.[58] As to the "untraining" of experienced pilots, the

---

[55] Matthews v. Allis-Chalmers, 35 FEP 1404 (ND Ill, 1984).

[56] Criswell v. Western Air Lines, Inc., 709 F.2d 544, 32 FEP 1204, 1211 (CA 9, 1983), aff'd, 472 U.S. ____, 37 FEP 1829 (1985).

[57] Smallwood v. United Air Lines, Inc., 661 F.2d 303, 26 FEP 1655 (CA 4, 1981), citing City of Los Angeles v. Manhart, 435 U.S. 702, 716, 17 FEP 395 (1978).

[58] Id., relying on 29 CFR §860.103(h) (1980).

court observed that there was no reliable evidence that the airline's "crew concept" would be impaired by the sole factor of hiring Flight Officers, starting as Second Officers, over the age of 35.[59]

In asserting business or economic necessity as a defense to a charge of age discrimination, the defending party must produce more than economic or statistical evidence showing that retaining members of the protected class will injure the business; since the ADEA provides for other statutory defenses, any employer attempting to plead the business/economic necessity defense will need to show that employees' *age* brings them within the BFOQ/RFOA exemptions. But using the claim of business necessity as the sole basis for asserting the statutory defenses will not be acceptable to the courts.

Proof of Pretext

Once the employee has established his prima facie case, and the employer has articulated a legitimate, nondiscriminatory reason for the employment decision, the employee then has the opportunity to show that the employer's proffered reason is in fact a pretext for the actual age discrimination. The Supreme Court clarified *McDonnell Douglas* in 1981 with *Texas Department of Community Affairs v. Burdine (Burdine)*,[60] concerning the employer's efforts to rebut the employee's prima facie case, and the employee's opportunity to show that the employer's proffered reason was pretextual. In *Burdine*, the Court said:

(1) Establishment of a prima facie case eliminates most common nondiscriminatory reasons for an individual's rejection and, in effect, creates a presumption that the employer engaged in the unlawful discrimination alleged;

(2) The employer seeking to rebut the prima facie case must only raise a genuine issue of fact as to whether it discriminated, by setting forth through admissible evidence the reasons for the rejection;

(3) Introduction of such evidence by the employer does not preclude the district court from considering evidence on which the prima facie case was based, as well as inferences properly drawn from such evidence, in considering whether the employer's explanation is pretextual;

(4) The employer's evidence should be evaluated in terms of whether it presents a legitimate reason for the employment decision and frames the factual issue with sufficient clarity so that the employee will have a full and fair opportunity to demonstrate pretext; and

(5) The employee whose prima facie case has been rebutted may show that the employer's proffered reason was not the true reason and may prove that he has been the victim of intentional discrimination by showing that the discriminatory reason more likely motivated the employer or by showing that the employer's proffered reason was not credible.[61]

---

[59]*Id. But see* Coburn v. Pan Am. Airways, 711 F.2d 339, 32 FEP 843 (CA DC, 1983), *cert. denied*, 464 U.S. 994 (1983).

[60]450 U.S. 248, 25 FEP 113 (1981).

[61]*Id.*

In establishing the respective burdens, *Burdine* also permitted the employer to choose among equally qualified candidates for employment/promotion, as long as the selection of one individual over another was not based on any unlawful consideration.[62]

Finally, the Supreme Court shed further light on the plaintiff's ultimate burden after the employer has articulated some legitimate nondiscriminatory reason for the employment decision. In *U.S. Postal Service Board of Governors v. Aikens*,[63] the Court held that the plaintiff ultimately bears the burden of persuading the trier of fact that his explanation is more likely or that the employer's proffered explanation is unworthy of credence. Under this reasoning, it appears that where both parties have met their burden, the court must decide which party's explanation of the employer's motive is the more believable. This is the latest pronouncement on what is becoming the *McDonnell Douglas-Burdine-Aikens* reasoning.

Proof of pretext may be demonstrated in many ways, both directly and inferentially, through circumstantial evidence. The Third Circuit has observed that an employee's successful demonstration that the employer's proffered reason was pretextual was itself equivalent to a finding that the employer *intentionally* discriminated, echoing *Burdine*.[64] In that case, the court noted that the employer had terminated the four oldest and most highly paid salesmen in the plaintiff's district, that the plaintiff's performance was superior to that of younger men who had been retained, and that an employer official told another discharged salesman who was the same age as the plaintiff that the employer was anxious to get younger and more aggressive people in the field; the court concluded that the employer's explanations and testimony were internally inconsistent and not credible.[65]

A district court has reasoned that an employer who presented a business justification for a discharge decision was not entitled to summary judgment, since such an explanation merely destroys the legally mandatory inference of discrimination arising from the employee's initial evidence, and joins the issues for resolution on all of the evidence by the trier of fact.[66] The Ninth Circuit has also ruled that an employee's assertion that he intends to prove pretext by challenging the credibility of the employer's witness on cross-examination is insufficient to produce specific, substantial evidence of pretext in the employer's explanation, and summary judgment was granted to the employer.[67]

Similarly, an airline that terminated its reservations supervisor during a RIF produced evidence that the RIF's purpose was to reduce costs and prevent individual hardship, according to the District of Columbia Circuit Court.[68] The supervisor failed to prove that the airline's proffered reason was pretextual, the court ruled; the fact that both employees terminated from that region were within the protected age group was pure coincidence, the airline's attempt to

---

[62]*Id.*

[63]460 U.S. 711, 31 FEP 609 (1983).

[64]Duffy v. Wheeling Pittsburgh Steel Corp., 735 F.2d 1393, 35 FEP 246 (CA 3, 1984).

[65]*Id.*

[66]Grecco v. Spang & Co., 527 F. Supp. 978, 31 FEP 360 (WD Pa, 1981).

[67]Steckl v. Motorola, Inc., 703 F.2d 392, 31 FEP 705 (CA 9, 1983).

[68]Coburn v. Pan Am. World Airways, *supra* note 59.

induce managers aged 55–65 to retire early was a fair attempt to reduce its costs, two younger employees employed as trainers were not included in the supervisor's peer group analysis because their positions were different from that of the supervisor, and evidence did not support the claim that there were inconsistencies between the prior evaluations and the RIF evaluation.[69]

The same court subsequently declared that a federal employee could prevail in his ADEA action by demonstrating that the federal agency's explanation for his nonpromotion was a sham and by offering additional circumstantial evidence of age discrimination in the agency, notwithstanding the claim that he could prevail only by both discrediting the agency's explanation and by providing particularized evidence of actual discrimination in the specific employment decision at issue.[70] The court added that the employee need not in all cases submit additional evidence concerning the particular employment decision at issue in order to show that age was a determining factor in the decision.[71] However, since the employee had in fact presented additional evidence of age discrimination within the agency, the court was not required to go into further detail on this point.

The means of showing pretext are as varied as the forms that age discrimination may take; it is incumbent on the plaintiff to convince the court through objective evidence that the proffered reason is simply not to be believed in any rational sense because of its context in the employment situation, under *McDonnell Douglas-Burdine-Aikens*.

Age as a Determining Factor

The courts have attempted to establish a balance in the degree of proof needed to establish age discrimination, once the *nexus* has been established. To that end, courts have refused to require employees to show that age was the *sole* factor for the employment decision,[72] but have required them to show that age was a *determining* factor ("but for" causation test) in the employment decision.[73] The Second Circuit was faced with a mixed motive discharge case, and a claim by both parties that the standard to be applied to the employee's proof of age discrimination was in conflict: the so-called "Loeb" rule of showing that age was a "causative" or "determinative" factor in the discharge, conflicted with the Laugesen/Cova standard that age was a "determining" factor that "but for" the employer's unlawful motive the employee would not have been discharged.[74] The Second Circuit reasoned, however, that there was no conflict: "If age discrimination was a 'factor . . . (which) made a difference,' then the employee's fortunes would have been 'different' without the

[69]*Id.*, 32 FEP at 846.

[70]Krodel v. Young, 748 F.2d 701, 36 FEP 468, 472 (CA DC, 1984).

[71]*Id.*, citing Burdine, *supra* note 60.

[72]Kelly v. American Standard, Inc., 640 F.2d 974, 984–85, 25 FEP 94, 102 (CA 9, 1981).

[73]Loeb v. Textron, Inc., 600 F.2d 1003, 20 FEP 29 (CA 1, 1979).

[74]Geller v. Markham, 635 F.2d 1027, 24 FEP 920, 925–26 (CA 2, 1980), citing Loeb v. Textron, *supra* note 73, Laugesen v. Anaconda, 510 F.2d 307, 10 FEP 567 (CA 6, 1975), and Cova v. Coca Cola Bottling Co., 574 F.2d 958, 17 FEP 448 (CA 8, 1978).

inatory action and age discrimination was therefore a 'but for' cause of the result that did take place.''[75]

The *McDonnell Douglas* standard, as refined by *Burdine* and *Aikens* (see this chapter, "The Prima Facie Case"), need not be applied where the employee produces direct evidence that the employer announced, admitted, or otherwise unmistakably indicated that age was a determining factor in the employee's treatment, according to the Fourth Circuit.[76] This same principle holds true where the employee produces circumstantial evidence that includes, but is not limited to, proof of his general qualifications, from which an inference of age discrimination may rationally be drawn independently of any presumption.[77] The court observed that the *McDonnell Douglas* proof scheme with its first stage presumption favoring claimants may be employed in resolving the motivational issue, but in some cases it would be unnecessary, and in other situations it would be improper.[78] An airline maintained a policy that age-60 captains seeking to downbid to the position of second officer to avoid mandatory retirement are the only employees not permitted to maintain employee status until a vacancy occurs. A district court ruled that this was sufficient to establish the likelihood that age is a "determining factor" in the airline's failure to consider the pilots' downbid applications and accommodate them in the same manner as it treats other employees.[79] In RIF situations, the Sixth Circuit has determined, a plaintiff must come forward with additional direct, circumstantial, or statistical evidence that "age was a factor" in his termination.[80] The District of Columbia Circuit has given the plaintiff credit for establishing his prima facie case and rebutting as pretextual the employer's proffered reason for the employment decision, by not requiring additional evidence concerning the particular employment decision at issue in order to demonstrate that age was a "determining factor" in the decision.[81] The federal agency had argued that it merely made a poor business judgment when it promoted the "better candidate," and that this is an insufficient basis on which to find age discrimination; however, the appeals court observed that the district court correctly found the proffered reason to be a sham and that the circumstantial evidence indicated that age was a "determining factor."[82]

Disparate Impact

The Second Circuit has observed that the disparate or adverse impact theory developed under Title VII can be applied to age discrimination cases involving nonscored objective criteria.[83] A school district maintained a facially neutral

---

[75]Geller v. Markham, *supra* note 74, 24 FEP at 926.

[76]Cline v. Roadway Express, 689 F.2d 481, 29 FEP 1365 (CA 4, 1982).

[77]*Id.*, 29 FEP at 1368.

[78]*Id.*

[79]Stone v. Western Air Lines, 544 F. Supp. 32, 32 FEP 1152 (CD Cal, 1982), *aff'd subnom.* Criswell v. Western Airlines, Inc., 709 F.2d 544, 32 FEP 1204 (CA 9, 1983), *aff'd*, 472 U.S. ____, 37 FEP 1829 (1985).

[80]LaGrant v. G & W Mfg. Co., 36 FEP 465, 468 (CA 6, 1984).

[81]Krodel v. Young, 748 F.2d 701, 36 FEP 468 (CA DC, 1984).

[82]*Id.*

[83]Geller v. Markham, *supra* note 74.

policy of not hiring teachers with more than five years of experience, the purpose being to reduce salary costs. But the plaintiff argued and the district court found that the policy had an adverse effect on older teachers to the degree that more than 92 percent of teachers within the protected age group were affected, while only 60 percent of teachers under age 40 were excluded by the policy.[84]

Similarly, another group of employees successfully argued that the statistical evidence showed that there was an unlawful motive in the application of the subjective judgments of supervisors in making layoff decisions, in view of the fact that workers in the range of 52 to 64 years old were selected, and this represented a pattern of discriminatory action.[85] The Tenth Circuit observed that the number of workers within the affected group of laid off employees was more than twice their percentage in the work force.[86]

An airline's policy of not considering downbid applications for the position of second officer by captains nearing the mandatory retirement age of 60 if no such position was open at the time of the bid establishes a prima facie case of disparate impact, according to a federal court, since age-60 captains seeking to downbid are the only individuals who are severed from the airline, rather than being allowed to maintain their employee status until such time as a vacancy occurs.[87] The court noted that the airline had arranged via the collective bargaining agreement to allow other second officers whose positions had been eliminated to maintain their employee status so that they could submit bids when openings occur.

An employee who challenged the employer's use of subjective criteria of "flexibility, production ability, and frequent oral communication" was required to show that these criteria produce a significant discriminatory impact on the protected class, according to the Ninth Circuit.[88] The court ruled that the employee had failed to offer any "statistically significant" evidence of disparate impact, where her statistical survey of the "five or six individuals doing basically the same job as clerical specialist" was not a reliable indication of a significant adverse impact on a protected group.[89] The court concluded that the employee's claim was in fact one of discriminatory treatment, notwithstanding the language of her complaint.

At least one authority has argued that the adverse impact doctrine should not be extended to ADEA actions, in view of the legislative history, inconsistent application of the statute to employees versus applicants, and other public policy considerations.[90]

---

[84]*Id.*

[85]EEOC v. Sandia Corp., 639 F.2d 600, 620–23, 23 FEP 799, 815–17 (CA 10, 1980).

[86]*Id.*

[87]*Supra* note 79.

[88]Yartzoff v. Oregon, 36 FEP 16 (CA 9, 1984).

[89]*Id.*

[90]Stacy, *A Case Against Extending the Adverse Impact Doctrine to ADEA*, Vol. 10, No. 3, EMPLOYEE REL. L.J. 437 (1985).

Defenses

The Act provides several defenses to a charge of unlawful age discrimination. Section 4(f) says that it is not unlawful for an employer, employment agency, or labor organization to:

"(1) Take any action otherwise prohibited . . . where age is a bona fide occupational qualification reasonably necessary to the normal operation of the particular business; or

"(2) Take any action otherwise prohibited . . . where the differentiation is based on reasonable factors other than age;

"(3) Observe the terms of a bona fide seniority system or any bona fide employee benefit plan . . . which is not a subterfuge to evade the purposes of the Act; or

"(4) Discharge or otherwise discipline an individual for good cause."[91]

The first defense, the bona fide occupational defense, is usually referred to as "BFOQ" and constitutes a true affirmative defense in that the charged party relying on a BFOQ defense is admitting that age played a part in the employment decision, but that there was some bona fide job requirement that precluded someone who is the plaintiff's age from filling those requirements.

The second defense, "reasonable factors other than age," is usually referred to as the "RFOA" defense, and it, like the fourth defense for "good cause," represents a claim that the employee/job applicant's performance, irrespective of age, was inadequate and justified the employment decision on those inadequacies.

The third defense, bona fide seniority systems or bona fide employee benefit plans, operate in the same manner as the BFOQ defense, where the charged party essentially concedes a prima facie case of age discrimination, but argues that there was a legitimate basis for the employment decision nonetheless. Because the "good cause" defense is more a creature of labor law than employment discrimination law, only the BFOQ, RFOA, bona fide seniority system, and bona fide employee benefit plan defenses will be discussed.

BFOQ Defense

The bona fide occupational qualification, or "BFOQ" defense, is probably the richest source of material for law review articles and litigation. Asserted as an affirmative defense, the BFOQ claim constitutes an admission by the charged party that age was in fact a determining factor in the employment decision. However, pursuant to the ADEA, the charged party also avers that age in this instance is "reasonably necessary to the normal operation of the particular business."[92] This statutory language constitutes the all important nexus between the charging party's age and the employer's legitimate basis for the employment decision. It is this nexus that Congress intended to require of the employer, in order to uphold an otherwise unlawful action against an employee or job applicant. And it is this nexus which is precisely the source of most confusion and litigation, since the validity of the employment decision

---

[91]29 U.S.C. §623(f).
[92]*Id.*

will stand or fall, depending on whether the trier of fact credits the proffered business reason or not. Incidentally, this "business" based reason for an employment decision should not be confused with a purely "economic" decision affecting members of the protected age group. (See this chapter at "Defense of Business or Economic Necessity.")

The charged party's responsibility to establish the nexus between the age of the charging party and the normal operation of the business arises from the charged party's claim of the BFOQ defense: if the employer wants this shield, he must prove he is entitled to it. An employer's failure to establish the nexus deprives the employer of the opportunity to use the BFOQ defense. This logical interpretation of the Act was the basis for a decision by the Fourth Circuit in 1981.

In *Smallwood v. United Air Lines*,[93] the Fourth Circuit examined the airline's policy against hiring pilots over age 35. The airline claimed that the policy was based on safety considerations, and that extensive medical examinations— far more intensive than those required by the Federal Aviation Administration—were effective in detecting potentially disabling medical conditions. However, the Fourth Circuit ruled:

> "Likewise, United's medical evidence cannot establish that its age requirements are a BFOQ . . . . Under United's pilot progression policy, Smallwood, if employed, would probably remain a Second Officer until his mandatory retirement at age 60.[7] It is undisputed that a significant number of United's pilots maintain Second Officer status from hire to mandatory requirement to age 60. Not only is there no significant evidence tending to prove "that all or substantially all persons within the class would be unable to perform safely and efficiently," *Arritt, supra*, but the employment of Smallwood would not create a new class or group of pilots in this respect—he would simply become part of a group of second officers 35 years of age or over, whose continued status as pilots strongly tends to disprove United's contention that the employment of pilots in this age group violates their air safety standards. Even were this not so, United's attempt to establish a BFOQ is further frustrated by the second prong of the Arritt test. United has provisions in place for the medical testing of its pilots of all ages. United's expert medical witness Dr. Kidera testified at trial that while the FAA mandates periodic physical examinations of all Flight Officers, United's company physical far exceeds the FAA's minimum requirements. Aimed at a preventive medicine approach, United includes extensive laboratory tests, blood screening, electrocardiograms, urinalysis, chest x-rays and diabetes screening. Examinations are given to Captains every 6 months and to First and Second Officers annually. The scope and depth of each examination is identical across each flight crew position. It was conclusively shown at trial that United's physical examination program was effective in detecting potentially disabling medical conditions, and that future cardiovascular problems could be detected with a high degree of predictability. These preventive medical examinations must have the same degree of predictability as to future medical disabilities for newly-hired 48-year-old pilots from other airlines as they would for career United pilots. In short, United's evidence at trial, while probative of the incidence of medical problems in pilots of advanced age and of the effectiveness of its own examination system, failed to show a relationship between a maximum age-at-hire limitation and airline safety. It has failed to show the impossibility or impracticality of dealing with applicants individually."[94]

---

[7][Footnote omitted.]

---

[93]661 F.2d 303, 26 FEP 1655 (CA 4, 1981), *cert. denied*, 456 U.S. 1007 (1982).
[94]*Id.*, 26 FEP at 1658–59.

The BFOQ defense usually arises in the context of public safety, and usually is proffered in the guise of some physiological problem, such as a physical inability to perform or a medical incapacity due to age. In order to defend against a charge of age discrimination under the BFOQ defense, an employer must meet a two-prong test; the burden is on the employer to show

> "(1) that the BFOQ is . . . reasonably necessary to the essence of the business . . .; and (2) that the employer has reasonable cause, i.e., a factual basis, for believing that all or substantially all persons within the class . . . would be unable to perform safely and efficiently the duties of the job involved, or that it is impossible or impractical to deal with persons over the age limit on an individualized basis."[95]

A large number of BFOQ cases involve the air line industry flight personnel and law enforcement and firefighter personnel, since these positions have obvious and significant public safety ramifications. The "safety factor" is the linchpin in these decisions: if the employer's evidence is sufficient to show some degree of decreased effectiveness or some degeneration in performance, the employer must then show that this affects the normal, i.e., "safe" operation of the business. However, this safety factor varies, with an air line pilot having a higher risk factor than a driver of a municipal trash collection truck. And the courts have recognized this disparity, in formulating the *nexus* standard of "reasonable necessity" and "essence of the employer's business." Interestingly enough, the first major test of the BFOQ defense involved bus drivers.

In *Usery v. Tamiami Trail Tours, Inc.*,[96] the Fifth Circuit upheld a bus company's policy against hiring individuals over age 40 for certain bus assignments based on the state of medical science at that time, and the employer's reasonable reliance on the available data. The court declared:

> "Tamiami introduced testimony by both medical and transportation experts. In particular the testimony of Dr. Harold Brandaleone, an eminent medical expert in the field of transportation and motor vehicle accidents, was heavily weighted by the Court. Dr. Brandaleone testified that while chronological age could not be isolated as a factor automatically indicating that an individual could not adjust to the rigors of the extra board schedule, medical science could not accurately separate chronological from functional or physiological age. According to him, (1) certain physiological and psychological changes that accompany the aging process decrease the person's ability to drive safely and (2) even the most refined examinations cannot detect all of these changes. In his opinion 40 years of age was by no means an arbitrary cutoff to enable bus companies to screen out such impairments.[31]
> "In addition to this medical testimony, Tamiami called Dr. Ernest G. Cox, former Safety Director for the Bureau of Motor Carriers in the Interstate Commerce Commission and later Deputy Director of the Bureau of Motor Carrier Safety in the Department of Transportation to explain the strains on intercity drivers and the importance of the driver's relationship to traffic safety. Dr. Cox expressed the unequivocal opinion that the maximum age qualification was essential to the normal and safe operation of intercity bus lines.
> "Lastly, Tamiami called five of its current drivers—both senior and extra board juniors—to describe their experiences with the driving conditions of the extra board and regular runs. It was clear from their testimony that acquiring

---

[95]Arritt v. Grisell, 567 F.2d 1267, 1271, 17 FEP 753 (CA 4, 1977).
[96]531 F.2d 224, 12 FEP 1233 (CA 5, 1976).

enough seniority to get off the extra board was a primary goal of every driver. Despite their experience, the regular run senior drivers emphatically believed that they could not return to the extra board and still maintain the safety of their passengers.

"In contrast to Dr. Brandaleone's medical testimony, the Government relied primarily on the rebuttal testimony of Dr. Abraham J. Mirkin, an expert on automotive accidents, who dismissed any relationship between age and one's ability to drive a vehicle safely, and Kenneth Pierson, Dr. Cox' successor as Deputy Director of the Bureau of Motor Carrier Safety of DOT, who believed that the physical examination, training program and road test that all new drivers are subjected to were sufficient to screen out those applicants of any age who would not be qualified to be safe bus drivers.

"The key question is whether a sufficient factual basis for Tamiami's case has been demonstrated by the catalogued strains and pressures of the extra board on the drivers who must serve it, the evidence regarding the inevitable physiological degeneration that accompanies age, and in particular the testimony of Dr. Brandaleone—which the District Judge was entitled to credit fully—that the available tests cannot distinguish those drivers not yet affected by the more crucial age-related accident-causing impairments like loss of stamina, etc. Whatever might have been our finding were we deciding this issue *de novo*, the District Court found that examinations cannot detect the relevant physiological and psychological changes "with sufficient reliability to meet the special safety obligations of motor carriers of passengers." Hodgson v. Tamiami Trail Tours, Inc., S.D. Fla., 1972, 4 E.P.D. ¶ 7795, at 6051, 4 FEP Cases 728 at 732. This is a finding of fact and, therefore, may not be set aside unless "clearly erroneous." Fed.R.Civ.P. 52(a). Because of the testimony of Dr. Brandaleone, we do not believe the District Court's finding can be so categorized.[32]" [97]

[31–32][Footnotes omitted.]

The Seventh Circuit has observed that the existence of an airline's claim of a BFOQ is determined by objective evidence concerning the role played by second officers and medical science's ability to detect and predict medical conditions in those over age 60, not by the airline's subjective beliefs or good faith.[98] The physical evidence produced through medical science can be a sufficient basis for an employer, and a reviewing court, to find an employment decision justified, or at least "reasonable" within the meaning of the BFOQ defense. The Seventh Circuit's recognition that objective evidence concerning the role of aggrieved individuals (second officers) and medical science's ability to detect and predict medical conditions in those over the age limit echoes the *Tamiami* court's deferral to any medical evidence that would support or rebut the employer's claim of having a reasonable basis for believing that its age limit was justified. The Seventh Circuit added an important caveat to its deliberations when it said: "a once valid BFOQ may lose its justification with advances in medical science."[99]

Similarly, the Ninth Circuit ruled, with approval, that

"the job qualifications which the employer invokes to justify his discrimination must be *reasonably necessary* to the essence of his business. The greater the safety factor, measured by the likelihood of harm and the probable severity of

---

[97]*Id*. at 236, 12 FEP at 1242–43.
[98]Monroe v. United Air Lines, 34 FEP 1622, 1627–28 (CA 7, 1984).
[99]*Id*. at 1630.

that harm in case of an accident, the more stringent may be the job qualifications designed to insure (safety)."[100]

Subsequently, the battle lines shifted to a detailed examination of the BFOQ language and what Congress intended by the term "reasonably necessary." The Ninth Circuit upheld jury instructions that the BFOQ defense was available only if the employer's behavior was "reasonably necessary"; the trial court did not err in rejecting the employer's contention that the "rational basis in fact" standard was sufficient. It concluded that the term "reasonably necessary" does not require a legal definition apart from its ordinary sense.[101]

In the public sector, a similar battle was being fought. A municipality that enforced a mandatory retirement age of 55 for its firefighters asserted the BFOQ defense, and used federal and state legislation to buttress its claim. But the Seventh Circuit rejected the defense, ruling:

(1) The existence of a federal law requiring U.S. Government firefighters to retire at age 55 does not automatically establish the municipality's BFOQ defense, where the two types of firefighters operate under different working conditions and perform significantly different job functions;

(2) Mandatory retirement schemes approved by Congress for federal government employees need only meet the rationality requirement of the Constitution, and are not subject to the strict requirements of the ADEA;

(3) State legislation setting age 55 as the "normal" retirement date for protective service employees for the purpose of determining pension eligibility is not automatically valid, in view of 1978 amendments to the Act abolishing the exception for compulsory retirement made pursuant to a bona fide retirement plan, since this would put the state and local governments in a better position under the Act than private employers, and it would require employees to refute the BFOQ defense;

(4) The municipality must show that the age limit is reasonably related to the "essential operations" of its business and must demonstrate either that a factual basis exists for believing that all or substantially all persons over the age limit would be unable to perform their job duties effectively or that it is impossible or impractical to determine job fitness on an individualized basis; and

(5) Neither a subjective belief that the aging process would take its toll particularly quickly on the physical and mental skills of protective service employees nor a need to have a definite and financially feasible age on which to base the retirement benefit formula supports the municipality's contention that age 55 is a valid BFOQ for retiring its firefighters.[102]

The Seventh Circuit added that neither economic factors nor any speculative or subjective belief about the lessening capability of older employees to handle the rigors of a physically demanding job can be the basis for a BFOQ, and the fact that the protective service is a safety-related business does not relieve the municipality from its burden of justifying the particular age limit adopted.[103]

[100]Harriss v. Pan Am. Airways, Inc., 649 F.2d 670, 676, 24 FEP 947 (CA 9, 1980), citing Usery v. Tamiami Trail Tours, Inc., *supra* note 96.

[101]Criswell v. Western Air Lines, 709 F.2d 544, 32 FEP 1204, 1209 (CA 9, 1983).

[102]Orzel v. City of Wauwatosa Fire Dep't, 697 F.2d 743, 30 FEP 1070 (CA 7, 1983).

[103]*Id.,* 30 FEP at 1078–79.

On June 17, 1985, the Supreme Court issued two rulings on the BFOQ defense, specifically addressing the meaning of "reasonably necessary," in the context of public safety considerations.

In the first decision, *Western Air Lines v. Criswell*,[104] the Supreme Court unanimously ruled that the BFOQ exception is extremely narrow. In that case, two captains sought to avoid the Federal Aviation Administration's retirement-at-60 rule by obtaining reassignment as flight engineers. The airline argued that safety made retirement at age 60 a BFOQ for flight engineers. The Court endorsed the standard applied in *Usery v. Tamiami Trail Tours*[105] that the age restriction must be "reasonably necessary" to further the overriding interest in public safety by showing that (1) a factual basis exists for believing that all or substantially all persons over the age limit would be unable to perform the duties of the job in question safely and efficiently or (2) determining job fitness of older employees on an individualized basis would be impossible or highly impractical.

The Court observed that the FAA's age-60 rule was adopted for safety reasons and is relevant to the BFOQ defense, but the rule is not conclusive. The FAA, Western, and other airlines all acknowledge that the requirements for the flight engineer position are less rigorous than for a pilot, the Court added.

The "reasonable necessity" standard does not mean "reasonableness," the Court determined. Because of the impossibility of resolving medical disputes with certainty, the airline contended that it need only establish a "rational basis" in fact for believing that persons lacking suitable job qualifications could not be identified on an individual basis. However, the Court discerned, this would amount to instructing the jury to decide the case in the airline's favor. The proposed standard is inconsistent with the structure of the ADEA, which contemplates that age discrimination cases will be resolved by a jury on a case-by-case basis, and also with the preference for individual evaluation expressed in the language and legislative history of the ADEA, the Court concluded.[106]

In the second decision, *Johnson v. Baltimore*,[107] the Supreme Court reversed the Fourth Circuit's decision and unanimously ruled that the City of Baltimore's municipal code requiring that firefighters retire as early as age 55 violates the ADEA. The municipal code established an age range of between 55 and 70 years old for mandatory retirement for its firefighters. There was no factual showing that age was a BFOQ for the firefighters, but the Fourth Circuit held that the city nonetheless was entitled to the BFOQ defense as a matter of law.[108] The court relied on the federal civil service statute which generally requires federal firefighters to retire at age 55, in holding that retirement at age 55 for state and local firefighters was proper.[109]

---

[104]472 U.S. ____, 37 FEP 1829 (1985).
[105]*Supra* note 96.
[106]*Supra* note 104.
[107]731 F.2d 209, 34 FEP 1839 (CA 4, 1983), *rev'd*, 472 U.S. ____, 37 FEP 1839 (1985).
[108]*Id.*
[109]*Id.*

The Supreme Court declared: "almost four decades of legislative history establish that Congress at no time has indicated that the federal retirement age for federal firefighters is based on a determination that age 55 is a bona fide occupational qualification."[110] A court facing an ADEA challenge to an age limit for firefighters would err if it gave "any weight, much less conclusive weight, to the federal retirement provision," the Court concluded.[111]

The proposed "rational basis in fact" standard would have given employers almost *carte blanche* in devising limits and rules that could be used as a pretext for age discrimination. Similarly, rejecting the federal firefighter retirement age prevents state and local agencies from circumventing the ADEA merely by pointing to a federal standard, without regard to whether the standard constitutes a BFOQ under the Act.

The Court has created a symmetry under the ADEA, since it has established that the BFOQ exception is to be read narrowly, and the "willful" violation standard for imposing liquidated damages is also to be read narrowly.[112]

Although the Supreme Court has illuminated the narrow scope of the BFOQ, there still remain questions over the meaning of the BFOQ within any particular occupation or business. A state police regulation requiring the mandatory retirement of all "uniformed" individuals age 50 and over provided the First Circuit with an opportunity to shed light on the meaning of what is a bona fide "occupational qualification" and the meaning of a "particular business." In *Mahoney v. Trabucco*,[113] the court said that "occupational qualification," in the context of a paramilitary uniformed force means a discrete and acknowledged vocation, rather than a desk assignment for an employee subject to all obligations and benefits of a quasi-military organization. A contrary interpretation permitting a particularistic analysis of the actual duties performed would raise immeasurable problems of morale, administration, litigation and adjudication, the court reasoned. The appeals court approved an approach that recognizes the need to focus not only on the "particular business" for whose normal operation the BFOQ may be reasonably necessary, but also on genuine and well recognized occupations within that business. This approach will prevent the state from indiscriminately lumping together under one classification, many distinct vocations and occupations for which a low mandatory retirement age would be unjustified.[114]

This analysis does not mean that the BFOQ for private employers is different from the BFOQ available to public employers; it does mean that, at least in the context of a paramilitary or quasi-military organization, the public employer must be careful to assert the BFOQ vis-à-vis a discrete and recognized vocation, while at the same time avoid any temptation to "lump together" in one classification distinct vocations and occupations where the low retirement age is unjustified.

Age Stereotyping.   An important aspect of setting policy, and one that was

---

[110]*Id.*, 37 FEP at 1845 n. 107.

[111]*Id.*

[112]TWA v. Thurston, 466 U.S. 926 (1984) and 469 U.S. _____ (1985), 36 FEP 977 (1985).

[113]35 FEP 97 (CA 1, 1984).

[114]*Id.* at 102. *See also* Heiar v. Crawford County, 746 F.2d 1190, 35 FEP 1458 (CA 7, 1984).

intended to be eliminated by passage of the ADEA, is age stereotyping. This involves a policy determination that a class of individuals—in this case individuals in a certain age group—share a common characteristic or series of traits that are identifiable and have a negative effect on ability to fulfill job requirements. In 1976, the Fifth Circuit observed that such "class discrimination" that is otherwise unlawful is valid under a BFOQ defense, "if all or substantially all members of a class do not qualify, or if there is no practical way reliably to differentiate the qualified from the unqualified applicants in that class."[115] *Tamiami* illustrates the circumstances where such a class-based determination is valid. Where a class-based policy determination is unsupported, or supported by subjective evidence, this constitutes age stereotyping.

A municipality's determination that its firefighters must retire at age 55 was defended on the basis of a BFOQ safety-related defense. The Seventh Circuit cogently warned that overuse of the BFOQ defense involves the risk of reintroducing on a broader scale the very age stereotyping that the Act was designed to prevent, because age stereotyping frees the employer from making individualized judgments regarding the ability of older workers.[116]

Subjective opinions or stereotyped hunches of the employer regarding the effect of age on an employee's ability to perform particular job skills are not sufficient to establish age as a BFOQ, according to a district court.[117] The court observed that the "general truism that physical capabilities decrease as age increases is not sufficient evidence by itself" to establish the BFOQ; the employer must demonstrate some "specific, objective, or factual basis for its hiring qualifications based on age."[118]

Courts will generally not give much weight to any intuitive or subjective basis for a classwide policy or rule; there must be some objective evidence that supersedes the proscription against age stereotyping, and at least raises a question of fact.

RFOA Defense

The defense of a "reasonable factor other than age" or "RFOA" defense[119] requires a factual determination, on a case-by-case basis. The EEOC regulations provide an insight into what the agency regards as acceptable, that is, "reasonable" elements for distinguishing between positions available to protected individuals and those not available.[120]

One of the earliest cases to be decided under the RFOA defense, *Stringfellow v. Monsanto Co.*,[121] involved, inter alia, mandatory retirement of six employees by an employer whose process for selecting such retirees was called into question. The district court found no violation, since the employer selected

---

[115]Usery v. Tamiami Trail Tours, Inc., 531 F.2d 224, 236, 12 FEP 1233, 1241 (CA 5, 1976).

[116]Orzel v. City of Wauwatosa Fire Dep't, 697 F.2d 743, 30 FEP 1070 (CA 7, 1983).

[117]EEOC v. Pennsylvania, 36 FEP 234, 237–38 (MD Pa, 1984).

[118]*Id.*, citing EEOC v. University of Tex. Health Sciences Center, 710 F.2d 1091, 32 FEP 994 (CA 5, 1983).

[119]29 U.S.C. §623(f)(1).

[120]29 CFR §1625.7(e).

[121]320 F. Supp. 1175, 3 FEP 22 (WD Ark, 1970).

the retirees after evaluating their ability and job performance according to established criteria ordinarily used for such purposes, and the evaluation was based upon "reasonable factors other than age." The plan of evaluation used by the employer was to differentiate in selecting personnel on the basis of performance and ability to perform the jobs remaining after plant reduction and shutdown of some operations. The court found that the employer's action was reasonable, and was necessary in light of the plant reduction.

A district sales manager was discharged in violation of the Act, according to a district court, since the employer's RFOA defense was not supported by the evidence. The court observed that although the manager did not meet projections set up for his district, he did as well as or better than the company as a whole, both in total sales and in regular sales.[122] The district court contrasted the *Stringfellow* decision[123] and that employer's elaborate evaluation system with the defendant in this case, and the absence of anything other than a single performance appraisal apparently written after the employer decided to terminate the manager.

The Eighth Circuit upheld a finding that the employer's discharge of four sales department employees over the age of 53, each with over 29 years of experience, was based on reasonable factors other than age. The employer had shown, according to the appeals court, that one employee was a supervisor for servicing a major customer and that customer had made various complaints; that a second employee had had prior difficulties in warehouse work and had no major supervisory responsibility; that a third employee lacked any clear responsibilities at the time of a company reorganization; and that the fourth employee had recently been blinded in one eye.[124]

The employer's sole evidence of its reasons for the discharges came from the subjective explanation of a newly appointed general sales manager. The appeals court declared that the ADEA does not require use of any formal evaluation procedures to establish as a matter of law that the discharges were for reasons other than age.[125]

An employer asserting the RFOA defense must prove "by a preponderance of the evidence" that its employment decision was based on "reasonable factors other than age," and cannot simply attempt to meet the *McDonnell Douglas* standard of articulating a legitimate, nondiscriminatory defense, the Ninth Circuit has ruled.[126] The airline attempted to benefit from the defense without carrying the proper burden, the appeals court observed.[127]

The RFOA defense is in fact very close substantively to the "good cause" defense. Both defenses are based on some objective, ascertainable characteristics of the employee/job applicant that constitutes a deficiency in fulfilling the requirements of the assigned job. RFOA cases tend to read like "for cause" cases, such as employment decisions based on productivity standards, perfor-

---

[122]Schulz v. Hickok Mfg. Co., 358 F. Supp. 1208, 5 FEP 1010 (ND Ga, 1973).

[123]Stringfellow v. Monsanto Co., *supra* note 121.

[124]Cova v. Coca Cola Bottling Co., 574 F.2d 958, 17 FEP 448 (CA 8, 1978).

[125]*Id.*, 17 FEP at 451.

[126]Criswell v. Western Air Lines, 709 F.2d 544, 32 FEP 1204, 1211 (CA 9, 1983), *aff'd on other grounds*, 472 U.S. _____, 37 FEP 1829 (1985).

[127]*Id.*, *but see* Marshall v. Westinghouse Elec. Corp., 576 F.2d 588, 17 FEP 1288 (CA 5, 1978).

mance evaluations, personality differences, dishonesty, and so forth. The difference between the RFOA defense and a "good cause" defense may in fact be only the breadth of the employer's burden: "good cause" opens a plethora of avenues for the diligent plaintiff to pursue, whereas the RFOA defense limits the employer's burden to what the case law in that circuit states is necessary to justify the employment decision under the ADEA.

Bona Fide Seniority System

Since the cases have distinguished between the bona fide seniority system defense and the bona fide employee benefit plan (and its amendments), the discussion of these defenses will proceed accordingly. The ADEA provides that it is not unlawful to "observe the terms of a bona fide seniority system," which is not a "subterfuge" to evade the purposes of the Act.[128] The 1978 amendments added the qualification that no such seniority system shall require or permit involuntary retirement of any employee under 70 on the basis of age. Prior to the amendments, employers could lawfully require employees under 65 years of age to retire, if the system was not a subterfuge. There have been few cases litigated on this defense, since most if not all seniority systems favor the longer term, and hence older, worker.

Shortly after the 1978 amendments, an employer lowered the "normal" retirement age in its mandatory retirement plan from age 65 to age 62. A district court ruled that the plan was a "subterfuge" to evade the purposes of the Act, since the Secretary of Labor's enforcement stance at the time of the age change was that the provision would not allow involuntary retirement, and the employer had presented no evidence that the early retirement change had any business purpose other than arbitrary age discrimination.[129]

An airline was not entitled to judgment notwithstanding the verdict (JNOV) in an action challenging its policy of refusing to permit 60-year-old captains and first officers from downbidding to second officer positions to avoid forced retirement, the Seventh Circuit has ruled.[130] The evidence is sufficient to support a finding that the airline administered its seniority system in a discriminatory manner, the court reasoned, and if the airline does not allow younger pilots any greater freedom in downgrading than is afforded to older pilots, the jury could consider whether the seniority system has a disparate impact on older pilots and evaluate any business necessity defense that the airline may raise.[131]

The Supreme Court said in 1985 that any seniority system that includes an airline's discriminatory policy of precluding captains who are disqualified by virtue of age from transferring to flight engineer positions is not "bona fide" for purposes of the ADEA.[132] The Court added that the bona fide seniority system defense was unavailable to the airline, even though the FAA's "age

---

[128]29 U.S.C. §623(f)(2).
[129]Marshall v. Eastern Air Lines, Inc., 474 F. Supp. 364, 20 FEP 908 (SD Fla, 1979).
[130]Monroe v. United Air Lines, Inc., 34 FEP 1622 (CA 7, 1984).
[131]Id. at 1632.
[132]TWA v. Thurston, 469 U.S. ___, ___, 36 FEP 977, 983 (1985).

60 rule" may have caused aggrieved employees involuntary retirement, where the airline's seniority plan "permitted" their involuntary retirement for purposes of the Act; their retirement was age-based, inasmuch as the captains disqualified for reasons other than age are allowed to bump less senior flight engineers.[133]

EEOC regulations establish guidelines for determining the "bona fides" of a seniority system:

> "(a) Though a seniority system may be qualified by such factors as merit capacity, or ability, any bona fide seniority system must be based on length of service as the primary criterion for the equitable allocation of available employment opportunities and prerogatives among younger and older workers.
>
> "(b) Adoption of a purported seniority system which gives those with longer service lesser rights, and results in discharge or less favored treatment to those within the protection of the Act, may, depending upon the circumstances, be a 'subterfuge to evade the purposes' of the Act.
>
> "(c) Unless the essential terms and conditions of an alleged seniority system have been communicated to the affected employees and can be shown to be applied uniformly to all of those affected, regardless of age, it will not be considered a bona fide seniority system within the meaning of the Act.
>
> "(d) It should be noted that seniority systems which segregate, classify, or otherwise discriminate against individuals on the basis of race, color, religion, sex, or national origin, are prohibited under Title VII of the Civil Rights Act of 1964, where that Act otherwise applies. The 'bona fides' of such a system will be closely scrutinized to ensure that such a system is, in fact, bona fide under the ADEA."[134]

Bona Fide Employee Benefit Plan

Finally, the Act provides that it is not unlawful for an employer to "observe the terms of a . . . bona fide employee benefit plan such as a retirement, pension, or insurance plan, which is not a subterfuge" to evade the purposes of the Act.[135] The 1978 amendments added the caveat that no such employee benefit plan shall excuse the failure to hire any individual, or require or permit the involuntary retirement of any individual because of age.

The bona-fide-employee-benefit-plan defense "is an affirmative defense and must be plead and proven by the defendant. The defendant must show that it (1) observes the terms of the plan; (2) the plan was a bona fide employee benefit plan and (3) it is not a subterfuge to evade the purposes of the ADEA."[136] It is not unlawful, though, to implement a plan allowing employees to elect early retirement at their own option, nor is it unlawful to require early retirement for reasons other than age.[137] The Act explicitly prohibits any "involuntary" retirement based on age, and litigation will usually address the degree of inducement placed upon a candidate for retirement, and when that inducement rises to the level of "involuntary" retirement.

---

[133]*Id.*, 36 FEP at 983–84.
[134]29 CFR §1625.8.
[135]29 U.S.C. §623(f)(2).
[136]Marshall v. Eastern Airlines, Inc., *supra* note 129, 20 FEP at 910.
[137]29 CFR §1625.9.

The Act excludes from the ban against involuntary retirement those individuals who are "bona fide executives" or who are in a "high policy making position."[138] The Second Circuit has affirmed a decision of a district court that an employer did not violate the ADEA when it involuntarily retired its chief labor counsel, since the labor counsel was neither a "bona fide executive" nor a "high policy making employee."[139] Congress intended the test for the exemption to be one of function, not of pay according to the court.[140] The evidence supports findings that the labor counsel was primarily an attorney doing legal work, that his supervisory duties were quite minimal and occupied a very small portion of his time, that the employer did not encourage or invite its house lawyers to play a dynamic policy-creating role, and that his role in connection with policy-formulation was minor, and did not rise to the level contemplated by the exemption, the court concluded.[141]

The EEOC has promulgated regulations stating that this exemption will not bar involuntary retirement if the prospective retiree is within two years of retirement and is entitled to a pension of at least $44,000 per year.[142] (In 1984, following passage of the Older Americans Act Amendments to the ADEA,[143] the EEOC amended the regulation, raising the income level necessary for an employee to be involuntarily retired from $27,000 to $44,000 per year.[144])

Spousal Health Care.   In 1982, Congress passed the Tax Equity and Fiscal Responsibility Act (TEFRA),[145] which added language to Section 4 of the Act.[146] The amendment required employers to provide health care coverage to spouses of employees age 65–69, if the employee received such coverage through an employer-sponsored plan. Under TEFRA, Medicare became the secondary payor to employer-sponsored group health insurance plans. The effect of the change in the law was to prohibit the common practice of "carving out" from the employer's plan those expenses that were covered by Medicare for employees who were eligible for the federal plan. Such employees, however, still could elect to have Medicare as their primary insurer, and the employer's plan as their secondary insurer.

In 1984, Congress passed and President Reagan signed the Deficit Reduction Act,[147] which clears up an area left cloudy by the TEFRA—the *age* of spouses entitled to coverage under an employer-sponsored plan. According to the House-Senate Conference Report accompanying the legislation (H.R. 4170), the amendment is intended to provide that "employers must offer group coverage to an employee who has not reached age 65 in cases where the employee has a spouse age 65 through 69 under the same circumstances as coverage is offered

---

[138]29 U.S.C. §631(c)(1).

[139]Whittlesey v. Union Carbide Corp., 742 F.2d 724, 35 FEP 1089 (CA 2, 1984), *aff'g* 567 F. Supp. 1320, 32 FEP 473 (SD NY, 1983).

[140]*Id.*, 35 FEP at 1090–91.

[141]*Id.*

[142]29 CFR §1627.17.

[143]Pub. L. No. 98–459, eff. 10–9–84.

[144]29 CFR §§1625.12 and 1627.17.

[145]Pub. L. No. 97–248, eff. 9–3–82.

[146]29 U.S.C. §623(g)(1) & (2).

[147]Pub. L. No. 98–369, eff. 7–18–84.

to employees with a spouse under the age of 65. In the case where such employee elects the employer plan, Medicare would be secondary.'' The congressional intent, according to the report, is that the individual eligible for Medicare, the older spouse in this case, should have an opportunity to decide whether to opt for the employer plan or the federal plan.

The Deficit Reduction Act Amendment to the ADEA became effective January 1, 1985. It reads as follows:

> "(g)(1) For purposes of this section, any employer must provide that any employee aged 65 through 69 and any employee's spouse aged 65 through 69 shall be entitled to coverage under any group health plan offered to such employee, and the spouse of such employee under age 65.
>
> "(2) For purposes of paragraph (1), the term "group health plan" has the meaning given to such term in section 162(i)(2) of the Internal Revenue Code of 1954.''

"Group health plan" is defined in the Internal Revenue Code as "any plan of, or contributed to by, an employer to provide medical care . . . to his employees, former employees, or the families of such employees or former employees, directly or through insurance, reimbursement, or otherwise."[148]

Waiver

Employers have been known to encourage former employees who may be potential plaintiffs to sign a release as to their right to sue. These releases are usually accompanied by the employer's offer of financial incentive to sign the release. In the ADEA context, the question is whether such a waiver bars the employee's subsequent action, and the only circuit court to answer the question did so in the negative, but then changed its mind.

In *Runyan v. National Cash Register Corp.*,[149] the employer's former assistant general counsel, who is a member of the Ohio bar, signed an unsupervised release of his ADEA rights. The attorney was 59 years old at the date of his termination, and he signed the release in exchange for an amendment to the consulting agreement he had with his employer; the amendment netted him an additional $12,000. He subsequently sued under the Act.

Applying Title VII analysis, the district court concluded that a general release knowingly signed by the attorney in 1977 constituted a complete bar to his claim that a bona fide dispute existed with respect to the reason for his termination. The court also found that the consideration the employee received was adequate and not at all contrary to public policy.[150]

The Sixth Circuit reversed, holding that the unsupervised release of the employee's statutory rights cannot serve to bar his ADEA action, even though he admittedly suspected at the time that the release was not valid and did not manifest that suspicion to his employer.[151] The appeals court applied the Fair Labor Standards Act, rather than Title VII, since the FLSA was expressly and

---

[148]26 U.S.C. §162(i)(2).

[149]573 F. Supp 1454, 33 FEP 322 (SD Ohio, 1983).

[150]*Id.*

[151]Runyan v. National Cash Register Corp., 759 F.2d 1253, 37 FEP 1086 (CA 6, 1985).

selectively incorporated into the ADEA.[152] In light of the FLSA legislative history and the historical development of that statute and the ADEA, the Sixth Circuit concluded that the principles governing FLSA waiver disputes also govern ADEA waiver disputes, and therefore, that the unsupervised release did not bar the employee's ADEA claim.[153]

But the court was not done. It next observed:

> "It is indeed difficult to gather any excitement over Runyan's claim. He is a long time member of the Ohio Bar, yet he took advantage of an amendment to the original consulting agreement that netted him approximately $12,000 in exchange for a release he believed to be of little or no value. As we interpret his deposition testimony, Runyan was quite confident that the release he signed would not be an acceptable bar to an ADEA claim.[9] We would suppose that a member of the bar would deal more forthrightly with his former employer. Nevertheless, his legal acumen aside, Runyan falls within the class of employees protected by the ADEA and, consequently must be afforded the same rights as any other ADEA claimant."[154]

---

[9][Footnote omitted.]

The court was obviously less than satisfied with the bona fides of the attorney's claim.

In June 1985, the court vacated its previous ruling and set the case for rehearing.[155] The tension between waiver of ADEA rights and the deception of this particular plaintiff has created a split within the circuit. Had the plaintiff been more forthright or less educated, or both, the court would certainly have had less difficulty using FLSA analysis to invalidate the release. These facts could lead the court into making an exception in the otherwise consistent law of nonwaiver of certain statutory rights. But there is an equally compelling need to protect the courts from the deluge of cases that would inevitably follow from a failure to support legitimate settlement efforts. And the need for EEOC supervision of such waivers must be weighed against the agency's resources.

---

[152]*Id.*, 37 FEP at 1089.

[153]*Id.*, 37 FEP at 1090.

[154]*Id.*, 37 FEP at 1090–91.

[155]Runyan v. National Cash Register Corp., 38 FEP 5 (CA 6, 1985), *vacating* 37 FEP 1086 (CA 6, 1985).

6

Legal Remedies

Remedial Scheme

The Age Discrimination in Employment Act follows a remedial scheme laid out in the Fair Labor Standards Act. Section 7(b) of the ADEA[1] incorporates Section 11(b) and parts of Section 16 of the FLSA.[2] Section 7(b) authorizes a private suit for unpaid wages plus an equal amount in liquidated damages, and authorizes the Secretary of Labor to sue for the same remedies, and for injunctive relief. This Section also provides that a court may grant such "legal or equitable relief" as will effectuate the purposes of the Act.

The grant of equitable relief under the ADEA created a conflict with the FLSA remedial scheme because, under FLSA case law, injunctive relief (which is a form of equitable relief) was not available to the private plaintiff. To resolve this dilemma, Congress passed Section 7(c) of the ADEA[3] which added the specific language authorizing "legal or equitable relief" for private actions.

The statutory grant of the right to sue for "legal or equitable" relief has its roots in the historical development of law and its merger with equity. During the Middle Ages, courts were divided into courts of law and courts of equity. Courts of law administered the law as established by the King and determined legal remedies, usually ascertained as a specific amount of money to compensate for the injury sustained. Courts of equity were called upon to decide disputes where the law was silent and where the legal remedies were inadequate to compensate the aggrieved individual.

The acknowledgment of this dichotomy guided the drafters of much social legislation to consider the propriety of either or both remedial schemes in devising laws such as the Fair Labor Standards Act, which provides for back pay, liquidated damages, attorney's fees, and injunctions. Because of the legislative and adjudicative experience gained through the administration of the FLSA, drafters of the ADEA had a clear idea of the variety of forms which both legal and equitable remedies could take. The breadth of such words as "wages" and "compensation" had provided much grist for the courts to consider, and it was deemed appropriate to rely on this experience in drafting the remedial provisions of the ADEA. The complexity of applying equitable relief became clear when the issue of reinstatement was raised, since it carries with it the additional indicium of continued employment tenure. But the courts

---

[1] 29 U.S.C. §626(b).
[2] 29 U.S.C. §§211(b), 216 (except for subsection (a)), and 217.
[3] 29 U.S.C. §626(c).

require an aggrieved employee to pursue legal remedies, or to demonstrate why legal remedies are inappropriate or inadequate, before attempting to obtain equitable relief.

Under the ADEA, amounts that are owed are deemed to be unpaid minimum wages or unpaid overtime compensation under the FLSA, according to Section 7(b) of the ADEA. The ADEA borrows heavily from the FLSA and even defines and limits "liquidated damages" according to the Wage Act: "liquidated damages shall be payable only in cases of willful violations."[4] The term "liquidated damages" is defined under Section 16(b) of the FLSA as an amount equal to unpaid minimum wages or unpaid overtime compensation. But in the context of unlawful hiring, layoff, discharge, involuntary retirement, or selection for transfer or training, the penumbra of rights and benefits inuring to the employee or job applicant exceeds minimum wages or overtime compensation. The ADEA vests jurisdiction in the courts to grant such equitable or legal relief necessary to effectuate the purposes of the Act, "including without limitation judgments compelling employment, reinstatement or promotion, or enforcing the liability for amounts deemed to be unpaid overtime compensation" under Section 7(b). These judgments and this enforcement authority represent the forms of equitable relief that Congress contemplated when it included that language in the Act. The Secretary (now the EEOC) is required to attempt to eliminate the allegedly discriminatory practice and to obtain voluntary compliance with the Act through "informal methods of conciliation, conference, and persuasion, before bringing any action" under Section 7(b). A private party is under no similar duty to seek conciliation before filing a complaint.

Back Pay Entitlement

The purpose of the ADEA remedial provisions is to restore aggrieved individuals to the "economic position they would have occupied but for the intervening unlawful conduct of the employers."[5] The Third Circuit has advised that the "touchstone" for fashioning legal and equitable remedies should be the "make whole" standard—i.e., that the employee should be made "whole," or as nearly restored to his former position as is judicially practicable.[6] But it should be noted that an adjudication of an unlawful employment practice does not *sine mora* entitle the prevailing plaintiff to the relief he seeks.[7] The plaintiff must establish that he is entitled to relief; that the relief sought is within the court's power and the congressional intent of the Act; that he has done nothing to aggravate, and everything reasonable to mitigate, the employer's damages; that any proffered reinstatement was either invalid or inadequate; and, in certain cases, that reinstatement at this point would be inappropriate. In fact, the Third Circuit in *Rodriguez* stated that the plaintiff was required to show that there

---

[4]29 U.S.C. §626(b).

[5]Rodriguez v. Taylor, 569 F.2d 1231, 16 FEP 533 (CA 3, 1977), *cert. denied*, 436 U.S. 913, 17 FEP 699 (1978).

[6]*Id.*

[7]Combes v. Griffin Television, Inc., 421 F. Supp. 841, 13 FEP 1455 (WD Okla, 1976).

were positions which he could perform but were denied to him. Of course, the employer has an opportunity to rebut the plaintiff's case on damages entitlement, but the important point is that a mere finding of unlawful age discrimination will not invariably lead to an award of damages or other requested relief.

Additionally, Sections 6 and 10 of the Portal-to-Portal Act,[8] incorporated into the ADEA under Section 7(e),[9] provide a possible limitation on back pay exposure in that an employer's good-faith reliance on, or actions in conformity with, any written Department of Labor regulation, order, ruling, or interpretation, may preclude liability for unpaid minimum wages or overtime compensation. (See this chapter, "Liquidated Damages.")

The Fifth Circuit denied relief to a prevailing plaintiff in *Marshall v. Airpax Electronics*,[10] when it ruled that the individual was within the protected group and was denied a position in violation of the ADEA, but was not entitled to injunctive relief, since no vacancy existed at the precise moment she applied for the position of executive secretary. Allegations in the complaint and concessions by the Secretary of Labor limited the action to alleged discrimination which may have occurred only on the day of the plaintiff's interview for the job. Other evidence indicated that the employer had made a good-faith, and for the most part highly successful, effort to hire members of the protected age group, and to comply with the federal government's directives on employment discrimination.

In 1982, the Supreme Court ruled in *Ford Motor Co. v. EEOC*[11] that a Title VII claimant's right to back pay was precluded by his rejection of the employer's unconditional offer of a "comparable" job. Although this case arose in a Title VII context, the Court iterated its long-held view that an injured party had an obligation to mitigate his damages to ensure that his claim was made in good faith. In an ADEA action, a district court in Alabama faced a similar situation where the plaintiff had rejected the employer's offer of a transfer to a comparable position in another city after he filed his Age Act charges with the EEOC, protesting his termination.[12] The court accepted the jury determination of unlawful age discrimination, but refused to award back pay under the *Ford Motor Co.* rationale. When the employer offered the comparable position in "conformity with the public policy favoring conciliation"[13] while the Commission was considering the charges, the court found that the employee's rejection of the offer constituted a relinquishment of any claim for back wages, illustrating once again that not all violations will lead to back pay awards.

Back Pay Under the Act

A prevailing plaintiff who seeks back pay must state specifically the relief requested, and must demonstrate the appropriateness both of the kind of relief

---

[8]29 U.S.C. §251-262.

[9]29 U.S.C. §626(e).

[10]595 F.2d 1043, 19 FEP 1286 (CA 5, 1979).

[11]458 U.S. 219, 29 FEP 121 (1982).

[12]Cowen v. Standard Brands, Inc., 572 F. Supp. 1576, 33 FEP 53 (ND Ala, 1983).

[13]*Id.*, 33 FEP at 57.

sought, and the need for the amount/degree of liability to be imposed on the defendant. The most frequently sought remedy is legal damages, also known as "money," for the wages lost as a result of the unlawful discrimination. Though the Act requires a plaintiff to seek "legal or equitable" relief, the injured employee may seek both forms of relief. The typical example of such relief would be an order by the court requiring the employer to pay the employee back pay and to reinstate him to his former or equivalent job. It is the dual compulsion of legal and equitable liability that most completely does justice to the injured employee and the offending employer. However, it is the "sting" of monetary liability that most completely deters the employer from engaging in such practices in the future. The monetary liability usually takes the form of back pay, encompassing the time and amounts of money that would have been earned by the employee during the discriminatory period absent the discrimination. But since most employees receive employment benefits in addition to their wages, it is this common grant of wages and benefits that make up the total calculation of "back pay."

What Constitutes Back Pay

Back pay generally encompasses wages lost as the result of the unlawful discrimination practiced upon the injured party. But wages are not always hourly or weekly earnings. In one instance, a district court ruled that the ADEA would cover "reasonably predictable lost commission income,"[14] in addition to regular wages, as part of lost wages in computing back pay. The court observed that the plaintiff—an account manager for the manufacturer—had an annual income from commissions that had remained fairly constant for the four years prior to his termination, and on that basis the lost commission income was deemed to be "reasonably predictable."[15] Though such compensation is normally considered to be too speculative, the courts have shown a willingness to hear and consider extrinsic factors.

In *Combes v. Griffin Television, Inc.*,[16] a district court in Oklahoma computed the back pay due an employee under the Act as of the day on which the employer implemented a new pay formula, using the new formula. The court reasoned that the new pay formula would have determined the employee's pay, if he had not been discharged on the day prior to its implementation. The court also determined that the plaintiff would have received a six-percent increase and cost of living increase, in addition to receiving company-paid health and life insurance, and included this in the back pay award.

A district court in West Virginia, applying the *Combes* rationale, ruled that the amount of back pay due an employee under the ADEA should be increased by the value of the pension benefits, health insurance, seniority, leave-time or other fringe benefits that he would have accrued during the back pay period absent the discrimination.[17]

---

[14]Buchholz v. Symons Mfg. Co., 455 F. Supp. 706, 16 FEP 1084 (ED Wis, 1978)
[15]*Id.*, 16 FEP at 1088.
[16]*Supra* note 7.
[17]Coates v. National Cash Register Co., 433 F. Supp. 655, 15 FEP 222 (WD Va, 1977).

In 1980, the Tenth Circuit struggled with the problem of an employer's defunct policy of requiring workers within the protected age group under the Act to wait longer for minimum salary increases than younger colleagues not covered by the Act. The employer's so-called "stretch out" policy had a "continuing effect," according to the appeals court, which was compensable as an element of damages. The court declared that there was little doubt that the "stretch out system had both overt and hidden age bias as an integral feature of its structure."[18]

An airline and a union adopted a contract provision requiring pilots retiring at the mandatory age of 60—but not pilots retiring earlier—to use up a percentage of their accrued vacation time before retirement. A district court in Minnesota determined that the resulting reduction in their lump-sum payments would not have occurred in the absence of the discriminatory clause in the contract. It ruled that the loss was in the nature of lost wages, and was therefore compensable under the Act.[19]

A long-time sales representative was terminated following the employer's decision to reduce its sales force. The Ninth Circuit ruled that the "wages lost" as the result of the employer's unlawful termination under the Act encompassed wages, pension benefits, and prejudgment interest.[20]

Pension benefits pose a particularly difficult problem since they are usually tied to the length of employment, and are affected by the court's decision on the issue of reinstatement. A female teacher within the protected age group successfully established that the employer's policy of refusing to hire as permanent teachers individuals with more than five years' experience violated the ADEA. Despite the Second Circuit's refusal to order reinstatement, the court nevertheless determined that the plaintiff fell within the category of entitlement to equitable relief, for the one-year period which she would have worked absent the unlawful practice. The court awarded her back pay, including pension rights, for the year that the jury determined that she would have worked, under a "make-whole" philosophy.[21]

The First Circuit has examined the three basic employment situations of reinstatement, nonreinstatement with vested benefits, and nonreinstatement where the plaintiff's pension benefits have not vested. It declared:

> "An award of pension benefits is plainly authorized under the ADEA. Congress intended that the calculation of 'amounts owing' to a prevailing plaintiff include 'items of pecuniary or economic loss such as wages, fringe, and other job-related benefits.' H. Conf. Rep. No. 95–950, 95th Cong., 2d Sess. 13, reprinted in [1978] U.S. CODE CONG. & AD. NEWS 528, 535. Pension benefits are part of an individual's compensation and, like an award of back pay, should be awarded under 29 U.S.C. §626(b). If a prevailing plaintiff is returned to the defendant's employment, this award will consist of payments to the pension fund on plaintiff's behalf, bringing plaintiff's pension interest to the level it would have reached absent discrimination.
>
> "When reinstatement is not ordered, any pension benefits due a prevailing

---

[18]Mistretta v. Sandia Corp., 639 F.2d 588, 24 FEP 316 (CA 10, 1980).

[19]EEOC v. Air Line Pilots Ass'n, 489 F. Supp. 1003, 22 FEP 1609 (D Minn, 1980), *rev'd and remanded on other grounds*, 661 F.2d 90, 26 FEP 1615 (CA 8, 1981).

[20]Kelly v. American Standard, Inc., 640 F.2d 974, 25 FEP 94 (CA 9, 1981).

[21]Geller v. Markham, 635 F.2d 1027, 24 FEP 920 (CA 2, 1980), *cert. denied*, 451 U.S. 945 (1981).

plaintiff normally should be liquidated as of the date damages are settled, *see Monroe v. Penn-Dixie Cement Corp.*, 335 F. Supp. 231, 235, 4 FEP cases 629, 631 (N.D. Ga. 1971), and should approximate the present discounted value of plaintiff's interest. Just as with back pay, the award should be computed as if plaintiff had been employed until the date damages are settled. Where the time from plaintiff's initial employment until that date does not meet the employer's vesting requirements, some pension award may still be appropriate—an employer need not be allowed to stand on requirements that plaintiff cannot meet because of the employer's own wrongful acts. In such cases, the district court will have to exercise its discretion carefully. At the least, a plaintiff will be entitled to whatever would have been paid into the pension fund on his behalf. At most, he will be entitled to be treated as a vested employee and to receive a pension award based on employment from when he was first hired until damages are settled or on the minimum vesting period. This is a matter of some technicality, however, and one that we leave largely to the trial court's discretion."[22]

These three formulae encompass most of the factors involved in computing pension benefits due following a finding of unlawful discrimination. However, they do not represent all the formulae which can be devised, nor do they resolve all issues which could arise.

One plaintiff was awarded pension benefits, computed as if he were entitled to work until the date of his planned retirement, rather than the date of his unlawful termination, some three years earlier. The court said that the employee was entitled to the difference between his back pay award and the unemployment compensation received, and to the pension benefits computed to his planned retirement date. However, it disallowed reimbursement for health insurance expenses, in light of the employee's admission that he did not get insurance after discharge because of the high cost of premiums.[23]

The Third Circuit has ruled that both unemployment benefits and pension plan benefits are not deductible from an ADEA back pay award, since both are collateral benefits designed to serve social policies independent of those served by back pay awards:

"More importantly, deducting pension benefits received by McDowell from his back pay award could potentially reduce the amount in liquidated damages to which he otherwise could be entitled while benefitting the employer by giving it a windfall—a result certainly not intended by the ADEA. This apparent inequitable result of mitigating the back pay award occurs because under the ADEA liquidated damages are measured by doubling the back pay award. See 29 U.S.C. §216(b). Consequently, for every dollar deducted from back pay a dollar is deducted from the liquidated damages award; thus, the employer would end up paying two dollars less in total damages for every dollar McDowell received in pension plan benefits or unemployment compensation benefits. Hence, even though McDowell would be made whole as to back pay (that is, he will not have suffered any net dollar loss), he would not get the full benefit of the liquidated damages provision.

"The employer, on the other hand, would end up paying less back pay than he would have spent in actual pay but for the discrimination. Additionally, if liquidated damages are deemed appropriate he would pay less liquidated damages than he would have been liable for paying, but for the pension benefits which McDowell received."[24]

---

[22]Loeb v. Textron, Inc., 600 F.2d 1003, 20 FEP 29 (CA 1, 1979).

[23]*Supra* note 14.

[24]McDowell v. Avtex Fibers, Inc., 740 F.2d 214, 35 FEP 371, 374–75 (CA 3, 1984).

Between the recognition that benefits would continue to accrue absent the employment discrimination, and the judicial notice of the effect on liquidated damages liablity of a reduction in benefits, it can be argued that courts will be reluctant to accept any employer requests for reduction/rejection of employee benefit claims.

How Back Pay Is Measured

The purpose of back pay is to make the employee "whole," to return him to that status which he would have been in absent the unlawful discrimination.

Once the scope of the elements of the back pay have been determined, the amount to be awarded should fully compensate the employee for the time in question. Unfortunately several formulae may be used, with differing results, depending on how the court determines the back pay period. This determination can run from the inception of the unlawful conduct to its elimination; from the inception to the date of the trial; or from the inception up to the date of the "final order."

In an early ADEA action, a federal court ruled that the employer's unlawful discharge of the plaintiff resulted in a back pay period beginning on the date of the discharge, and ended on the trial date.[25] Another court reasoned: "The damages should properly equal the difference between the value of the compensation by way of salary together with other specific monetary benefits . . . to which plaintiff would be entitled had he remained employed by defendant until the trial date. Put more plainly, money damages in a case under the Age Discrimination Act must be liquidated as of the date of judgment."[26]

However, another court ruled that the back pay period commenced with the nearest date *after* the date of the application for employment, where a younger applicant was hired, and the back pay liability continued until the discrimination was eliminated.[27] Yet another federal court reasoned that the employer's unlawful conduct began the back pay period, and the employee's action of accepting or declining a valid reinstatement offer, or offer of a "comparable position" terminated the back pay liability.[28]

Back pay under the Fair Labor Standards Act has consistently been awarded, despite the absence of precise determinations of the amount in question. Because of the remedial provisions of the FLSA, and the mandate of Section 11(c) of the Act that the employer maintain adequate and accurate payroll and work records, the courts have allowed the employee to establish the amount of unpaid compensation due, if the evidence is sufficient to create a "reasonable inference" of that amount; the employer has the opportunity to rebut by clear and unmistakable evidence the inferences drawn from the employee's evidence. But in the absence of adequate records—itself a violation of the FLSA—the employer is usually unable to rebut this inference.[29]

---

[25]Brennan v. Ace Hardware Corp., 495 F.2d 368, 7 FEP 657 (CA 8, 1974).

[26]Monroe v. Penn-Dixie Cement Corp., 335 F. Supp. 231, 4 FEP 629 (ND Ga, 1971).

[27]EEOC v. Goodyear Tire & Rubber Co., 22 FEP 786 (WD Tenn, 1980).

[28]Coates v. National Cash Register, 433 F. Supp. 655, 15 FEP 222 (WD Va, 1977).

[29]Anderson v. Mount Clemens Pottery Co., 328 U.S. 680, 5 WH Cases 347 (1946); Hodgson v. Humphries, 454 F.2d 1279, 20 WH Cases 444 (CA 10, 1972); Donovan v. Simmons Petrol Corp., 26 WH Cases 935 (CA 10, 1983).

In view of this remedial purpose and case law, courts administering ADEA remedies have interpreted evidence concerning any dispute over the back pay period in a broad, inclusive manner consistent with the remedial purpose of the ADEA, rather than a restrictive approach. To that end, courts have not been reluctant to extend the back pay period to reach the date of "final order" on the complaint. A typical case where the court will extend the back pay period to this date involves reinstatement to the same job, or a comparable position. The employee's desire for and/or acceptance of reinstatement can be seen as support for extending the back pay period to the date of judgment.[30] An employee who prevailed in his ADEA action and sought "front pay" (an amount the employee would have earned up to a specific date, such as retirement, in the absence of the unlawful age discrimination), while preserving his right to reinstatement, was awarded back pay up to the date of trial, and denied any prospective damages in view of the reinstatement issue.[31] An employer that unlawfully demoted an employee was ordered to compensate him on a monthly basis in an amount equal to the earnings of the person who presently held that job, until the employer reinstated him.[32]

Though it could be argued that the variety of forms which may be devised to calculate the back pay period is limited only by the imagination of the plaintiff's attorney, the courts are experienced in and sensitive to the use of the "make whole" philosophy which underlies most statutory remedial schemes. Employers have attempted to end their back pay liability by pointing to a particular time within the back pay period during which the employer made a valid reinstatement offer to the employee of the same or a comparable job;[33] the employee counters that the reinstatement offer was invalid, either because the job being offered was not in fact available, or because the comparable job was not in fact "comparable." Generally, though, the time frame of the back pay period can be established through extrinsic evidence.

Interim Compensation

The back pay award is not intended to constitute a "windfall" to the employee by compensating him over and above the amount he would have received in the absence of unlawful conduct. Following termination, however, a discharged employee may derive income from such sources as interim employment, layoff allowance or severance pay, self-employment earnings, and unemployment compensation.

Echoing *Buchholz v. Symons Manufacturing Co.*,[34] that "reasonably predictable" commission income could be an element of back pay, a district court in West Virginia reduced a back pay award by the amount of severance pay received and amounts earned by the employee, or the amounts "earnable with

---

[30]Schulz v. Hickok Mfg. Co., 358 F. Supp. 1208, 5 FEP 1010 (ND Ga, 1973).

[31]Grecco v. Spang & Co., 566 F. Supp. 413, 32 FEP 850 (WD Pa, 1983).

[32]Spagnuolo v. Whirlpool Corp., 548 F. Supp. 104, 32 FEP 1372 (WD NC, 1982).

[33]Orzel v. City of Wauwatosa Fire Dep't, 697 F.2d 743, 30 FEP 1070 (CA 7, 1983).

[34]445 F. Supp. 706, 16 FEP 1084 (ED Wis, 1978).

reasonable diligence."[35] The crucial consideration for many courts appears to be whether the employee would have received the particular compensation in question in the absence of the unlawful discrimination. For example, one court determined that vacation pay is "earned" income, and is not paid on the occurrence of termination.[36] Another court allowed the employer to set off against its back pay liability the amount received by the employee as severance pay, because this amount was occasioned by termination, and would not have otherwise been received by the employee in the absence of termination. The court conceded that severance pay may be measured by the length of past service; nevertheless, it is payment occasioned by an involuntary termination. It reasoned that if the employee is to be returned to his original position—the essence of the make-whole remedy—then this amount should be deducted from the back pay award.[37]

A troublesome element of the back pay consideration is unemployment compensation. The Fifth Circuit has declared that unemployment compensation benefits received during the interim period need not be deducted from the back pay award, since this was a collateral benefit akin to collateral losses, which are also not compensated for in measuring the back pay owing to an employee.[38] However, the Third Circuit took exception to the Fifth Circuit's reasoning that refusal to set off such collateral benefits would not make an employee more than whole. The Third Circuit stated "alternate employment income" is surely a direct benefit compared to unemployment compensation, and therefore, an employee is in fact made "more than whole" if he obtains current back pay for two jobs which he could not have simultaneously performed.[39] The inference is clear that the unemployment compensation would not have been received in the absence of the unlawful age discrimination. Other courts have struggled with the propriety of offsetting unemployment compensation from back pay liability on various theories, with conflicting results. The Ninth Circuit has ruled that it is not an abuse of a trial court's discretion to reduce the back pay award by the unemployment compensation received during the back pay period.[40] The Tenth Circuit has ruled in conformity with the Fifth Circuit's decision not to offset this compensation, on the theory that this is a collateral benefit of the employment relationship.[41] A district court in Tennessee determined that back pay shall be reduced by interim earnings "from any source," unemployment compensation, and the amount that could have been earned by the employee in the exercise of reasonable diligence.[42] The court reasoned that:

> "Forms of public assistance other than unemployment compensation should not

[35]Coates v. National Cash Register Co., 433 F. Supp. 655, 15 FEP 222 (WD Va, 1977). *See also* EEOC v. Goodyear Tire & Rubber Co., *supra* note 27.

[36]Monroe v. Penn-Dixie Cement Corp., *supra* note 26.

[37]Laugesen v. Anaconda Co., 510 F.2d 307, 10 FEP 567 (CA 6, 1975).

[38]Marshall v. Goodyear Tire & Rubber Co., 554 F.2d 730, 15 FEP 139 (CA 5, 1977).

[39]Rodriguez v. Taylor, 569 F.2d 1231, 16 FEP 533 (CA 3, 1977), *cert. denied*, 436 U.S. 913, 17 FEP 699 (1978).

[40]Naton v. Bank of Cal., 649 F.2d 691, 27 FEP 510 (CA 9, 1981).

[41]Mistretta v. Sandia Corp., 639 F.2d 588, 24 FEP 316 (CA 10, 1980).

[42]EEOC v. Goodyear Tire & Rubber Co., 22 FEP 786 (WD Tenn, 1980).

be deducted from a discriminatee's recovery. The basis for this distinction is three-fold. First, unemployment compensation is more closely analogous to interim earnings. Second, as an employee the defendant has contributed to the fund from which unemployment compensation is paid. Finally the Court deems it unwise to entertain the administratively unwieldy issue of determining what welfare benefits a discriminatee would not have received had he been hired by defendant."[43]

Unemployment compensation is regarded by many courts as a "collateral benefit" of the employment relationship, since the employer pays into the state fund on behalf of his employees. It is seen as a form of (social) insurance to which the employee is entitled on a vested basis, per pay period. However, this approach conflicts head-on with the concept of "make whole" and unjust enrichment, where not offsetting the unemployment compensation results in a windfall to the employee, but offsetting the income reduces the deterrent effect on the employer of engaging in such conduct. The courts have not reached a consensus on this dilemma, and in the absence of some authoritative pronouncement from the Supreme Court, inconsistent and unpredictable results may be expected to continue.

Front Pay

The question whether prospective damages are recoverable under the ADEA has been the subject of considerable discussion by the courts, since there is no specific reference in the statutory language to such a remedy. The "legal or equitable" relief to be granted in terms of the "make whole" philosophy augers in favor of such a remedy, where the facts would indicate that an award of front pay is otherwise appropriate.

A prevailing plaintiff who was awarded back pay from the date of his discharge to the date of trial argued that he was also entitled to future prospective damages (i.e., front pay), to some date in the future—possibly to the age of retirement—as a substitute for the equitable remedy of reinstatement. The Third Circuit declined to decide whether future damages could be awarded under the ADEA, because the employee's refusal to consider reinstatement removed the issue of front pay from the court's consideration.[44] The appeals court reasoned that any basis for calculating front pay would include the amount the employee would have received had he continued to be employed by the employer. The employee's argument that he was entitled to future damages in lieu of reinstatement presupposed that he wanted to be reinstated, according to the court, but at pretrial the employee had specifically disclaimed any desire to be reinstated. The court concluded that the issue of front pay was not properly before it for determination.

Applying the same reasoning, a district court in Pennsylvania ruled that an employee seeking reinstatement may not also seek lost future wages, where such a remedy would enable him to recover twice for the same injury. The court noted that the Act's failure to specify an award of prospective damages

---

[43]*Id.* at 788. *See also* Note, "Set-offs Against Back-Pay Awards Under the Federal Age Discrimination in Employment Act," 79 Mich. L.R. 1113.

[44]Wehr v. Burroughs Corp., 619 F.2d 276, 22 FEP 994 (CA 3, 1980).

as an element of its remedial scheme appeared to foreclose such an award.[45] The court stated:

"It is important first to note that although plaintiff seeks to recover prospective damages, he has indicated in a reply brief that his prayer for relief should not be read as foreclosing the request that he be reinstated in his former job. This Court is specifically empowered by section 626(b) to order reinstatement of a successful plaintiff in his former job. Such reinstatement clearly would stop any further damages to the plaintiff. Since reinstatement is a remedy being sought by the plaintiff and it would, if granted, bring an end to further damages to the plaintiff, lost future wages should not also be recoverable because that would enable the plaintiff to recover twice for the same alleged injury.[1]

"Also, section 626(b) indicates that the ADEA is to be enforced in accordance with the powers, remedies and procedures of the Fair Labor Standards Act (FLSA).[2] In actions brought under the FLSA, the awarding of damages beyond those specifically provided for in the statute repeatedly has been denied. *See*, for instance, *Martinez v. Behring's Bearings Service, Inc.*, 501 F.2d 104, 105, 21 WH Cases 980 (5th Cir. 1974), where it was held that there was no private right of damages for an employer violation of 29 U.S.C. §215(a)(3). The Court, after deciding that Congress did not see fit to specifically provide for such a remedy, concluded that it would be improper for a court to add a remedy by implication to those specifically enumerated in the FLSA. *See also Powell v. Washington Post Co.*, 267 F.2d 651, 14 WH Cases 140 (D.C. Cir. 1959).

"Since section 626(b) specifically incorporates the enforcement powers, remedies and procedures of the FLSA, it seems that in action under the ADEA the awarding of damages beyond those specifically enumerated in the statute is to be denied. Because the award of prospective damages is not specified as a remedy under the ADEA, it appears to be a remedy that is foreclosed.[3] *See also Ginsberg v. Burlington Industries, Inc.*, 500 F. Supp. at 700. Consequently, plaintiff will not be permitted to introduce at trial any evidence as to damages for wages lost subsequent to the time of trial. Only evidence as to losses occurring up to the date of trial shall be admissible."[46]

[1-3][Footnotes omitted.]

Refusal by a court to award front pay does not mean necessarily that the employee is without a remedy. As the *Grecco* court mentioned, the prevailing plaintiff will often have the opportunity to be reinstated, or reinstatement will have been declined.[47] In such circumstances, front pay would clearly be over-compensation to the injured party, notwithstanding any arguments that the refusal to accept reinstatement is the result of the employer's unlawful conduct. In the absence of express statutory language, or convincing legislative history, the courts will not award front pay if the result would constitute more than a make-whole remedy.

Two discriminatees were successful in establishing before the court that reinstatement was inappropriate and should not be relied upon. The court noted that the plaintiffs had secured alternate employment, and in view of their current salary levels from termination and the additional award of liquidated damages, any damage award in lieu of reinstatement (i.e., front pay) would be inappro-

---

[45]Grecco v. Spang & Co., 566 F. Supp. 413, 32 FEP 850 (WD Pa, 1983).

[46]*Id.*, 32 FEP at 850–51.

[47]*Id.*, 32 FEP at 851 n.3.

priate, since it was not necessary to return the plaintiffs to the economic status they would have occupied but for their discharges.[48]

One employee was awarded front pay to the date on which he would have retired under normal conditions, while another plaintiff was denied front pay based on his disingenuous pursuit of reinstatement and his inadequate work performance. Neither court found the lack of statutory language specifying front pay to be a hindrance in awarding this remedy.[49]

A seminal case on front pay is a decision by the federal district court for the Southern District of New York. That court stated that it had the power to compensate a discharged employee for the economic injury he sustained as a result of the employer's violation of the ADEA, and that the employee was entitled to be paid lost salary that he would have earned up to the date of his retirement.

KOYEN v. CONSOLIDATED EDISON CORP.

560 F. Supp. 1161, 31 FEP 488 (SD NY, 1983)

. . .

C. Prospective Damages

Plaintiff has withdrawn his request for reinstatement and in lieu thereof seeks an award of damages for future loss of earnings and other benefits from the date of judgment to his 70th birthday, when he no longer will be a member of the ADEA's protected class. Whether damages for future loss of earnings may be awarded under the ADEA has not been passed upon by our Court of Appeals, and district court rulings within the circuit are in conflict.[32] Similarly, appellate and district courts elsewhere have taken both sides on this issue.[33] Those that have rejected such claims have done so principally for two concerns: (1) doubt as to the court's power to grant future loss of earnings, and (2) the speculative nature of an award. The first concern arises out of the incorporation of the remedial enforcement provisions of the FLSA into the ADEA, resulting in a "model of imprecision."[34] Under the FLSA the employer is liable to the employee for "unpaid minimum wages . . . or overtime compensation"[35] and, as already noted, when a litigant prevails, that amount is automatically doubled by its provision for liquidated damages. The ADEA, after appropriate references to the FLSA, correlated the two statutes by stating:

Amounts owing to a person as a result of a violation of this chapter shall be deemed to be unpaid minimum wages or unpaid overtime compensation for purposes of sections 216 and 217 of this title: *Provided*, That liquidated damages shall be payable only in cases of willful violations of this chapter.[36]

Significantly, this ADEA enforcement section contains a provision not included in the FLSA, to wit:

In any action brought to enforce this chapter the court shall have jurisdiction to grant such legal or equitable relief as may be appropriate to effectuate the purposes of this chapter, including without limitation judgments compelling employment, reinstatement or promotion, or enforcing the liablity for amounts deemed to be unpaid minimum wages or unpaid overtime compensation under this section.[37]

The manifest purpose of this broad grant of legal and equitable power is to enable

---

[48]Robb v. Chemtron Corp., 17 FEP 1535 (SD Tex, 1978); *see also* Pavlo v. Stiefel Laboratories, Inc., 22 FEP 489 n.16 (SD NY, 1979).

[49]Naton v. Bank of Cal., *supra* note 40; Ginsberg v. Burlington Indus., Inc., 500 F. Supp. 696, 24 FEP 426 (SD NY, 1980). *But see* Jaffee v. Plough Broadcasting Co., 19 FEP 1194 (D Md, 1979) *and* Covey v. R.A. Johnston Co., 19 FEP 1188 (D Md, 1977) where front pay was declined as too speculative.

the courts to fashion whatever remedy is required to fully compensate an employee for the economic injury sustained by him. The power so granted is sufficient to authorize an award of future loss of earnings in appropriate cases. To deny that authority would defeat a purpose of the Act to make a victim of discrimination "whole" and to restore him to the economic position he would have occupied but for the unlawful conduct of his employer.[38] To deny such authority would remove a deterrent force against future violations.[39]

Similarly, the Court does not agree with those holdings which deny future damages solely because of the prospect of speculative and windfall awards. The courts which have adopted that view emphasize their concern in the instance of a discharged employee who may be at the lower scale of the protected class (40 years of age)[40] and where an award may encompass a decade or more during which the employee, had he not been unlawfully discharged but continued in his employment, "might or might not get raises, reductions, fired or incapacitated."[41] However, that extreme situations may be envisioned does not warrant denial of relief in appropriate cases. The problem is more imaginary than real. Courts and juries are not without experience in assessing damages for future loss of earnings in breach of employment contract and personal injury cases. Each can readily be decided upon its individual facts. A discharged employee, however much he may be aggrieved by his alleged wrongful termination, cannot sit idly by. He is under a duty to mitigate damages by making reasonable efforts to obtain gainful employment in an available market.[42] It is not difficult to determine the availability of employment opportunities, the period within which one by reasonable efforts may be re-employed, the employee's work and life expectancy, the discount tables to determine the present value of future damages and other factors that are pertinent on prospective damage awards. The mere fact that damages may be difficult of computation should not exonerate a wrongdoer from liability. "The most elementary conceptions of justice and public policy require that the wrongdoer shall bear the risk of the uncertainty which his own wrong has created."[43] Moreover, to restrict the employee to losses sustained from the date of discharge to the date of the return of the verdict or entry of judgment would encourage the employee to delay the judgment date as long as possible. It would serve to encourage tactics of delay in order to obtain the benefit of increased verdicts by the mere passage of time.

It has already been noted that plaintiff originally sought, and then withdrew his request for, reinstatement and now seeks damages for loss of future salary. The defendant urges that the withdrawal of his request for reinstatement bars any future monetary award. Some courts have taken this view and held that where a discharged employee fails to request or withdraws a request for reinstatement, he automatically waives his right to prospective damages."[44] This Court does not agree. To foreclose prospective damage awards under that concept would mean that the employee is left with no choice but to seek reinstatement, a remedy which in particular cases may be undesirable or unwarranted considering both the employee's or employer's interests.[45]

. . .

[32–45][Footnotes omitted.]

A final note on front pay: the Tenth Circuit has ruled that its availability turns on the nonavailability of reinstatement, and that reinstatement is in fact the "preferred" remedy, even if the discriminatee prefers front pay.[50]

Duty to Mitigate Damages

Entitlement to an award of damages requires the plaintiff to come before the court at least with "clean hands." The injured employee must therefore

---

[50]Blim v. Western Elec. Co., 731 F.2d 1473, 34 FEP 757 (CA 10, 1984); EEOC v. Prudential Federal Sav. & Loan Ass'n, 741 F.2d 1225, 35 FEP 783 (CA 10, 1984).

show that he has attempted to minimize his injury, and the employer's liability, by following all reasonable means of obtaining alternate, substantially equal employment. As one noted legal authority has written:

> "Where one person has committed a tort, breach of contract, or other legal wrong against another, it is incumbent upon the latter to use such means as are reasonable under the circumstances to avoid or minimize the damages. The person wronged cannot recover for any item of damage which could thus have been avoided."[51]

Since many employers attempt to minimize their liability by offering ADEA plaintiffs alternate jobs, litigation arises as to whether these proffered jobs are in fact valid reinstatement offers to the same or substantially equal jobs sufficient to eliminate any post-offer liability against the employer. The employer has the burden of showing that the employee failed to mitigate his damages.[52] One method of doing this would be to show that the employee's efforts to find alternate work, or his decision to switch professions, was not made in good faith.[53]

SPAGNUOLO v. WHIRLPOOL CORP.

548 F. Supp. 104, 32 FEP 1372 (WD NC, 1982), aff'd in relevant part, 717 F.2d 114, 32 FEP 1382 (CA 4, 1983)

Mc MILLIAN, District Judge.

. . .

The principal question is the question of reinstatement.

The job the plaintiff had was a regional supervisory job with headquarters in Charlotte. As Builder Sales Manager he supervised five other salesmen (the number of salesmen in the present job is about ten) and was a part of the management of the sales and distribution of Whirlpool products in the states of North Carolina and South Carolina. He traveled, almost exclusively in the two Carolinas, twenty to twenty-five percent of his time. His territory and customers were familiar. During one period under his management his department accounted for something like two-thirds of the profits that Whirlpool made in its national operation. He was an officer in the Charlotte Home Builders' Association and was active in the home builders' associations of both North Carolina and South Carolina. He was eligible for the "Brintnall" award, which was given annually to the best sales manager in Whirlpool's entire nationwide operation; plaintiff had won that award on two occasions. He was eligible for other such awards.

Defendant offers to make plaintiff a "National Account Manager" for Manufactured Housing. In this position plaintiff would call upon the headquarters of builders of manufactured housing in the hope of developing a new market for Whirlpool products. (Whirlpool re-entered the Manufactured Housing market about two years ago after a period during which it had sold no products directly to the industry because it was unable to do so profitably.) Plaintiff would be required to spend about seventy-five percent of his time traveling all over the country to call on customers directly. As National Account Manager he would supervise no one and would not even have a secretary of his own. The prospects for future advancement in this position are uncertain; unlike Builder Sales Managers, no National Account Manager has ever been promoted.

---

[51]C. McCormick, HANDBOOK ON THE LAW OF DAMAGES 127 (1935).
[52]Cline v. Roadway Express, Inc., 689 F.2d 481, 488–89, 29 FEP 1365 (CA 4, 1982).
[53]*Id.*

In terms of compensation, the "salary points" and the approximate level of promised earnings in the two jobs in question are about the same. However, Sales Managers have opportunities to win bonuses and prizes and to take desirable trips which are not available in the job that has been offered. These items have substantial financial value.

In the new job, plaintiff would be removed entirely from his old friends and customers and would have to break new trails among untried and hitherto unsold potential customers. Also, his transfer at age 59 from a supervisor's job in this community to a traveling salesman's job all over the country would have the obvious effect of making him a living demonstration of the penalties suffered by one who tangles with Whirlpool management, even when plaintiff is so obviously right, as a twelve-person jury long ago found him to be.

In summary of the above, and all the other evidence which may not be mentioned above, the job proposed by defendant would:

(a) Banish plaintiff from his lifelong home and put him on the road for the rest of his employment days;

(b) De-grade him from a supervisory position into the role of a traveling salesman, pure and simple;

(c) Require him to travel three-fourths or so of his time instead of one-fifth to one-fourth of his time as formerly;

(d) Separate plaintiff from his old friends and customers and start him hammering on strange doors in strange lands, dealing with strange people, carrying out a strange selling program which has yet to be substantially tested; and

(e) Remove him from the opportunity for desirable vacation trips and competition for cash prizes and bonuses of substantial amounts, and from the opportunities to attend conventions and make trips with customers which were part of his job heretofore.

I am unable to conclude that the offered job comes close to being "equal" within the meaning of the December 11, 1979 judgment.

Defendant has argued that even if the reinstatement offer does not satisfy the court's original order, plaintiff must accept the proffered job as a means of mitigating the substantial damages that have accrued. Defendant's memorandum of Law on Contested Issues at 5-6. Defendant recognizes, however, that "a discrimination victim may refuse to accept other employment that is . . . essentially different from that in which he was previously employed." *Id.* at 4, citing *Brown v. Colman-Cocker Co.*, 16 FEP Cases 1046, 1051 (W.D. N.C. 1975).

As discussed above, the offered position of national traveling salesman is, in the judgment of the court, "essentially different" from plaintiff's old job of regional supervisor and common law principles of mitigation therefore do not require that plaintiff accept the offer of reinstatement. *See Florence Printing Co. v. NLRB*, 376 F 2d 216, 65 LRRM 2047 (4th Cir.), *cert. denied*, 389 U.S. 840, 66 LRRM 2307 (1967).

. . .

An employee seeking to establish his right to recover for a violation under the ADEA must show that he has attempted to limit the employer's liability by doing what he reasonably could to secure interim/alternate employment, i.e., "mitigate damages." This concept is well-established in other areas of law such as tort and contract law. Its application in statutory law is well-documented, and applying it to ADEA cases is logical. The requirement of mitigating one's damages in ADEA cases enables the plaintiff to show that he has exercised reasonable diligence in good faith to secure work; if such work was located, the employer's back pay liability will be set off accordingly. If such work proved to be unavailable, then the plaintiff's efforts are his proof as to entitlement to an award of monetary relief. In the normal circumstances, the employee is required to show that he was unsuccessful in locating work that was comparable in skill, effort, and pay. Most courts have determined that ADEA plaintiffs must show reasonably diligent efforts to obtain suitable alternate employment before the duty to mitigate requirement will have been met.[54]

Though the employee need only make "reasonable" efforts to mitigate damages due to the employer's unlawful conduct, the employee also cannot know how a court will regard his efforts months or years later. Courts have not been willing, or perhaps have been unable, to establish a bright line between "adequate" versus "inadequate" diligence. The Third Circuit has described the employer's burden in rebutting the employee in terms of a two-pronged test: the employer must show that the employee failed to exercise "reasonable" diligence and that there was a "reasonable" likelihood of finding comparable work with the exercise of such diligence.[55] Since the employer is the party attempting to reduce or eliminate his monetary liability, the burden is properly on him to overcome the employee's evidence. And since the court will presumably have determined that the employer violated the Act—at least in a bifurcated proceeding—the employer contests this portion of the trial from a weaker stance. The test of "reasonableness," though widely used in other areas of law such as torts, may not always adequately consider the employee's aggrieved state of mind, the local employment situation, and other extrinsic factors which affect the determination of the reasonable nature of the employee's conduct, notwithstanding every effort to bring such facts to the court's attention. It can be argued that the test, because of its amorphous nature, does not facilitate the task of weighing the evidence in terms of what the employee may have thought was "reasonable" at the time.[56]

Although one authority suggests that scarcity of available jobs in the labor market and the likely futility of the job search are irrelevant considerations on the issue of mitigating damages, the proffered cases arise under the Taft-Hartley Act, rather than either the FLSA or the ADEA.[57] The courts have not definitively answered the question whether such factors are in fact irrelevant, and it is arguable whether the law would require the doing of a futile act.

The "bottom line," according to the Tenth Circuit, is that the plaintiff need only show reasonable effort to mitigate, rather than a higher standard. The employer has the burden to show that the employee did not make reasonable efforts to secure employment,[58] and that there was a reasonable likelihood that the employee would have found comparable work with the exercise of reasonable diligence.[59]

---

[54]Jackson v. Shell Oil Co., 702 F.2d 197, 31 FEP 686 (CA 9, 1983); Orzel v. City of Wauwatosa Fire Dep't, 697 F.2d 743, 30 FEP 1070 (CA 7, 1983); Koyen v. Consolidated Edison Corp., 560 F. Supp. 1161, 31 FEP 488 (SD NY, 1983); Coates v. National Cash Register Co., 433 F. Supp. 655, 15 FEP 222 (WD Va, 1977) ("reasonable diligence").

[55]Wehr v. Burroughs Corp., 619 F.2d 276, 22 FEP 994 (CA 3, 1980).

[56]Jackson v. Shell Oil Co., *supra* note 54.

[57]Herbert C. Snyder, Jr. (Barnes & Thornburg), "Recent Developments and Trends in ADEA Remedies," citing NLRB v. The Madison Courier, Inc., 505 F.2d 391, 87 LRRM 2440 (CA DC, 1974) and American Bottling Co., 116 NLRB 1303, 38 LRRM 1465 (1956), delivered before the Labor Law Section of the American Bar Association, Annual Meeting-1983, Atlanta, Ga.

[58]EEOC v. Sandia Corp., 639 F.2d 600, 627, 23 FEP 799, 820–21 (CA 10, 1981).

[59]Wehr v. Burroughs Corp., 619 F.2d 276, 278 n.3, 22 FEP 994, 995 (CA 3, 1980).

Pre- and Post-Judgment Interest

The awarding of interest to a successful ADEA plaintiff is based on FLSA case law.[60] The FLSA cases involve recovery for labor previously performed. However an ADEA claim requires reimbursement for wages lost after termination of employment. Under the provisions of 29 U.S.C. Section 626(b), any amounts recoverable under the Age Act are "deemed to be unpaid minimum wages or unpaid overtime . . . (as in FLSA)." Based on that statutory language, courts have rejected employer claims that awarding interest on the back pay award is inequitable, and have awarded such interest.[61] One appeals court has declared that "In assuring equitable relief under the ADEA, the loss of use of this money during the period payments were withheld from (the plaintiff) should be compensated by payment of interest."[62] However, the lost wages must be "accrued and owing" within the meaning of Section 626(b) of the Act.[63]

The Ninth Circuit, citing its own precedent, differentiated between liquidated damages ("a substitution for punitive damages and intended to deter intentional violations") and prejudgment interest, which is intended to compensate "the loss of use of this money during the period payments (are) withheld from plaintiffs."[64]

Prejudgment interest generally is not allowed under the ADEA if liquidated damages have been awarded.[65] An employee's failure to request prejudgment interest before the jury precludes a subsequent request before the trial judge.[66]

Liquidated Damages

The availability of liquidated damages depends on a showing of a "willful violation" of the ADEA.[67] A district court in Virginia instructed the jury to find a willful violation if the acts were "done voluntarily and intentionally, and with the specific intent to do something which is forbidden by law."[68] An unlawfully discharged employee failed to establish that the employer acted with knowledge of the illegality of its conduct, according to a district court in New York, and therefore, the employee was not entitled to liquidated damages because he failed to impugn the integrity of the employer's unsatisfactory evaluations of his performance or to support any claim that his supervisors were motivated by ill will or hostility toward him.[69]

---

[60]McClanahan v. Mathews, 440 F.2d 320, 324–26, 19 WH Cases 1051 (CA 6, 1971); Holtville Alfalfa Mills v. Wyatt, 230 F.2d 398, 401, 12 WH Cases 635 (CA 9, 1955).

[61]Hodgson v. First Federal Sav. & Loan Ass'n, 455 F.2d 818, 820, 4 FEP 269 (CA 5, 1972).

[62]Kelly v. American Standard, Inc., 640 F.2d 974, 25 FEP 94 (CA 9, 1981).

[63]*Supra* note 61.

[64]Criswell v. Western Air Lines, 709 F.2d 544, 32 FEP 1204, 1214 (CA 9, 1983), citing Kelly v. American Standard, Inc., *supra* note 62.

[65]Kolb v. Goldring, Inc., 694 F.2d 869, 30 FEP 633 (CA 1, 1982); Spagnuolo v. Whirlpool Corp., 641 F.2d 1109, 25 FEP 376 (CA 4, 1981), *cert. denied*, 454 U.S. 860 (1981).

[66]*Id.*

[67]Wehr v. Burroughs Corp., *supra* note 59.

[68]Coates v. National Cash Register Co., 433 F. Supp. 655, 15 FEP 222 (WD Va, 1977).

[69]Koyen v. Consolidated Edison Corp., 560 F. Supp. 1161, 31 FEP 488 (SD NY, 1983).

Requirement of Willfulness

Although willfulness is required under the Act for an award of liquidated damages, Congress did not define the term ''willful'' and the legislative history sheds no clear light on what was intended. Under the ADEA, the term has been defined variously as ''voluntarily and intentionally, and with the specific intent to do something the law forbids; that is to say, with bad purpose either to disobey or to disregard the law'';[70] ''employer 'knew' or showed 'reckless disregard' as to whether its conduct was prohibited by ADEA'';[71] and ''voluntary and intentional . . . reckless in not knowing . . . reckless disregard.''[72]

The ''basic divergence'' in the meaning of ''willfulness'' involves the element of specific intent, that is, knowledge of the illegality of the act of discrimination. One court reasoned that knowledge

> ''is an essential element to support an award of liquidated damages. The very fact that Congress, aware that in the instance of a FLSA violation there was an automatic doubling of the pecuniary charge, specified that liquidated damages in the ADEA cases could be recovered ''*only* in instances of *willful* violations,'' leaves no room to doubt that more was required than proof that age was a determining factor for plaintiff's discharge—that more is, a 'specific intent; an intent which goes beyond the mere intent to do the act'—an intent to violate the law.''[73]

Because of the gravity of the liquidated damages penalty, courts have found the logic of the *Koyen* decision on employer knowledge to be persuasive.

However, the question of what constitutes ''willfulness'' was finally settled by the Supreme Court in the following case:

TWA, INC. v. THURSTON

465 U.S. 1065, 36 FEP 977 (1985)

. . .

III

A

Section 7(b) of the ADEA, 29 U.S.C. §626(b), provides that the rights created by the Act are to be ''enforced in accordance with the powers, remedies, and procedures'' of the Fair Labor Standards Act. *See Lorillard v. Pons*, 434 U.S., at 579, 16 FEP Cases, at 886 (1978). But the remedial provisions of the two statutes are not identical. Congress declined to incorporate into the ADEA several FLSA sections. Moreover, §16(b) of the FLSA, which makes the award of liquidated damages mandatory, is significantly qualified in ADEA §7(b) by a proviso that a prevailing plaintiff is entitled to double damages ''only in cases of willful violations.'' 29 U.S.C. §626(b). In this case, the Court of Appeals held that TWA's violation of the ADEA was ''willful,'' and that the respondents therefore were entitled to double damages. 713 F.2d, at 957, 32 FEP Cases, at 1197. We granted certiorari to review this holding.

---

[70]Loeb v. Textron, Inc., 600 F.2d 1003, 1020 n.27, 20 FEP 29 (CA 1, 1979), citing E. Devitt & C. Blackmar, Federal Jury Practice & Instructions, Section 14.06, at 384 (3rd Ed. 1977).

[71]Goodman v. Heublein, Inc., 654 F.2d 127, 131, 25 FEP 645 (CA 2, 1981).

[72]Blackwell v. Sun Elec. Corp., 696 F.2d 1176, 1184, 30 FEP 1177 (CA 6, 1983).

[73]Koyen v. Consolidated Edison, *supra* note 69.

The legislative history of the ADEA indicates that Congress intended for liquidated damages to be punitive in nature. The original bill proposed by the administration incorporated §16(a) of the FLSA, which imposes criminal liability for a willful violation. *See* 113 CONG. REC. 2199 (1967). Senator Javits found "certain serious defects" in the administration bill. He stated that "difficult problems of proof . . . would arise under a criminal provision," and that the employer's invocation of the Fifth Amendment might impede investigation, conciliation, and enforcement. 113 CONG. REC. 7076 (1967). Therefore, he proposed that "the [FLSA's] criminal penalty in cases of willful violation . . . [be] eliminated and a double damage liability substituted." *Ibid.* Senator Javits argued that his proposed amendment would "furnish an effective deterrent to willful violations [of the ADEA]," *ibid.*, and it was incorporated into the ADEA with only minor modification, S. 788, 90th Cong., 1st Sess. (1967).

This Court has recognized that in enacting the ADEA, "Congress exhibited . . . a detailed knowledge of the FLSA provisions and their judicial interpretation . . . ." *Lorillard v. Pons*, 434 U.S. 575, 581, 16 FEP Cases 885, 887 (1978). The manner in which FLSA §16(a) has been interpreted therefore is relevant. In general, courts have found that an employer is subject to criminal penalties under the FLSA when he "wholly disregards the law . . . without making any reasonable effort to determine whether the plan he is following would constitute a violation of the law." *Nabob Oil Co. v. United States*, 190 F.2d 478, 479, 10 WH Cases 318 (CA 10), *cert. denied*, 342 U.S. 876, 10 WH Cases 465 (1951); *see also Darby v. United States*, 132 F.2d 928, 3 WH Cases 23 (CA 5, 1943).[19] This standard is substantially in accord with the interpretation of "willful" adopted by the Court of Appeals in interpreting the liquidated damages provision of the ADEA. The court below stated that a violation of the Act was "willful" if "the employer . . . knew or showed reckless disregard for the matter of whether its conduct was prohibited by the ADEA." 713 F.2d, at 956, 32 FEP Cases, at 1197. Given the legislative history of the liquidated damages provision, we think the "reckless disregard" standard is reasonable.

The definition of "willful" adopted by the above cited courts is consistent with the manner in which this Court has interpreted the term in other criminal and civil statutes. In *United States v. Murdock*, 290 U.S. 389 (1933), the defendant was prosecuted under the Revenue Acts of 1926 and 1928, which made it a misdemeanor for a person "willfully" to fail to pay the required tax. The *Murdock* Court stated that conduct was "willful" within the meaning of this criminal statute if it was "marked by careless disregard [for] whether or not one has the right so to act." *Id.*, at 395. In *United States v. Illinois Central R.*, 303 U.S. 239 (1938), the Court applied the *Murdock* definition of "willful" in a civil case. There, the defendant's failure to unload a cattle car was "willful," because it showed a disregard for the governing statute and an difference to its requirements. *Id.*, at 242–243.[20]

The respondents argue that an employer's conduct is willful if he is "cognizant of an appreciable possibility that the employees involved were covered by the [ADEA]." In support of their position, the respondents cite §6 of the Portal-to-Portal Act of 1947 (PPA), 29 U.S.C. §255(a), which is incorporated in both the ADEA and the FLSA. Section 6 of the PPA provides for a 2-year statute of limitations period unless the violation is willful, in which case the limitations period is extended to three years. 29 U.S.C. §255(a). Several courts have held that a violation is willful within the meaning of §6 if the employer knew that the ADEA was "in the picture." *See, e.g., Coleman*

---

[19]Courts below have held that an employer's action may be "willful," within the meaning of §16(a) of the FLSA, even though he did not have an evil motive or bad purpose. See Nabob Oil Co. v. United States, 190 F.2d 478, 10 WH Cases 318 (CA 10, cert. denied, 342 U.S. 876, 10 WH Cases 318 (1951). We do not agree with TWA's argument that unless it intended to violate the Act, double damages are inappropriate under §7(b) of the ADEA. Only one court of appeals has expressed approval of this position. See Loeb v. Textron, Inc., 600 F.2d 1003, 1020 n.27, 20 FEP Cases 29, 41 (CA 1 1979).

[20]The definition of "willful" set forth in Murdock and Illnois Central has been applied by courts interpreting numerous other criminal and civil statutes. See e.g., Alabama Power Co. v. Federal Energy Regulatory Comm'n, 584 F.2d 750 (CA 5 1978); F.X. Messina Construction Corp. v. Occupational Safety & Health Review Comm'n, 505 F.2d 701 (CA 1 1974).

v. Jiffy June Farms, Inc., 458 F.2d 1139, 1142, 20 WH Cases 321 (CA 5 1971), *cert. denied*, 409 U.S. 948, 20 WH Cases 937 (1972); *EEOC v. Central Kansas Medical Center*, 705 F.2d 1270, 1274, 31 FEP Cases 1510, 1512 (CA 10 1983). Respondents contend that the term "willful" should be interpreted in a similar manner in applying the liquidated damages provision of the ADEA.

We are unpersuaded by respondents' argument that a violation of the Act is "willful" if the employer simply knew of the potential applicability of the ADEA. Even if the "in the picture" standard were appropriate for the statute of limitations, the same standard should not govern a provision dealing with liquidated damages.[21] More importantly, the broad standard proposed by the respondents would result in an award of double damages in almost every case. As employers are required to post ADEA notices, it would be virtually impossible for an employer to show that he was unaware of the Act and its potential applicability. Both the legislative history and the structure of the statute show that Congress intended a two-tiered liability scheme. We decline to interpret the liquidated damages provision of ADEA §7(b) in a manner that frustrates this intent.[22]

---

[21]The Courts of Appeals are divided over whether Congress intended the "willfulness" standard to be identical for determining liquidated damages and for purposes of the limitations period. Compare Spagnuolo v. Whirlpool Corp., 641 F.2d 1109, 1113, 25 FEP Cases 376, 379 (CA 4), cert. denied, 454 U.S. 860, 26 FEP Cases 1688 (1981) (standards are identical), with Kelly v. American Standard, Inc., 640 F.2d 974, 979, 25 FEP Cases 94, 97 (CA 9 1981) (standards are different).

[22]The "in the picture" standard proposed by the respondents would allow the recovery of liquidated damages even if the employer acted reasonably and in complete "good faith." Congress hardly intended such a result.

The Court interpreted the FLSA, as originally enacted, as allowing the recovery of liquidated damages any time that there was a violation of the Act. See Overnight Motor Transportation Co. v. Missel, 316 U.S. 572, 2 WH Cases 47 (1942). In response to its dissatisfaction with that harsh interpretation of the provision, Congress enacted the Portal-to-Portal Act of 1947. See Lorillard v. Pons, 434 U.S. 575, 581–582 n.8, 16 FEP Cases 885, 887 (1978). Section 11 of the PPA, 29 U.S.C. §260, provides the employer with a defense to a mandatory award of liquidated damages when it can show good faith and reasonable grounds for believing it was not in violation of the FLSA. Section 7(b) of the ADEA does not incorporate §11 of the PPA, contra Hays v. Republic Steel Corp., 531 F.2d 1307, 12 FEP Cases 1654 (CA 5 1976). Nevertheless, we think that the same concerns are reflected in the proviso to §7(b) of the ADEA.

Standard of Proof.   Since the characteristic of age is different from race or creed, the form of prejudice and the form of proof may be different. As the Fifth Circuit stated: "replacement of an older employee by a younger worker does not raise the same inference of improper motive that attends replacement of a black by a white person in a Title VII case."[74] In age discrimination cases, "the judgment may be wrong, but it does not connote willfulness absent direct or circumstantial evidence to support the charge."[75]

As an indication of the type of proof that is inadequate to support a claim of "willful" violation, in pursuit of liquidated damages, the Supreme Court's decision in *TWA, Inc. v. Thurston* is illustrative. The Court observed that the employer "acted reasonably and in good faith in attempting to determine whether their plan would violate the ADEA."[76] The Court reasoned:

"There is no indication that TWA was ever advised by counsel that its new transfer policy discriminated against captains on the basis of age.

"There simply is no evidence that TWA acted in 'reckless disregard' of the

---

[74]Marshall v. Goodyear Tire & Rubber Co., 554 F.2d 730, 736, 15 FEP 139 (CA 5, 1977), citing Laugesen v. Anaconda Co., 510 F.2d 307, 311–12 n.4, 10 FEP 567 (CA 6, 1975).

[75]*Supra* note 69.

[76]TWA, Inc. v. Thurston, 469 U.S. ____, 36 FEP 977 (1985); *see also* Prudential Fed. Sav. & Loan Ass'n v. EEOC, ____U.S. ____, 36 FEP 1168 (1985).

requirements of the ADEA. The airline had obligations under the collective-bargaining agreement with the Airline Pilots Association. In an attempt to bring its retirement policy into compliance with the ADEA, while at the same time observing the terms of the collective-bargaining agreement, TWA sought legal advice and consulted with the Union. Despite opposition from the union, a plan was adopted that permitted cockpit employees to work as "flight engineers" after reaching age 60. Apparently TWA officials and the airline's attorneys failed to focus specifically on the effect of each aspect of the new retirement policy for cockpit personnel. It is reasonable to believe that the parties involved, in focusing on the larger overall problem, simply overlooked the challenged aspect of the new plan.[23] We conclude that TWA's violation of the Act was not willful within the meaning of §7(b), and that respondents therefore are not entitled to liquidated damages."[77]

---

[23][Footnote omitted.]

Court Discretion. The Second Circuit has rejected the employer's argument that Section 7(b) of the ADEA, by incorporating FLSA procedures, also incorporates the procedural aspects of the Portal-to-Portal Act (PPA) concerning the good-faith defense to liquidated damages liability.[78] The appeals court relied on *Lorillard v. Pons*, wherein the Supreme Court "pointedly observed" that the ADEA selectively adopts only some of the procedural changes that the PPA made applicable to the FLSA: Section 7(e) (29 U.S.C. Section 626(e)(1976)) specifically incorporates Sections 6 and 10 of the PPA (29 U.S.C. Sections 225 and 259)(1976)), concerning statute of limitations and reliance on agency rulings, but not Section 11 (29 U.S.C. 260)(1976), the liquidated damages provision (the so-called "doctrine of selective incorporation").[79] Following *Lorillard v. Pons*, and the addition of Section 7(c)(2) to the ADEA (29 U.S.C. Section 626(c)(2)(Supp. II 1978)), the issue of court discretion in awarding liquidated damages for willful violations would appear to have been settled.

However, the Supreme Court may have left room for such discretion in the wake of *TWA v. Thurston*, by failing to spell out with particularity the elements of willful intent.[80] The Court rejected the employer's argument that liquidated damages could be imposed only when there was a finding of specific intent to violate the ADEA, but this leaves open the question of precisely what type of intent is required to trigger the finding of a "willful" violation. District courts may be confused in determining whether their prior standards are viable under *TWA v. Thurston*. The Seventh Circuit indicated that the standard for determining willfulness should be the employer's state of mind at the time the alleged discrimination occurred.[81] But the Fourth Circuit regarded this decision as providing only "some judicial support" for the proposition that the absence of intent makes an employer's action other than willful.[82] The Supreme Court's decision in *TWA v. Thurston* raises at least two important questions: what

---

[77]TWA, Inc. v. Thurston, *supra* note 76, 465 U.S.____, 36 FEP at 987.

[78]*Supra* note 71.

[79]*Id.*, citing Lorillard v. Pons, 434 U.S. 575, 16 FEP 885 (1978).

[80]*Supra* note 76. *See also* McDowell v. Avtex Fibers, Inc., 740 F.2d 214, 35 FEP 371 (CA 3, 1984).

[81]Syvock v. Milwaukee Boiler Mfg. Co., 665 F.2d149, 27 FEP 610 (CA 7, 1981.

[82]Crosland v. Charlotte Hosp., 686 F.2d 208, 29 FEP 1178, 1184 (CA 4, 1982).

constitutes "intent" under the ADEA; and whether *Thurston* precludes all of the approaches previously adopted by the lower courts.[83] And the answers to these questions may require the courts to exercise even more discretion.

Claim of Good-Faith Belief

The First Circuit has stated that it did not accept the claim that a specific finding as to the employer's good faith under Section 11 of the Portal-to-Portal Act was required before liquidated damages may be awarded in an ADEA case.[84] Citing the selective incorporation doctrine enunciated by the Supreme Court in *Lorillard v. Pons*,[85] the First Circuit ruled that a finding of a good-faith belief by the employer was unnecessary to the imposition of liquidated damages. This reasoning was adopted in *Wehr v. Burroughs Corp.*,[86] which also contained a well articulated discussion on the meaning of "willfulness." But any confusion noted by the *Wehr* court as to the various standards for determining when willful violations have occurred was settled by the Supreme Court in *TWA, Inc. v. Thurston*.[87] Suffice to say that the defense of a good-faith belief is insufficient to preclude imposition of an award of liquidated damages, if the requisite state of mind is found.

Compensatory Damages

In 1977, a court found that damages for pain and suffering were allowable under the ADEA, on the grounds that:
(1) The ADEA, like Title VIII of the Civil Rights Act of 1968 creates a new statutory tort, and the existence of such a statutory right implies the existence of necessary and appropriate remedies;
(2) The ADEA shares the "make whole" purpose of Title VII of the Civil Rights Act of 1964 and emotional and psychological losses occasioned by age discrimination were clearly recognized by Congress in its deliberations on ADEA;
(3) Compensatory damages for pain and suffering have been found appropriate in other discrimination contexts, including employment and housing; and
(4) Cases denying damages awards for pain and suffering in Title VII cases have been premised on that statute's express limitation of relief to equitable remedies, but the ADEA contains specific allowance of legal relief.[88]

However, the Act was subsequently amended in 1978, and it has been noted that the statute as originally enacted, and subsequent amendments are silent

---

[83]"Standard forDetermining Willfulness of Violation of ADEA," 118 Analysis 5, at 9 (1-14-85), *Labor Relations Reporter* (BNA 1985).

[84]Loeb v. Textron, Inc., 600 F.2d 1003, 1020, 20 FEP 29, 41–42 (CA 1, 1979).

[85]434 U.S. 575, 16 FEP 885 (1978).

[86]619 F.2d 276, 22 FEP 994 (CA 3, 1980).

[87]TWA, Inc. v. Thurston, 469 U.S. _____, 36 FEP 977 (1985).

[88]Coates v. National Cash Register Co., 433 F. Supp. 655, 15 FEP 222 (WD Va, 1977).

on the issue of compensatory damages for pain and suffering. The Conference report accompanying the 1978 amendments indicates congressional disapproval of such awards, though, on the ground that liquidated damages provide full relief for damages, such as emotional or psychological distress, that are difficult to prove.[89]

The circuit courts have consistently rejected claims for compensatory damages.[90]

Punitive Damages

A claim for punitive damages is essentially a request that the court "punish" the offending party for its misconduct. The request is usually based on the emotional distress aspect of pain and suffering (see this chapter, "Compensatory Damages") but courts of appeals have uniformly rejected requests for "emotional distress" punitive damages.[91] The basis for rejecting such claims rests on the supposition that the statutory scheme of reinstatement, lost wages and benefits, liquidated damages, and attorney fees is sufficient to make the plaintiff whole.[92] However, the Ninth Circuit in *Kelly v. American Standard, Inc.*,[93] allowed the plaintiff to pursue damages for emotional distress under the Washington State Law Against Discrimination (Wash. Rev. Code Ann. §49.60)(Supp. 1980), since it regarded emotional distress as an "appropriate element of damage recovery" under that statute.

It is safe to say that the absence of any legislative intent to create a punitive effect upon an ADEA violator and the presence of a full statutory scheme to make the injured party whole have defeated attempts to obtain punitive damages under the federal Age Act. But counsel should be warned to consider the application of the state statutes to their actions.

Attorney's Fees

Section 7(b) of the ADEA incorporates Section 16(b) of the Fair Labor Standards Act to the effect that a prevailing plaintiff in an Age Act suit is entitled to "reasonable attorney's fee to be paid by the defendant and costs of action." The difficulty arises when there is a dispute over what constitutes a "reasonable" attorney's fee, and what are the "costs" of the action as contemplated by the statute.

In a non-ADEA case, the Tenth Circuit determined the amount of an award of attorney's fees by considering the following factors: "(1) the number of

---

[89]H.R. Conf. Rep. No. 950, 95th Cong. 2d Sess. 14, reprinted in 1978 U.S. CODE CONG. & AD. NEWS 528, 535.

[90]*Supra* note 86; Slatin v. Stanford Research Institute, 590 F.2d 1292, 18 FEP 1475 (CA 2, 1979); Hill v. Spiegel, Inc., 708 F.2d 233, 31 FEP 1532 (CA 6, 1983); Perrell v. Financeamerica Corp., 726 F.2d 654, 33 FEP 1728 (CA 10, 1984).

[91]*Supra* note 86; Walker v. Petit Constr. Co., 605 F.2d 128, 129–130, 20 FEP 993 (CA 2, 1979), *modified sub nom.* Frith v. Eastern Air Lines, Inc., 611 F.2d 950, 25 FEP 87 (1979); Slatin v. Stanford Research Institute, *supra* note 90; Vasquez v. Eastern Air Lines, Inc., 579 F.2d 107, 17 FEP 1116 (CA 1, 1978); Rodriguez v. Taylor, 569 F.2d 1231, 16 FEP 533 (CA 3, 1977).

[92]Kelly v. American Standard, Inc., 640 F.2d 974 n.14, 25 FEP 94 (CA 9, 1981).

[93]*Id.*, 25 FEP at 101.

hours the attorney used in preparing and arguing the claim; (2) the novelty and complexity of the case; (3) the skill and preparedness of the attorney; (4) the resulting judgment; and (5) awards in similar cases."[94]

This set of criteria has been applied in ADEA cases by several courts.[95]

Reasonableness

The first step in determining a reasonable fee is to calculate the "lodestar" amount—that is, the reasonable number of hours devoted to pursuing the claim multiplied by the reasonable hourly rate.[96] The Third Circuit has ruled that the district court is required to determine "not only the number of hours actually devoted to the successful claims, but also whether it was reasonably necessary to spend that number of hours in order to perform the legal services for which compensation is sought."[97] This is the "reasonably necessary" aspect of the reasonableness test.

Application of the "reasonably necessary" standard has resulted in a district court ruling that a law firm representing an individual against his former employer will be compensated for time that the firm spent in reviewing the case file after another law firm voluntarily withdrew from the case, and for the second firm's use of a large number of persons who worked on the case; however, the second firm was not allowed to recover fees for time spent in unsuccessful pursuit of state law claims or for time spent in responding to the employer's motion for sanctions.[98]

Another aspect of the reasonableness of an attorney's fee is the hourly rate. Use of a paralegal to perform routine administrative or clerical tasks has been regarded as an efficient use of a law firm's time, even at the paralegal's rate of $27.50 per hour, since an attorney's rate for such tasks would be wasteful.[99] In a non-ADEA context, the Third Circuit has established the principle that a district court may consider an attorney's unethical conduct as a factor in determining a reasonable fee.[100] The reasonable value of an attorney's services also affect the determination of what the reasonable fee should be. The hourly rate of two attorneys was reduced by the Third Circuit upon evidence that there was an overcharge scheme, and a third attorney was receiving compensation where no services had been performed.[101]

Some courts of appeals have denied recovery to plaintiffs for any work on unsuccessful claims.[102] Prevailing plaintiffs generally should receive a fee

---

[94]Taylor v. Safeway Stores, Inc., 524 F.2d 262, 268, 11 FEP 449, 452 (CA 10, 1975).

[95]E.g., see Coates v. NCR, supra note 88.

[96]Wehr v. Burroughs Corp., 477 F. Supp. 1012, 22 FEP 982 (ED Pa, 1979), citing Lindy Bros. Builders, Inc. of Philadelphia v. American Radiator & Standard Sanitary Corp., 487 F.2d 161 (CA 2, 1973) ("Lindy I"). See also Detroit v. Grinnell, 495 F.2d 470, 473 (CA 2, 1974).

[97]Hughes v. Repko, 578 F.2d 483, 487 (CA 3, 1978).

[98]Wehr v. Burroughs, 477 F. Supp. 1012, 22 FEP 982 (ED Pa, 1979), aff'd as modified, 619 F.2d 276, 22 FEP 994 (CA 3, 1980).

[99]Id.

[100]Prandini v. National Tea Co., 585 F.2d 47, 18 FEP 700 (CA 3, 1978).

[101]Id.

[102]Bartholomew v. Watson, 665 F.2d 910, 914 (CA 9, 1982); Muscare v. Quinn, 614 F.2d 577, 579–81 (CA 7, 1980); Hughes v. Repko, supra note 97.

based on hours spent on all "nonfrivolous" claims, according to other courts.[103] Recovery of a fee for hours spent on unsuccessful claims depends, to other courts, on the "nexus" between those hours expended and the success achieved.[104]

"Lodestar" Adjustments

An award of attorneys' fees is not conditioned on a plaintiff's *complete* success either at trial or on appeal, to receive attorneys' fees.[105] However, the Supreme Court has ruled that the extent of success is a critical factor in determining the amount of the award, under the Civil Rights Attorney's Fees Awards Act of 1976 (42 U.S.C. Section 1988): "The amount of the fee, of course, must be determined on the facts of each case."[106] The Court was interpreting a statute that was designed to enhance plaintiffs' rights to bring civil rights litigation, to attract competent counsel, and to avoid a windfall for counsel in pursuing attorneys' fees.

The Court cited the House Report which accompanied the legislation, for the criteria to be applied in determining the "reasonable" fees to be awarded to successful plaintiffs in civil rights litigation:

> "The twelve factors are: (1) the time and labor required; (2) the novelty and difficulty of the questions; (3) the skill requisite to perform the legal service properly; (4) the preclusion of employment by the attorney due to acceptance of the case; (5) the customary fee; (6) whether the fee is fixed or contingent; (7) time limitations imposed by the client or the circumstances; (8) the amount involved and the results obtained; (9) the experience, reputation, and ability of the attorneys; (10) the 'undesirability' of the case; (11) the nature and length of the professional relationship with the client; and (12) awards in similar cases."[107]

The Court pointed out that the Act was designed to overcome the discouraging effect of the "American Rule"—each party in a lawsuit ordinarily shall bear its own attorney's fees unless there is express statutory authorization to the contrary. It concluded, based on the Senate Report, that a prevailing plaintiff " 'should ordinarily recover an attorney's fee unless special circumstances would render such an award unjust.' "[108]

However, the Age Act specifically provides for an award of attorneys' fees, and it may appear at first blush to be unnecessary or irrelevant to examine Supreme Court pronouncements under the Civil Rights Attorney's Fees Awards Act on this issue. The crucial point of this examination is that in *Hensley v. Eckerhart*, the Court stated in a footnote:

> "The legislative history of Section 1988 indicates that Congress intended that

---

[103]Sherkow v. Wisconsin, 630 F.2d 498, 504–05, 23 FEP 939, 943–44 (CA 7, 1980); Northcross v. Board of Educ. of Memphis City Schools, 611 F.2d 624, 636 (CA 6, 1979), *cert. denied*, 447 U.S. 911 (1980).

[104]Copeland v. Marshall, 641 F.2d 880, 891–92 n.18, 23 FEP 967, 975 (CA DC, 1980)(en banc); Lamphere v. Brown Univ., 610 F.2d 46, 47, 21 FEP 824, 825 (CA 1, 1979).

[105]Cancellier v. Federated Dep't Stores, 672 F.2d 1312, 28 FEP 1151 (CA 9, 1981), *cert. denied*, 459 U.S. 859 (1982).

[106]Hensley v. Eckerhart, 461 U.S. 424, 31 FEP 1169 (1983).

[107]*Id.*, citing H.R. Rep. No. 94–1558 (1976); Johnson v. Georgia Highway Express, Inc., 488 F.2d 714, 7 FEP 1 (CA 5, 1974).

[108]*Id.*, citing S.Rep. No. 94–1011, p.4 (1976) (quoting Newman v. Piggie Park Enterprises, 390 U.S. 400, 402 (1968).

'the standards for awarding fees be generally the same as under the fee provisions of the 1964 Civil Rights Act.' S. Rep. No. 94-1011, p. 4 (1976). *The standards set forth in this opinion are generally applicable in all cases in which Congress has authorized an award of fees to a "prevailing party."* (emphasis supplied)[109]

It becomes clear that the Court established a policy for determining the propriety of awarding attorneys' fees in civil rights litigation. The Court intended to "paint with a broad brush," as evidenced by the delimiting language of "all cases in which Congress has authorized an award of fees" to a prevailing plaintiff.

Following this decision, one source noted that several issues remained unanswered:

(1) whether current rates should be used to account for inflation, whether an inflation adjustment should be made to historical rates, or whether inflation should be considered at all;
(2) whether locally prevailing rates or national rates should be applied;
(3) whether market rates should be awarded to attorneys whose retainers require fee payments at a lower rate; and
(4) whether fees may be awarded for time spent in other proceedings that had an effect on the lawsuit.[110]

The Court had an opportunity to clarify some of these issues in 1984. Again in a non-ADEA context, the Court interpreted the Civil Rights Attorneys' Fees Award Act to the effect that:

(1) The "prevailing market rates in the relevant community," and not the cost-related standard, are to be used in calculating fees awards;
(2) An upward adjustment of the "lodestar" amount of attorneys' fees is permissible in proper circumstances;
(3) The quality of representation may justify an upward adjustment of the "lodestar" amount only in rare cases in which the fee applicant offers specific evidence to show that the quality of service rendered was superior to what reasonably should be expected in light of the hourly rates charged and that the success was exceptional;
(4) The results obtained normally should not provide an independent basis for an upward adjustment of the "lodestar" amount, where acknowledgement of this factor generally will be subsumed within the other factors used to calculate a reasonable fee; and
(5) The number of persons benefited is not a consideration of significance in calculating a fees award under Section 1988.[111]

The Court settled the issue of whether and when adjustments to the lodestar amount may be made: "where a plaintiff has obtained excellent results, his attorney should recover a fully compensatory fee. Normally this will encompass all hours reasonably expended on the litigation, and indeed in some cases of

---

[109]Hensley v. Eckerhart, *supra* note 106, 31 FEP at 1172–73 n.7.

[110]"Extent of Success as Critical Factor in Award of Attorney's Fees to Prevailing Party," 113 Analysis 17, *Labor Relations Reporter* (BNA 1983).

[111]Blum v. Stenson, 465 U.S. 886, 34 FEP 417 (1984).

exceptional success an enhancement award may be justified.''[112] It also conceded the difficulty in defining what constitutes a prevailing rate:

> ''We recognize, of course, that determining an appropriate 'market rate' for the services of a lawyer is inherently difficult. Market prices of commodities and most services are determined by supply and demand. In this traditional sense there is no such thing as a prevailing market rate for the service of lawyers in a particular community. The type of services rendered by lawyers, as well as their experience, skill and reputation, varies extensively—even within a law firm. Accordingly, the hourly rates of lawyers in private practice also vary widely. The fees charged often are based on the product of hours devoted to the representation multiplied by the lawyer's customary rate. But the fee usually is discussed with the client, may be negotiated, and it is the client who pays whether he wins or loses. The §1988 fee determination is made by the court in an entirely different setting: there is no negotiation or even discussion with the prevailing client, as the fee—found to be reasonable by the court—is paid by the losing party. Nevertheless, as shown in the text above, the critical inquiry in determining reasonableness is now generally recognized as the appropriate hourly rate. And the rates charged in private representations may afford relevant comparisons.
>
> ''In seeking some basis for a standard, courts properly have required prevailing attorneys to justify the reasonableness of the requested rate or rates. To inform and assist the court in the exercise of its discretion, the burden is on the fee applicant to produce satisfactory evidence—in addition to the attorney's own affidavits—that the requested rates are in line with those prevailing in the community for similar services by lawyers of reasonably comparable skill, experience and reputation. A rate determined in this way is normally deemed to be reasonable, and is referred to—for convenience—as the prevailing market rate.''[113]

The Court acknowledged the practical considerations in setting a prevailing rate, but did not retract from the underlying policy considerations of the Civil Rights Attorneys' Fees Award Act, as enunciated in *Hensley*.

The District of Columbia Circuit Court of Appeals has ruled that a law firm's customary rate is presumptively reasonable as an hourly rate for attorneys' fees purposes.[114] The employer sought to establish the appropriate amount for attorneys' fees awards as the rate actually charged by the firm in similar cases, while the employees sought to establish it as the ''prevailing community rate.'' The appeals court based its decision on the inherent reliability of the law firm's traditional billing practices and billing structure, rejecting the ''community'' approach.[115]

Because the Age Act provides for attorney's fees and costs ''of the action'' (29 U.S.C. Section 216(b)), a plaintiff's request for compensation for services and appearances by his attorney and the paralegal before the Equal Employment Opportunity Commission (EEOC) prior to the commencement of the lawsuit were denied.[116] The court was persuaded by the absence of the word ''proceeding'' in the statute, and the analysis of the U.S. Court of Appeals for the District of Columbia in an ADEA action.[117]

---

[112]*Id.*, 34 FEP at 423, citing Hensley v. Eckerhart, *supra* note 106, at 31 FEP 1174; *see also* Monroe v. United Air Lines, 565 F. Supp. 274, 34 FEP 1599 (ND Ill, 1983).

[113]*Id.*, 34 FEP at 421 n.11.

[114]Laffey v. Northwest Airlines, 35 FEP 1609 (CA DC, 1984).

[115]*Id.*

[116]Koyen v. Consolidated Edison Co., 560 F. Supp. 1161, 31 FEP 488 (SD NY, 1983).

[117]*Id.*, 31 FEP at 495, citing Kennedy v. Whitehurst, 690 F.2d 951, 957, 29 FEP 1373 (CA DC, 1982).

The district court disallowed the request for pre-action representation, and proceeded to lecture the attorney for his services once the action had commenced:

> "Time is only of relative importance. Allowances should be granted for time reasonably and necessarily required in the adequate representation and advance of the client's interests and one may not indulge in the luxurious practice of law at the expense of the other side."[118]

The court reduced the attorney's "lodestar" amount of $25,000 to $20,000, in view of evidence that time was "generously expended" with respect to some activities, but it then increased the amount to $30,000 to take into account all relevant factors, including the contingency nature of the retainer. There is an inherent tension between the contingency arrangement as a factor for adjusting the "lodestar" amount, and the need to use attorney's services in an efficient manner.

The most elaborate explanation of the "lodestar" approach in employment discrimination cases was rendered by the U.S. Court of Appeals at Washington, D.C. The case was brought under Title VII, and although the appeals court settled on the "prevailing market rate" which it later rejected in *Laffey v. Northwest Airlines*,[119] the court failed to establish a procedure for determining that rate, other than to declare that it was a function of a "multiplicity of factors."[120]

"Lodestars" have been adjusted for everything from novel issues to contingency arrangements to complex litigation; they have been adjusted downward for duplication of effort and for failure to document research. The only aspect of the "lodestar" that has not and will not change is the "multiplicity of factors" that the Washington, D.C. appeals court noted. These factors can be expected to continue to flourish, and to provide more litigation for civil rights, particularly ADEA, lawyers.

Fees and Costs

Aside from attorneys' fees, the issue of costs can be very important to a prevailing plaintiff, since the scope of these expenses can be sufficient to eclipse a substantial portion of many awards, including liquidated damages awards. Courts have rejected claims for the cost of travel, meals, hotels, or expenses in obtaining depositions, or expenses incidental to preparation of a case, or for an expert's report that was neither used nor referred to in trial.[121] This has led hard-nosed practitioners to attempt to enter into evidence or to have witnesses mention even the most extraneous reports, for purposes of justifying the cost under the case law.

Billable costs for determining fees include time spent in preparing a petition for the award of attorneys' fees, but attorneys should be wary of inefficiency

---

[118]*Id.*, 31 FEP at 496. (Footnotes omitted.)

[119]*Supra* note 114.

[120]Copeland v. Marshall, 641 F.2d 880, 23 FEP 967 (CA DC, 1980) (en banc).

[121]Ginsberg v. Burlington Indus., Inc., 500 F. Supp. 692, 702, 24 FEP 426, 430 (SD NY, 1980).

or duplication in the preparation of materials in support of these petitions.[122] Also allowed are fees for the transcript of an expert witness's deposition, where the deposition was taken at the employer's request and by court order during trial; disallowed costs include "LEXIS" research, telephone calls, travel, expenses, meals, exhibits, and any nontestifying witness unless a stipulation made the testimony unnecessary.[123] Within the court's discretion are such items as costs for transcript preparation, clerk's fees, and use of the U.S. Marshals Service.[124] For a comprehensive list of what fees and costs may be assessed in federal practice, consult 28 U.S.C. Sections 1911–1929.

Exceptions to Recovery

As with every rule, there are exceptions. Although the Age Act specifically provides for an award of reasonable attorneys' fees and costs, courts have found it necessary to carve out exceptions to this otherwise mandatory provision. Common-law doctrines for disallowing recovery include "unclean hands," estoppel, and sovereign immunity. Under the case law, courts have recognized bad faith, governmental immunity, and the nonprofit nature of the plaintiff as bases for rejecting claims for recovery, or for imposing liabilities.

Bad Faith.   The common-law rule is that "each party should bear the costs of its own legal representation."[125] However, a recognized exception to this rule is the "bad faith" exception which allows an award of fees to a party when an "opponent has acted in bad faith, vexatiously, wantonly or for oppressive reasons."[126] A district court in Texas ruled that an employer who prevailed in an ADEA action brought by the EEOC was entitled to attorneys' fees under the bad-faith exception, where the EEOC failed to make an objective evaluation of its case, pursued new theories relentlessly up to and during trial, and appeared "incredibly unprepared."[127] After a five-day jury trial, the employer was vindicated in one hour, and he subsequently sought to recover for attorney's fees and expenses, including expert witness fees. The court observed initially that such a motion against the EEOC is governed by the Equal Access to Justice Act, which provides in part:

> "The United States shall be liable for such fees and expenses to the same extent that any other party would be liable under the common law or under the terms of any statute which specifically provides for such an award."[128]

The court concluded that this action was "one of the weakest employment discrimination cases ever pursued to trial" before the court, and that the EEOC was proceeding in bad faith.[129] The court also granted the defendant's request

---

[122]Wehr v. Burroughs Corp., 477 F. Supp. 1012, 22 FEP 982 (ED Pa, 1979), *aff'd as modified*, 619 F.2d 276, 22 FEP 994 (CA 3, 1980).

[123]*Id.*

[124]*Supra* note 121.

[125]F.D. Rich Co., Inc. v. U.S. *ex rel.* Industrial Lumber Co., 417 U.S. 116, 129 (1974).

[126]*Id.*

[127]EEOC v. Western Elec. Co., 33 FEP 1259 (SD Tex, 1983).

[128]28 U.S.C. §2412(b).

[129]*Supra* note 127, 33 FEP at 1260–61.

for expert witness fees, finding that exceptional circumstances existed: "when an unfounded action or defense is maintained in bad faith, vexatiously, wantonly, or for oppressive reasons."[130]

A district court ruled that no attorney's fees at all would be awarded to counsel for an individual who settled his ADEA action against the employer, where counsel persisted in maintaining that the individual's back wages would come to over $57,000, even though it quickly became evident that they would amount to no more than $8,200.[131] The attorney never sought to inspect any of the documents that he claimed were critical, he took no depositions, and he failed to appear and to produce the individual for deposition-taking, the court noted.[132]

On appeal, the Seventh Circuit affirmed, on the basis of counsel unreasonably prolonging the litigation, his refusal to settle the case earlier for an amount only slightly less than the amount ultimately agreed to, his assertion that the employer could pay more, and the inadequacies of his fee schedule.[133]

It is clear that the bad-faith exception cuts both ways: it can serve as a basis for imposing fees and costs against an ill-founded prosecution, and it can preclude a plaintiff who ostensibly "prevails" in his ADEA suit from obtaining an award of attorneys' fees and costs.

Administrative Proceedings.   Because the Age Act provides for attorney's fees and costs "of the action," a plaintiff's request for compensation for services by his attorney are generally disallowed if the services were performed before the commencement of the action.[134] The U.S. Court of Appeals for the District of Columbia acknowledged the claims of a federal government employee that an award of fees for administrative legal services might contribute to the resolution of age discrimination complaints through agency processes and that this enhancement of the role of administrative proceedings might obviate frequent recourse to federal courts for relief.[135] Because the employee was a federal government worker, Section 15 of the Act controlled her right to recover. Section 15, unlike Section 7 for private sector employees, does not contain the incorporation language concerning the Fair Labor Standards Act remedial scheme of Section 16. Federal courts are simply empowered to grant prevailing parties who are federal employees such relief *"as will effectuate the purposes"* of the Act.[136]

Under this statutory construction, the D.C. Circuit Court noted that the 1978 amendments to the ADEA contained a new subsection (f) which essentially divorced the public and private sector enforcement schemes: "Any personnel action of any department, agency, or other entity referred to in subsection (a) of this section shall not be subject to, or affected by, any provision of this

---

[130]*Id.*, citing Kinneor Wead Corp. v. Humble Oil & Refining Co., 441 F.2d 631 (CA 5, 1971).

[131]Vocca v. Playboy Hotel, 519 F. Supp. 900, 29 FEP 1083 (ND Ill, 1981).

[132]*Id.*

[133]Vocca v. Playboy Hotel, 29 FEP 1139 (CA 7, 1982).

[134]Koyen v. Consolidated Edison Co., 560 F. Supp. 1161, 31 FEP 488 (SD NY, 1983).

[135]Kennedy v. Whitehurst, 690 F.2d 951, 29 FEP 1373 (CA DC, 1982).

[136]29 U.S.C. §633a(c).

chapter, other than the provisions of section 631(b) of this title and the provisions of this section."[137]

The court discerned, under the rationale of *Lehman v. Nakshian*, that there are different rights and remedies for federal and private sector employees under the ADEA.[138]

The court ultimately rejected the employee's contention that an award of fees for *administrative* legal services "effectuates the purposes of the ADEA since administrative proceedings under the Act are not a "pervasive and integral part of the overall scheme of enforcement."[139]

United States as Defendant. The language of Section 15(f) of the Act making almost all private-sector portions of the Act inapplicable to an action against the federal government, was found not to preclude an award of attorneys' fees to a prevailing plaintiff who was a government worker, since Section 15(a) of the Act was interpreted as a waiver of sovereign immunity, Section 15(c) authorizes relief "as will effectuate the purposes of this chapter," and this goal cannot be reached if age discriminatees have to pay attorneys' fees.[140] Congress passed Section 15(f) to:

> "remove discriminatory barriers against employment of older workers in government jobs at the Federal and local government levels as it has and continues to do in private employment."[141]

However, the district court in this case was faced with the express disallowance of incorporation of the FLSA remedial scheme into the ADEA for federal workers under this provision. Its solution was to read the "effectuate the purposes of this chapter" language of Section 15(c) as a mandate to determine the appropriate remedies by reading the ADEA as a whole.[142] The court concluded that the incentive for private employers to refrain from discriminating should not be lessened for the federal government, and that federal employees should not be made less than whole if private sector employees were made whole. On that basis, the federal government's immunity to attorneys' fees liability fell.

Nonprofit Legal Services Corporation. The Legal Services Corporation Act[143] bars recipient organizations from using federal funds "to provide legal assistance with respect to any fee-generating case (except in accordance with guidelines promulgated by the Corporation)." Under the enabling regulations, legal services organizations should not compete with private practitioners, but if no private attorneys are willing to accept a particular fee-generating case,

---

[137]29 U.S.C. §633a(f).

[138]*Supra* note 135, citing Lehman v. Nakshian, 453 U.S. 156, 26 FEP 65 (1981).

[139]*Id.*, 29 FEP at 1383–84. *See also* Swain v. Secretary, 27 FEP 1434 (D DC, 1982); Koyen v. Consolidated Edison Co., *supra* note 134.

[140]Krodel v. Young, 576 F. Supp. 390, 33 FEP 701 (D DC, 1983).

[141]H.R. Rep. No. 913, 93rd Cong., 2d Sess. (1974) at 40–41.

[142]Krodel v. Young, *supra* note 140, 33 FEP at 704, citing DeFries v. Haarhues, 488 F. Supp. 1037, 25 FEP 393 (CD Ill, 1980). *See also* Copeland v. Marshall, 641 F.2d 880, 23 FEP 967 (CA DC, 1980)(en banc).

[143]42 U.S.C. §2996f(b)(1).

legal aid offices may furnish counsel.[144] A fee-generating case is one that "reasonably may be expected to result in a fee for legal services from an award to a client, from public funds, or from the opposing party."[145] In view of the mandatory nature of attorneys' fees award under the ADEA, there is no bar to such awards under the Age Act. However, the enabling legislation also limits the authority of these legal services corporations to handle fee-generating or contingent fee cases, and it was this distinction that the Third Circuit had to address.

The appeals court, ruling on a municipality's appeal of an award of attorneys' fees under the ADEA to such a legal services corporation, upheld the district court's reasoning:

> "There is no logical reason to lessen defendant's burden simply because an indigent plaintiff obtains representation by an entity such as CLS. The extent of defendant's liability should not depend upon the ability of plaintiff to hire private counsel. Because CLS is publicly financed, reimbursement to it for the time and effort its attorneys and staff expended in vindicating the rights of plaintiff individually and the plaintiff class is all the more compelling. By awarding reasonable fees to CLS, its limited resources will be increased to expand its present services, or conversely, the same services may be rendered with less expenditure of public funds. In either event, the public benefits, and at no greater expense to defendants than if plaintiffs had privately retained an attorney."[146]

The Supreme Court has applied similar reasoning in setting the rate of payment for attorneys' fees to be awarded to a legal services corporation.[147]

Who Is Liable for Fees

As a final note on the matter of attorneys' fees, it should be pointed out that the Ninth Circuit has determined that only employers are liable for such fees. The reason, according to the court, is that the fee provisions of the FLSA, as it is incorporated into the ADEA, refers to the entity against which fees may be assessed as the "employer."[148] The employee's union intervened in opposition to a proposed consent decree settling the employee's ADEA action against the employer. The court declined the employee's invitation to look to policy considerations beyond the FLSA. The union was not acting as the employee's employer nor has it been charged with discrimination, the court noted, therefore rendering inapplicable the policy considerations underlying the shifting of the duty to the employer to pay the attorneys' fees of an employee who has been subjected to discrimination. The court concluded that imposing a fee award against the union would only punish it for performing an act it was under a duty to do—the representation of all members in the bargaining unit, and that if Congress wishes to expand fee awards as against nonemployers under the ADEA, "it is free to do so."[149]

---

[144]45 CFR §§1609.4 and 1609.5.

[145]45 CFR §1609.3.

[146]Rodriguez v. Taylor, 420 F. Supp. 894, 14 FEP 609 (ED Pa, 1976), aff'd in part, rev'd in part, 569 F.2d 1231, 16 FEP 533 (CA 3, 1977), cert. denied, 436 U.S. 913 (1978).

[147]Blum v. Stenson, 465 U.S. 886, 34 FEP 417 (1984).

[148]Richardson v. Alaska Airlines, Inc., 750 F.2d 763, 36 FEP 986 (CA 9, 1984).

[149]Id.

On the other hand, frivolous claims against an employer that prevails in an ADEA action will result in attorneys' fees against not only the employees involved, but also their attorney. The court observed that the attorney for the employees had knowledge of all the necessary facts early on in the litigation, if not before the suit was filed, and could have continued such groundless claims only in "bad faith" and with complete disregard for the valuable time and resources of the court.[150] The court concluded that the attorney's conduct of the case involved a "willful abuse of the judicial process."[151]

Criminal Penalties

Section 10 of the Act[152] provides that anyone who forcibly resists, opposes, impedes, intimidates, or interferes with a duly authorized representative of the EEOC while it is engaged in the performance of duties under the Act shall be punished by a fine of not more than $500 or by imprisonment for not more than one year, or both, *provided*, that no person shall be imprisoned under this section except when there has been a prior conviction under this section. To date, this section has not provided the basis for litigation.

---

[150]Steinberg v. St. Regis/Sheraton Hotel, 583 F. Supp. 421, 34 FEP 745 (SD NY, 1984).

[151]*Id.*, citing Roadway Express, Inc. v. Piper, 447 U.S. 752, 766 (1980).

[152]29 U.S.C. §629.

7

Equitable Remedies

Injunctions

In Chapter 6, we saw the scope of legal remedies, the various forms they can take, and the myriad issues that can arise in calculating a fair award. But one can easily envision a situation where legal (i.e., "money") remedies are inadequate to redress the injury, and a dollar award fails to make the plaintiff "whole." In such situations, courts have devised and imposed the extraordinary remedy of an equitable order, which requires the courts essentially to supervise the post-judgment compliance with its order. The order can take several forms, such as retroactive/prospective injunctions, reinstatement, hiring/promotion, retraining or relocating, and retroactive seniority with accrued benefits.

Scope of Injunctive Relief

An early case involved an injunction against a savings and loan association that barred it from violating the Act by discriminating in the hiring of tellers and teller-trainees. The Fifth Circuit ruled in *Hodgson v. First Federal Savings & Loan Association*,[1] that the order must be modified so as to forbid discrimination without specifying particular job categories, since there was evidence tending to show that the employer had a youth-oriented policy with respect to other jobs in addition to the teller and teller-trainee positions. The court reasoned that there was no legal justification to limit the injunction to a particular job category in which the violation occurred. With regard to the "compartmentalizing" of a corporation under such an injunction, the court noted:

> "The injunctive processes are a means of effecting general compliance with national policy as expressed by Congress, a public policy judges too must carry out—actuated by the spirit of the law and not begrudgingly as if it were a newly imposed fait of a presidium."[2]

The court applied FLSA case law on remedies, and the broad public policy considerations behind the FLSA and the ADEA, to conclude that limiting the injunction to the particular job category in which the violations actually occurred would not effectuate the policies of the ADEA. Such a "piece-meal"

---

[1]455 F.2d 818, 4 FEP 269 (CA 5, 1972).
[2]*Id.*, 4 FEP at 275, citing Mitchell v. Pidcock, 299 F.2d 281, 286, 15 WH Cases 338 (CA 5, 1962).

resolution would require plaintiffs to engage in constant litigation, and would provide employers with substantial loopholes in the Act's enforcement scheme.

The appeals court also examined the district court's limiting language in the injunction:

> "Such injunction is not to be construed to prohibit the Defendant institution, however, from refusing to hire tellers within the protected age bracket of this act who *for whatever reason* may not have the necessary qualifications to perform the job of a teller."[3]

The Fifth Circuit regarded this language as allowing the employer to use advanced age to serve as a job disqualification if, in the judgment of the defendant, youth were deemed a required "qualification" for a particular job. The court correctly discerned that this language was an addition to the statutory exclusions for "bona fide occupational qualifications" and "reasonable factors other than age." But since the injunction was intended to prohibit the employer from violating Section 4, and since Section 4(f) contains the only exceptions to the statutory prohibitions on age discrimination, the court ordered that this language be stricken from the injunction.[4] This decision by the Fifth Circuit reaffirmed the principle of statutory construction that exceptions are to be narrowly construed; the district court's loose interpretation and/or flippant inclusion of this expansive language was contrary to the clear language and intent of the framers of the ADEA, notwithstanding what the district court may have intended by that language.

Private sector and public sector employers are equally vulnerable to injunctions, but the language of the injunction will be crafted to take into account facts particular to the specific employer and the events giving rise to the violation.[5] The companywide approach taken by the Fifth Circuit in *First Federal Savings & Loan Association* was based on an underlying rationale that the injunction should reach all areas that may arguably be the site of future violations in the absence of a broad injunction. In a subsequent case, the Fifth Circuit found that a nationwide injunction was an overly broad remedy, in view of the facts that the ADEA action was the result of a discharge of a single individual and there was no showing of any company policy or practice of age discrimination.[6] The Ninth Circuit has determined that a substantial monetary judgment provided an adequate deterrent to future violations, thus obviating the need for injunctive relief.[7] And a district court properly granted "class-wide" injunctive relief against an airline, despite the claim that the court lacked jurisdiction to do so because the action was not a class action, where the employer's treatment of three flight-deck crew members who brought the action

---

[3]*Id.*, 4 FEP at 276 (emphasis supplied by Fifth Circuit).

[4]*Id.*

[5]Hodgson v. Approved Personnel Servs., 529 F.2d 760, 764, 11 FEP 688, 691 (CA 4, 1975), and Hodgson v. Poole Truck Line, Inc., 4 FEP 265 (SD Ala, 1972).

[6]Marshall v. Goodyear Tire & Rubber Co., 554 F.2d 730, 15 FEP 139 (CA 5, 1977).

[7]Cancellier v. Federated Dep't Stores, 672 F.2d 1312, 28 FEP 1151 (CA 9), *cert. denied*, 459 U.S. 859 (1982).

was under a classwide age-based policy applicable to all flight-deck crew members.[8]

Retroactive vs. Prospective Application

An injunction can be drafted in such a way as to reach both the employer's past and future conduct under the Age Act proscriptions. Prospective injunctions, usually ordering some affirmative compliance or conduct of the employer, of necessity require court supervision of its order and, therefore, a continued claim on the court's resources. Consequently, courts have traditionally been reluctant to issue such injunctions, absent compelling need. Such a need will generally be demonstrated through the facts of the case. For example, the Fourth Circuit has ruled that a promise not to violate the Act which was made after the commencement of the action was not a sufficient basis for denying the injunction, in view of the employer's prior broken promises.[9]

Under the Taft-Hartley Act,[10] prospective injunctions are issued where the employer's conduct provides a reasonable basis for believing that future violations will occur. Such injunctions have been of two varieties: a limited injunction enjoining the commission of specific kinds of unfair labor practices, the commission of which gave rise to the unfair labor practice findings; and the broad enjoining of any or all violations of the Act in the future. The employer who violates the broad injunction may face a contempt of court citation instigated by an NLRB attorney; the Board has a greater need for this type of injunction, since by statute it must seek court enforcement of its orders where compliance is not voluntary. However, the federal courts have not adopted the bifurcated approach to prospective injunctions devised by the NLRB. The courts do not have a need to compel compliance under threat of a contempt citation, since noncompliance would directly result in such a citation without the need for a full-blown contempt proceeding. In addition, employers facing a proposed injunction that sweeps broadly would vehemently oppose such language on grounds of overbreadth and due process.

Nevertheless, the courts have found it necessary in some situations to issue broad injunctions against employers whose violations of the ADEA indicate that the broad-brush approach is needed. An early extension of the injunction beyond the actual violation occurred when an employer was found to have violated the Act by refusing to hire a job applicant from the protected age group for a truck driver position. The district court enjoined this conduct, and compelled the employer to disgorge ("enjoined from withholding") unpaid minimum wages and overtime compensation due the applicant,[11] reminiscent of FLSA case law. Similarly, another district court has ruled that the employer's youth-oriented program that statistically showed a program of systematic age discrimination was the real reason for the discharge of three foremen; it issued

---

[8]Criswell v. Western Airlines, 514 F. Supp. 384, 29 FEP 350 (CD Cal, 1981), aff'd, 709 F.2d 544, 32 FEP 1204 (CA 9, 1983).

[9]Hodgson v. Approved Personnel Servs., Inc., *supra* note 5.

[10]29 U.S.C. §§141–169 (1984).

[11]Hodgson v. Poole Truck Line, Inc., *supra* note 5.

a broad injunction covering all employees, rather than one limited to supervisory personnel, and reaching hiring and job classifications as well.[12]

An employment agency that violated the ADEA by using discriminatory terms in its "help-wanted" advertisements was enjoined "only against future conduct which actually violates Section 4(e) of the Act."[13] The district court had refused to issue any injunction, but the Fourth Circuit apparently felt that since some of the language used in the ads was clearly violative of the Act and the agency did not stop its use of the prohibited advertisements until after the action was filed, the injunction was necessary. The appeals court noted that the agency had been informed by a U.S. Wage-Hour Division compliance officer, prior to the initiation of the action at the district court, that the ads in question violated the Labor Department's Interpretive Bulletin No. 860, and the agency had promised to refrain from future use of such ads. This broken promise was found by the court to be an indication that the agency's knowing violation of the ADEA created a situation warranting injunctive relief. Because of the plethora of terms such as "boy," "girl," "recent high school grad," and so forth, which had been used in the ads, the court attached an appendix to its decision, with the intention of providing guidance to the district court in the formulation of a proper injunction. The appeals court attempted to suggest a prospective injunction, limited by "conduct" which actually violates the Act. This type of injunction is clearly intended to regulate future conduct, but its scope is to be determined by the district court under the Fourth Circuit's guidance.

An employer that violated the ADEA by amending its retirement plan to lower the "normal" retirement age from 65 to 62 under Section 4(f)(2)[14] was enjoined from violating Section 4(a) of the Act ("prohibited employer practices").[15] Such a broad, apparently prospective injunction was appropriate under the facts of this case, according to the court, because

> "Economy of administrative effort dictates that 'after an employer has once violated the Act he should bear his own responsibility for the future.' "[16]

The courts consistently turn to the case law developed under the Fair Labor Standards Act, the remedial scheme of which was selectively incorporated into the ADEA, for assistance in determining the proper basis and scope of injunctive relief.

Whether the courts select a broad or narrow injunction, or whether the injunction is limited to past conduct or is designed to regulate future conduct, the FLSA case law will provide a basis for examining the facts in relation to the remedy sought. As noted in Chapter 5, the FLSA, and by extension the ADEA, were not intended to be punitive, notwithstanding the liquidated damages provision of both statutes. Injunctive relief for the injured plaintiffs will

---

[12]Hodgson v. Ideal Corrugated Box Co., 10 FEP 744, 751 (ND WVa, 1974).

[13]Hodgson v. Approved Personnel Servs., Inc., *supra* note 5.

[14]29 U.S.C. §623(f)(2) (1984).

[15]Marshall v. Eastern Air Lines, Inc., 474 F. Supp. 364, 370, 20 FEP 908, 912 (SD Fla, 1979).

[16]*Id.*, 20 FEP at 912, citing Goldberg v. Cockrell, 303 F.2d 811, 814, 15 WH Cases 496 (CA 5, 1962).

be crafted in light of the make-whole standard, in an effort to avoid any "windfall" to the prevailing plaintiffs, and in consideration of the nonpunitive philosophy of the original drafters of the legislation. Courts will avoid over-broad or onerous injunctions, as much for "administrative economy" as for the rights of the parties, in light of what Congress intended.

Reinstatement

As noted in Chapter 6 (see "Mitigation of Damages"), reinstatement is an appropriate form of equitable relief, wherein the injured employee successfully seeks to be put back into his former job or one that is substantially equal to his former position in the event that his former job is not available. Whether the employer discharged the employee or terminated the individual under the guise of a reduction-in-force ("RIF"), the prevailing plaintiff who seeks rein-statement may be entitled to this remedy under appropriate circumstances. It should be noted, of course, that a significant percentage of discriminatees will not be willing to return to the very work site at which they were originally discriminated against, and this fact of human nature will have an impact on the plaintiff's formulation of his prayer for relief. Conversely, employers may offer reinstatement to a position that is facially equal to the former position but which may involve subtle factors that make the position something other than "substantially equal." Counsel for the plaintiff has the obligation to ferret out these subtle differences in establishing the bona fides of the plaintiff's reason for any refusal of a reinstatement offer.

Section 7(b) of the Act specifically addresses the issue of reinstatement:

> "In any action brought to enforce this chapter the court shall have jurisdiction to grant such legal or equitable relief as may be appropriate to effectuate the purposes of this chapter, including without limitation judgments compelling em-ployment, reinstatement or promotion, or . . . ."[17]

The trial court has clear discretion to grant or deny any request for rein-statement, including a request made by a former employee of the federal government.[18] However, reinstatement carries with it a "penumbra" of rights, usually referred to as "fringe" benefits, which are affected by the employee's decision regarding any reinstatement offer. These accompanying rights include promotion, retroactive seniority, retraining, and so on. But one important aspect of reinstatement involves the issue of "bumping."

The courts, guided by Supreme Court decisions concerning the rights of "innocent, third parties,"[19] have been sensitized to the situation where an age discriminatee seeks reinstatement and the employer must "bump" an incum-bent who is innocent of wrongdoing, and may have been on the job for a considerable period. To date, however, only the Fourth Circuit has explicitly stated that relief under the ADEA does not extend to bumping incumbent

---

[17]29 U.S.C. §626(b) (1976).

[18]Polstroff v. Fletcher, 452 F. Supp. 17, 25, 17 FEP 123, 129 (ND Ala, 1978).

[19]City of Los Angeles v. Manhart, 435 U.S. 702, 723, 17 FEP 395 (1978); Teamsters v. U.S., 431 U.S. 324, 14 FEP 1514 (1977).

employees.[20] An issue of this importance will undoubtedly require Supreme Court review.

But the issue of reinstatement at the expense of an incumbent employee provides a more immediate concern for the employer: What constitutes a "valid" offer of reinstatement for purposes of tolling the back pay period and limiting the employer's liability? Unfortunately, the employer who merely offers the employee his "old" job back, or a similar one if the prior position is filled, may not necessarily satisfy the requirement of offering a "valid" reinstatement offer.

Valid Offer

It is well settled that an employee is not required to accept an offer of reinstatement to a position essentially different from his former position.[21]

In *Coates v. National Cash Register Co.*,[22] a district court awarding injunctive relief to two age discrimination plaintiffs against their employer who operates nationwide observed that if it ordered "employment," the employer could conceivably reemploy the plaintiffs in any of its offices in the nation; as an alternative, the court said it could order "reinstatement." The court added that a review of cases decided under the ADEA and other employment discrimination legislation revealed almost no discussion of the meaning of "reinstatement." It reasoned: "The *normal* definition of this word would clearly justify this court's ordering that plaintiffs be *reinstated in their original positions*" at the prior work site.[23] Although national corporations have repeatedly asserted their prerogative of transferring employees at will, the court stated that under the ADEA the transfer of an employee to an inferior job or to a less desirable place on account of age is just as discriminatory as the actual discharge on account of age.[24] Once age discrimination is established, it concluded, the type of injunctive relief granted must vary according to the facts of each case.[25]

This decision succinctly states both what reinstatement is and what it is not:

(1) Reinstatement is the return of the plaintiffs to "their original positions" at the original work site;
(2) Reinstatement is not the return of the plaintiffs to an "inferior job or to a less desirable place on account of age."[26]

The court acknowledged that the facts of each case will determine the type of injunctive relief granted. But it is this fact-specific approach which leads to unpredictable results, despite the presence of standard equitable principles and work rules.

In the *Coates* case, the district court ultimately ordered reinstatement of the employees to their former positions in their prior workplace, with all benefits,

---

[20]Spagnuolo v. Whirlpool Corp., 717 F.2d 114, 32 FEP 1382 (CA 4, 1983).
[21]Spagnuolo v. Whirlpool Corp., 641 F.2d 1109, 25 FEP 376 (CA 4, 1981).
[22]433 F. Supp. 655, 15 FEP 222 (WD Va, 1977).
[23]*Id.*, 15 FEP at 231.
[24]*Id.*
[25]*Id.*
[26]*Id.* at 231.

seniority, and job status that they would have accrued had the discharges never occurred. Had the court found the employer's reinstatement offer to be valid, it is doubtful that the plaintiffs' refusal to accept the offer would have resulted in such a favorable disposition for them. Although the court had clearly carved out the hemispheres of what is and what is not a "valid" offer of reinstatement, the analysis begs the real question: How does one determine whether a job offer is "inferior" or "less desirable"?

An important issue in evaluating the validity of a reinstatement offer concerns the granting of retroactive seniority. (See this chapter at "Retroactive Seniority.") In *Ford Motor Co. v. EEOC*,[27] the Supreme Court was faced with the question of whether an employer must offer retroactive seniority in its reinstatement offer in order to have made a "valid" offer of reinstatement for purposes of tolling the back pay period. The case involved discrimination under Title VII, and the court ruled that retroactive seniority need not be part of the reinstatement offer, because this would threaten the interests of other, innocent employees by disrupting the established seniority hierarchy. The Court reasoned:

"Although Title VII remedies depend primarily upon the objectives discussed above, the statute also permits us to consider the rights of "innocent third parties." *City of Los Angeles Department of Water & Power v. Manhart*, 435 U.S. 702, 723, 17 FEP Cases 395, 404 (1978). *See also Teamsters v. United States*, 431 U.S. 324, 371–376, 14 FEP Cases 1514, 1534–1536 (1977). The lower court's rule places a particularly onerous burden on the innocent employees of an employer charged with discrimination. Under the court's rule, an employer may cap backpay liability only by forcing his incumbent employees to yield seniority to a person who has not proven, and may never prove, unlawful discrimination. As we have acknowledged on numerous occasions, seniority plays a central role in allocating benefits and burdens among employees.[28]

"In light of the 'overriding importance' of these rights, *American Tobacco Co. v. Patterson*, 456 U.S.—,—, 28 FEP Cases 713, 719 (1982) (quoting *Humphrey v. Moore*, 375 U.S. 335, 346, 55 LRRM 2031 (1964)), we should be wary of any rule that encourages job offers that compel innocent workers to sacrifice their seniority to a person who has only claimed, but not yet proven, unlawful discrimination.

"The sacrifice demanded by the lower court's rule, moreover, leaves the displaced workers without any remedy against claimants who fail to establish their claims. If, for example, layoffs occur while the Title VII suit is pending, an employer may have to furlough an innocent worker indefinitely while retaining a claimant who was given retroactive seniority. If the claimant subsequently fails to prove unlawful discrimination, the worker unfairly relegated to the unemployment lines has no redress for the wrong done him. We do not believe that ' "the large objectives" ' of Title VII, *Albemarle Paper Co. v. Moody*, 422 U.S. 405,

"[28]Seniority may govern, "not only promotion and layoff, but also transfer, demotion, rest days, shift assignments, prerogative in scheduling vacation, order of layoff, possibilities of lateral transfer to avoid layoff, 'bumping' possibilities in the face of layoff, order of recall, training opportunities, working conditions, length of layoff endured without reducing seniority, length of layoff recall rights will withstand, overtime opportunities, parking privileges, and [even] a preferred place in the punchout line." Franks v. Bowman Transportation Co., 424 U.S. 747, 766–767, 12 FEP Cases 549, 556 (1976) (quoting Stacy, Title VII Seniority Remedies in a Time of Economic Downturn) 28 Vand. L. Rev. 487, 490 (1975)).

[27]458 U.S. 219, 29 FEP 121 (1982).

416, 10 FEP Cases 1181, 1187 (1975) (citation omitted), require innocent employees to carry such a heavy burden.[29]

"[29]In addition to the rights of innocent employees, the rule urged by the EEOC and adopted by the court below burdens innocent employers. An innocent employer—or one who believes himself innocent—has the right to challenge in court claims he considers weak or baseless. The approach endorsed by the lower court undermines this right by requiring the employer, if he wishes to offer some relief to the claimant and toll the mounting backpay bill, to surrender his defense to the charge that the claimant is entitled to retroactive seniority. If the employer offers the claimant retroactive seniority as well as a job, and then prevails at trial, he will have no recourse against the claimant for the costs of the retroactive seniority that the claimant erroneously received. The rule urged by Ford permits the parties to stem the ongoing effects of the alleged discrimination without compelling either claimant or employer to compromise his claims or surrender his defenses. Cf. Moro Motors Ltd., 216 NLRB 192, 193, 88 LRRM 1211 (1975) ('were [an employer] required to offer to an employee, allegedly discharged for discriminatory reasons, reinstatement *with accrued back pay*, the [employer's] right to litigate the issue of whether the discharge was unlawful would for all practical purposes be nullified') (emphasis in original); National Screen Products Co., 147 NLRB 746, 747–748, 56 LRRM 1274 (1964)."[28]

Though the *Ford Motor Co.* decision is under Title VII and not ADEA, there is no reason to think that the Court's sweeping language was limited to that statute; the decision very likely was intended to send a signal to the lower courts deciding employment discrimination cases. As the Fourth Circuit observed:

"the similarities between the language of the provisions authorizing equitable relief in ADEA, see 29 U.S.C. Sec. 626(b), and Title VII, see 42 U.S.C. Sec. 2000e-5(g), and the congruence of purpose behind the equitable relief—to put the injured party back into the position he would have been in but for the discrimination—make appropriate the application of the teachings of Title VII reinstatement cases to ADEA reinstatement questions."[29]

Under *Ford Motor Co.*, reinstatement offers and retroactive seniority are different issues; and *Spagnuolo* makes clear that Title VII case law is analogous in most cases to ADEA reinstatement questions.

A decision by the Seventh Circuit draws into focus just how close to full reinstatement an offer can be and still be deficient in terms of the bona fides of the offer. A city firefighter who had been involuntarily retired at age 55 in violation of the Act refused to accept the city's conditional offer of reinstatement to his former job. The reinstatement offer was expressly conditioned on the firefighter's taking and passing a physical examination arranged by the city. The firefighter followed his attorney's advice not to accept the city's offer based on the belief that acquiescence in the demand for a physical exam might be detrimental to the prosecution of his discrimination suit. The Seventh Circuit agreed with the firefighter in his concern that acceptance of the city's conditional offer could jeopardize his legal position.[30] The appeals court observed that:

(1) The city had not agreed to stipulate that the firefighter was physically capable of performing all firefighting duties, even though the firefighter had taken and "passed with flying colors" a physical just four months prior to the action;

---

[28]*Id.*, 29 FEP at 130.

[29]Spagnuolo v. Whirlpool Corp., *supra* note 20, 32 FEP at 1386 n.3, *aff'g in part, rev'g in part, and remanding*, 548 F. Supp. 104, 32 FEP 1372 and 550 F. Supp. 432, 32 FEP 1377 (WD NC, 1982).

[30]Orzel v. City of Wauwatosa Fire Dep't, 697 F.2d 743, 30 FEP 1070 (CA 7, 1983).

(2) The city apparently was unwilling to back up its offer of reinstatement with a written agreement to retain the firefighter at least until age 60;

(3) The city continued to assert that it was inclined to "reterminate" the firefighter as soon as any legal decision appeared to give it the right to do so; and

(4) The city had earlier withdrawn a settlement offer that the firefighter had apparently accepted, on the ground that the city's employment relations committee, which had extended the offer, had no authority to make binding settlement offers.[31]

Under these circumstances, the court concluded, it was not unreasonable for the firefighter, on advice of counsel, to refuse the city's conditional offer to return to work. The tenuous, conditional nature of the reinstatement, and the city's prior conduct diluted the bona fides of the reinstatement offer, even though the offer was to his former position at the same workplace.

But what about a reinstatement offer to a position that ostensibly is "superior" to the employee's former position? Such a situation was addressed by the Fourth Circuit in *Spagnuolo v. Whirlpool Corp.*[32] The district court had held that the position of "national account manager" which the employer had offered to a former "regional sales manager" was not equal in "stature, compensation, future prospects and responsibility"[33] to the prior position. The employer's demotion of the plaintiff and fusion of his duties with that of a co-worker were sufficient justification to require the employer to reinstate him to the position that he would have held after his former position had been combined with the other job, even though the reinstatement would require demotion of the co-worker. It reasoned that the "stigmatizing" effects of a *wholesale, companywide bumping* of incumbents that barred such a remedy in *Patterson v. American Tobacco Co.*, were absent in the present adjudication.[34] And this fact did not obviate the failure of the employer to make a bona fide offer of reinstatement.

The Fourth Circuit noted on appeal that "the comparability of any alternative position must be judged by a broad range of factors, and not merely any one criterion alone."[35] It affirmed the district court on this issue.

Suffice to say that the reinstatement offer, to be valid, must withstand a high degree of judicial scrutiny. The offer will be examined against the working conditions, pay, and prospects for advancement of the prior job, in addition to the "fringes" such as bonuses, opportunities to win trips, and degree of personal anguish that may accompany an assignment. As with other aspects of the law, the "title" of the position being offered will not be determinative as to whether the position is in fact substantially equal to the prior position. The offer will also be examined in light of the employer's past conduct, bona fide efforts to comply with the Act, and any conditions placed on the offer.

---

[31]*Id.*, 30 FEP at 1081.

[32]Spagnuolo v. Whirlpool Corp., 717 F.2d 114, 32 FEP 1382 (CA 4, 1983).

[33]Spagnuolo v. Whirpool Corp., 548 F. Supp 104, 32 FEP 1372, 1372 (WD NC 1982).

[34]*Id.*, 32 FEP at 1376, citing Patterson v. American Tobacco Co., 535 F.2d 257, 267–269, 12 FEP 314 (CA 4), *cert. denied*, 429 U.S. 920, 13 FEP 1808 (1976).

[35]*Id.*, 32 FEP at 1384, citing Williams v. Albermarle City Bd. of Educ., 508 F.2d 1242, 1243, 10 FEP 585 (CA 4, 1974) (en banc).

In general, the courts expect to see unconditional offers of reinstatement to the same or a substantially equal position to meet this hurdle.

When Reinstatement Is Inappropriate

If there is evidence that the employer and the discriminatee cannot work together in a harmonious, professional manner, then reinstatement would be an erroneous solution.[36] When the employee's attitude toward returning to work is negative and the employer has shown disdain for the employee's competence, the courts are again unwilling to compel them to reestablish a relationship.[37] A realistic appraisal of the day-to-day working relationship that exists in a workplace is necessary to make an accurate projection as to whether certain individuals are able and willing to resume working together. In many cases, the original taint of the discriminatory conduct precludes ever reestablishing a viable employer-employee arrangement.

Aside from these attitudinal considerations, such factors as the individual's ability to perform the work upon reinstatement,[38] or the employee's current earning power and legal damages,[39] would be contrary to the discriminatee's best interests. However, an employer's loss of "confidence" in his chief labor counsel who was terminated in violation of the Age Act would not be a sufficient basis, standing alone, to preclude reinstatement.[40]

An employee's failure specifically to seek reinstatement makes such an order improper, according to one court.[41] And the original employment relationship (i.e., part-time or temporary hire) may be determinative on the issue of reinstatement.[42]

Hiring and Promotion

An employer's decision to refuse to promote or hire an individual that is found to violate the Act creates the same or similar problems in the remedial stage of litigation as is created by a reinstatement remedy: the interim period between the violative conduct and the remedial order may have allowed the employer to place another person in the job in question. The difficulty arises when a court must weigh the rights of the discriminatee against the rights of a comparatively "innocent" individual who has a job because of the employer's misconduct. If the employer's work force/financial situation allows for the creation or maintenance of one more position on a particular staff, then the difficulty is decreased, but oftentimes the employer must face the prospect of

---

[36]Combes v. Griffin Television, Inc., 421 F. Supp. 841, 846–47, 13 FEP 1455, 1459–60 (WD Okla, 1976).

[37]Ginsberg v. Burlington Indus., Inc., 500 F. Supp. 696, 699, 24 FEP 426, 427–28 (SD NY, 1980).

[38]Houghton v. McDonnell Douglas Corp., 627 F.2d 858, 23 FEP 757 (CA 8, 1980).

[39]Robb v. Chemetron Corp., 17 FEP 1535 (SD Tex, 1978).

[40]Whittlesey v. Union Carbide Corp., 567 F. Supp., 1320, 32 FEP 473 (SD NY, 1983), aff'd, 742 F.2d 724, 35 FEP 1089 (CA 2, 1984).

[41]Seidel v. Chicago Sav. & Loan Ass'n, 544 F. Supp. 508, 34 FEP 297 (ND Ill, 1982).

[42]Geller v. Markham, 635 F.2d 1027, 1036, 24 FEP 920, 926 (CA 2, 1980), cert. denied, 451 U.S. 945, 25 FEP 847 (1981).

hiring a discriminatee at the risk of exposing himself to liability by terminating the individual hired or promoted in place of the discriminatee.

A district court has ruled that a U.S. Veterans Administration hospital disregarded a requirement of its affirmative action plan to seek out, identify, and assist "underutilized" employees, in an action alleging age and sex discrimination, and that the reason a 57-year-old employee was not selected for a certain position was due to the hospital's failure to assist her in preparing her application.[43] The court ordered that the employee was entitled to be promoted to the position, to be "red circled" if the position had been filled and to be given the next comparable position. Similarly, the U.S. Postal Service violated the Act when it failed to select a 50-year-old clerk for the position of letter sorting machine (LSM) supervisor who had supervisory experience and superior ratings for the most part in all categories in which she was evaluated, and instead selected an employee with no prior supervisory experience and who was between 25 and 30 years of age.[44] The court ordered the Postal Service to promote the discriminatee to the first LSM supervisory position or comparable supervisory position to become vacant.[45]

With regard to an action seeking an injunction against a government employer that failed to hire an individual within the protected age group, the First Circuit has determined that the Eleventh Amendment to the Constitution permits federal courts to enjoin state officials to conform future conduct to requirements of federal law; it ruled that there was no constitutional bar shielding the Commonwealth of Puerto Rico from an order requiring it to hire a 43-year old job applicant who passed a physical examination and qualified in all of the customary tests for the position of firefighter.[46] The appeals court noted that the applicant sought an injunction that would have required the commonwealth to reclassify him presently, and to hire him as a firefighter in the future, and regarded this as a "classic form of prospective remediation."[47]

It need only be said briefly that the issues and orders which arise in the context of reinstatement following a finding of a violation of the ADEA also pertain frequently to remedies of hiring and promotion.

Reduction in Force

The reduction in force ("RIF") is generally the result of a business decision to retrench, that is, to cut costs in an effort to stave off a severe financial crisis, though it is problematic whether the RIF itself is a severe financial crisis. But where the RIF is conducted in a manner that violates the ADEA, the discriminated employees are entitled to seek redress. The problem is that the employer may not be in a position to rehire any individuals for the foreseeable future. But the best way to avoid a RIF-related charge of age discrimination is to anticipate it prior to conducting the RIF.

---

[43]Jones v. Cleland, 466 F. Supp. 34, 25 FEP 390 (ND Ala, 1978).

[44]DeFries v. Haarhues, 488 F. Supp. 1037, 25 FEP 393 (CD Ill, 1980).

[45]Id.

[46]Muniz Ramirez v. Puerto Rico Fire Serv., 715 F.2d 694, 32 FEP 1239 (CA 1, 1983).

[47]Id.

An employer that operated a federally-owned research facility did not violate the Act when it terminated an employee within the protected age group as part of a RIF resulting from congressional budgetary cuts, according to a district court, since the employer considered age as a factor in attempting to save the jobs of older workers and did not use this factor adversely in evaluating the employee's services.[48] The court observed that the employer had established a system to evaluate the qualifications of each employee at the facility, and one standard of evaluation was that personnel with long company experience who were over 40 years of age should be given the most consideration for retention.[49] This philosophy is in direct contrast to that of most employers facing RIF decisions, who apply the "soft landing" or "least painful" criterion—RIF terminations are imposed on those employees who can most afford to bear the RIF via alternative forms of income such as Social Security, pension, spousal income, and so forth.[50] In one case, an employer that conducted a RIF which violated the ADEA was ordered to reinstate former employees in the classification which had been occupied, notwithstanding that the former employees had stated that they would not accept any reinstatement offers, the Tenth Circuit ruled.[51] And a district court in Illinois decided that an employer's objective evaluation criteria justified the decision to RIF an employee within the protected age group.[52] The court noted that statistical evidence indicated that the RIF affected younger employees more severely than older employees, and that the older employee's performance on a certain project relative to the younger employee's performance was a legitimate basis for deciding whom to keep, particularly in view of the older employee's managerial shortcomings: "The Age Discrimination in Employment Act . . . was not intended as a vehicle for judicial review of business decisions."[53]

If the RIF is conducted according to an objective, easily identifiable series of tests or criteria, and if the employer is sensitive to the issue of the disparate impact that a RIF may have on a particular age group, the possibility of avoiding an ADEA charge is increased, though by no means ensured.

Retroactive Seniority

The reinstatement or hire/promotion of an employee who has successfully maintained his ADEA action carries with it the attendant employment concern for fringe benefits, particularly retroactive seniority. The Supreme Court first faced this issue in a non-ADEA context, and answered affirmatively that discriminatees who were injured by the employer's unlawful conduct were entitled to retroactive seniority.[54] The Court had earlier stated that rightful-

---

[48]Gill v. Union Carbide Corp., 368 F. Supp. 364, 7 FEP 571 (ED Tenn, 1973).

[49]*Id.*

[50]B. Schlei & P. Grossman, EMPLOYMENT DISCRIMINATION LAW (2nd ed.: Washington, D.C.: The Bureau of National Affairs, Inc., 1983), p. 531, and 532, at note 274.

[51]EEOC v. Sandia Corp., 649 F.2d 1383, 23 FEP 799 (CA 10, 1980).

[52]Matthews v. Allis-Chalmers, 35 FEP 1404 (ND Ill, 1984).

[53]*Id.*, 35 FEP at 1406, citing Kephart v. Institute of Gas Technology, 630 F2d 1217, 1223, 23 FEP 1412 (CA 7, 1980), *cert. denied*, 450 U.S. 959, 24 FEP 1827 (1981).

[54]Teamsters v. U.S., 431 U.S. 324, 14 FEP 1514 (1977).

place seniority relief could be denied on the basis of "unusual adverse impact," but the Seventh Circuit has said that this does not mean either that such impact must reflect only factors unrelated to the impact of the remedy on the incumbents or that only the discharge of the incumbents will constitute "unusual adverse impact."[55] The courts, following the Supreme Court's lead, have analyzed the issue of retroactive seniority in terms of its effect on innocent, third parties. The Supreme Court refined its position on retroactive seniority in 1984, when it reexamined its decision in *Teamsters v. U.S.*,[56] that a court can award competitive seniority only when the beneficiary of the award has actually been a victim of discrimination; the Court said that such an award must be consistent with Title VII's policy of providing make-whole relief to *actual* victims of discrimination, but may not provide preferential treatment to *nonvictims*.[57] Although these cases arose in a non-ADEA context, they are the definitive word by the Supreme Court on the issue of retroactive seniority in an employment discrimination action. ADEA equitable remedies are to a substantial degree an outgrowth of Title VII.[58] Since the Court made no effort to limit its holding, even though it was clearly interpreting Title VII, there is a sound basis in regarding the Court's pronouncements under Title VII as reaching to other federal employment discrimination laws, including the ADEA.

Retraining

A frequently employed alternative to the RIF is the prospect of retraining employees to economically viable positions. In the context of new technology or a new plant, employees may be entitled to such retraining as of right. An early example of the right to such training instruction occurred in a 1977 decision of a district court. The employer was found to have violated the Age Act by discharging two employees because of a lack of training, and the court ordered reinstatement to their former jobs with all benefits, seniority, and job status that would have accrued in the absence of the unlawful discrimination; the employer was also ordered to place the employees on an accelerated training schedule so as to place them at a training level comparable to younger employees and to alleviate the "training obsolescence" that they suffered as a result of the age discrimination.[59]

An airline whose policy prohibiting second officers from working after the age of 60 and prohibiting other flight officers from transferring at age 60 to second officer positions was found to violate the Act and was ordered, inter alia, to provide the usual and customary training necessary for the second officer position for each flight officer who elected to remain employed as a second officer after the age of 60.[60] However, another airline was successful in proving that a similar order would be detrimental to the safe operation of

---

[55]Romasanta v. United Air Lines, 717 F.2d 1140, 32 FEP 1545 (CA 7, 1983), citing Franks v. Bowman Transp. Co., 424 U.S. 747, 12 FEP 549 (1976).

[56]Teamsters v. U.S., *supra* note 54.

[57]Firefighters Local 1784 v. Stotts, 467 U.S. 561, 34 FEP 1702 (1984).

[58]Spagnuolo v. Whirlpool Corp., 641 F.2d 1109, 25 FEP 376 (CA 4, 1981).

[59]Coates v. National Cash Register Co., 433 F. Supp. 655, 15 FEP 222 (WD Va, 1977).

[60]Monroe v. United Air Lines, 34 FEP 1610, 1612 (ND Ill, 1983).

its aircraft because it used the flight officer position to train future pilots and the possibility existed that so many ex-captains would become flight officers that the training position would be blocked and safety possibly endangered.[61] The airline presented two expert witnesses who testified that the presence of senior ex-captains in the flight officer position created a possible hazardous situation and that it was impossible to determine which ex-captains would pose a safety hazard.[62] Although this particular remedy involves the issue of the BFOQ defense, the ultimate point is that the training/retraining remedy is not always available, and the facts of each case will determine whether the prevailing plaintiff can get this remedy.

Declaratory Relief

Yet another aspect of "equitable" relief is the remedy of a court declaration concerning disputed rights. In a typical case, one party to a dispute will file an action seeking a pronouncement from the court as to the legal status of the dispute, i.e., whether the moving party or the opposing party has the right to act. In an ADEA action, however, the moving party must show some injury-in-fact, must demonstrate that he has "standing" to bring the action, and must show that the issue is ripe for judicial determination. Otherwise, the moving party has not brought an "issue" ("case or controversy") before the court, and any judicial determination will merely be advisory or in anticipation of an injury. This is contrary to Article III of the Constitution.[63] (See Chapter 4, "ADEA Enforcement Procedures," at "Private Action" for further discussions on these issues.)

The Second Circuit has ruled on an attempt to obtain a declaratory judgment under the ADEA.[64] It observed that the Act protects the rights of "person(s) aggrieved"—individual employees and applicants for employment—between 40 and 70 years of age.[65] The court noted that the union seeking a declaratory judgment was attempting not to vindicate some "associational right" of its members, but to use the Act to cut off the rights of older workers.[66] Aside from the fact that the purpose of the ADEA would be frustrated by the union's declaratory action, the action would also by-pass the statutory procedure provided for in the Act: prior filing of a charge of unlawful discrimination with the EEOC beginning a process of "conciliation, conference, and persuasion."[67] The court declared that a "potential ADEA defendant cannot be permitted to invoke the declaratory judgment procedure 'to preempt and prejudge issues that are committed for initial decision to an administrative body.' "[68]

It is clear that a proper plaintiff may seek a declaratory judgment under the

---

[61]Johnson v. American Airlines, 36 FEP 321 (CA 5, 1984).

[62]Id., 36 FEP at 325.

[63]Von Aulock v. Smith, 548 F. Supp. 196, 197, 32 FEP 1244 (D DC, 1982).

[64]Air Line Pilots Ass'n v. Trans World Airlines, 713 F.2d 940, 32 FEP 1185 (CA 2, 1983).

[65]29 U.S.C. §§ 623(a)–(e), 626(c)(1), and 631 (1984).

[66]Supra note 64, 32 FEP at 1192, citing 29 U.S.C. §626(d); see also 633(b) (1984).

[67]Warth v. Seldin, 422 U.S. 490, 500 (1975).

[68]Id., 32 FEP at 1193, citing Utah PSC v. Wycoff Co., Inc., 344 U.S. 237, 241, 246 (1952).

ADEA if the purpose of the action is to "promote employment of older persons" within the meaning of 29 U.S.C. Section 621(b) of the Act, and if the cause of action "arises under" the ADEA.[69] But beyond these requirements, parties seeking to obtain declaratory relief under the ADEA are in uncharted waters; court reluctance to by-pass the Act's procedural requirements will usually increase the difficulty of obtaining such relief.

---

[69]*Id.*

8

Administration of the ADEA

Administration

Section 6 of the Age Discrimination in Employment Act (ADEA) provides that the Secretary of Labor has the power to appoint agents and employees and to pay for technical assistance "to assist him in the performance of his functions" under the Act and to "cooperate with and furnish technical assistance" to employers, labor organizations, and employment agencies to aid in effectuating the purposes of the Act.[1] Because Section 7 of the Act[2] governs recordkeeping, investigation, and enforcement under the ADEA, Section 6 can be regarded as controlling all preenforcement aspects of administering the Act.

In 1977, Congress passed the Reorganization Act[3] which authorized the President to consolidate aspects of the executive branch to execute the laws of the land more effectively. On July 1, 1979, those responsibilities of the Labor Secretary were transferred to the Equal Employment Opportunity Commission (EEOC) under President Carter's Reorganization Plan No. 1.[4] At that time, the Commission expressed its intent to "provide continuity, to the extent possible, in the processing of charges under the ADEA and Title VII."[5]

Following a convoluted series of events that included a Supreme Court decision and an amendment to Title 5 of the U.S. Code, the EEOC's authority to administer and enforce the ADEA was affirmed. (See Chapter 1, "EEOC Role.")

As discussed in Chapter 1, currently the EEOC is in charge of investigations (with and without the filing of a charge), processing of administrative charges under the ADEA, conciliation, and complaint filing in federal district court. The Commission is also responsible for conducting various studies and reporting to Congress on the results of those studies.

Filing With the EEOC

A charging party must file a charge with the EEOC within 180 days of the unlawful practice.[6] Section 14, which defines the federal-state relationship,

---

[1] 29 U.S.C. §625 (1984).
[2] 29 U.S.C. §626 (1984).
[3] 5 U.S.C. §§901–912 (1984).
[4] 3 CFR 321 (1985).
[5] 46 FED. REG. 9970 (1981).
[6] Section 7(d)(1), 29 U.S.C. §626(d)(1) (1984).

also recognizes "deferral states"—states which have their own EEOC-type administrative body.[7] The federal ADEA encourages use of these state agencies under Section 7(d)(2),[8] which extends the filing period in these "deferral states" to 300 days after the violation has occurred or within 30 days after the individual receives notice of the termination of the state proceedings, whichever is earlier. As a result of the recognition of deferral state forums, there has grown out of administrative practice the "180/300-day" filing limit, which reflects charge-filing practices directly with the EEOC (180 days) or following state agency filing (300 days).

After a charge is filed with the EEOC within the filing period, the complainant must wait 60 days before bringing a civil action in court.[9]

The purpose of this waiting period is to allow the agency to attempt voluntary compliance through informal methods of conciliation, as is required under the Act.

(Procedural regulations of the EEOC's charge-filing process appear at 29 Code of Federal Regulations Section 1626. See Appendix B.)

OSCAR MAYER & CO. v. EVANS

441 U.S. 750, 19 FEP Cases 1167 (1979)

. . .

Petitioner argues that §14(b) mandates that in States with agencies empowered to remedy age discrimination in employment (deferral States) a grievant may not bring suit under the ADEA unless he has first commenced a proceeding with the appropriate state agency. Respondent, on the other hand, argues that the grievant has the option of whether to resort to state proceedings, and that §14(b) requires only that grievants choosing to resort to state remedies wait 60 days before bringing suit in federal court. The question of construction is close, but we conclude that petitioner is correct.

Section 14(b) of the ADEA was patterned after and is virtually *in haec verba* with §706(b) of Title VII, 42 U.S.C. §2000e-5(c).[2] The relevant portion of §706(b) reads as follows:

"In the case of an alleged unlawful employment practice; occurring in a State, . . . which has a . . . law prohibiting the unlawful employment practice alleged and establishing or authorizing a State . . . authority to grant or seek relief from such a practice . . ., no charge may be filed . . . by the person aggrieved before the expiration of sixty days after proceedings have been commenced under the State . . . law unless such proceedings have been earlier terminated . . . ."

Congress intended through §706(b) to screen from the federal courts those problems of civil rights that could be settled to the satisfaction of the grievant in "a voluntary and localized manner." *See* 110 CONG. RECORD 12725 (June 4, 1964) (remarks of Sen. Humphrey). The section is intended to give state agencies a limited opportunity to resolve problems of employment discrimination and thereby to make unnecessary resort to federal relief by victims of the discrimination. *See* Voutsis v. Union Carbide Corporation, 452 F.2d 889, 4 FEP Cases 74 (CA 2 1971). Because state agencies cannot even attempt to resolve discrimination complaints not brought to their attention, the section has been interpreted to require individuals in deferral States to resort to appropriate state proceedings before bringing suit under Title VII. *See* Love v. Pullman

---

[7]29 U.S.C. §633 (1984).
[8]29 U.S.C. §626(d)(2) (1984).
[9]*Id.*

Co., 404 U.S. 522, 4 FEP Cases 150 (1972): Olson v. Rembrandt Printing Co., 511 F.2d 1228, 10 FEP Cases 27 (CA 8 1975).[3]

Since the ADEA and Title VII share a common purpose, the elimination of discrimination in the workplace; since the language of §14(b) is almost *in haec verba* with §706(b) and since the legislative history of §14(b) indicates that its source was §706(b), we may properly conclude that Congress intended that the construction of §14(b) should follow that of §706(b). *See* Northcross v. Board of Education of the Memphis City Schools, 412 U.S. 427, 428 (1973). We therefore conclude that §14(b), like §706(b), is intended to screen from the federal courts those discrimination complaints that might be settled to the satisfaction of the grievant in state proceedings. We further conclude that prior resort to appropriate state proceedings is required under §14(b), just as under §706(b).

. . .

Respondent notes a second difference between the ADEA and Title VII. Section 14(a) of the ADEA, 29 U.S.C. §633(a), for which Title VII has no counterpart, provides that upon commencement of an action under ADEA, all state proceedings are superseded. From this respondent concludes that it would be an exercise in futility to require aggrieved persons to file state complaints since those persons may, after only 60 days, abort their involuntary state proceeding by filing a federal suit.

We find no merit in the argument. Unless §14(b) is to be stripped of all meaning, state agencies must be given at least some opportunity to solve problems of discrimination. While 60 days provides a limited time for the state agency to act, that was a decision for Congress to make and Congress apparently thought it sufficient. As Senator Dirksen told the Senate during the debates on §14(b)'s predecessor, §706(b) of Title VII:

"[A]t the local level . . . many cases are disposed of in a matter of days, and certainly not more than a few weeks. In the case of California, FEPC cases are disposed of in an average of about 5 days. In my own State it is approximately 14 days." 110 CONG. REC. 13087 (June 9, 1964).

[2-3][Footnotes omitted.]

In *Oscar Mayer*, the employee was involuntarily retired after 23 years of work. On March 10, 1976, he filed a notice of intent to sue his employer under the ADEA with the U.S. Department of Labor. The employee charged that he had been forced to retire because of his age in violation of the Act. At that time, the employee also inquired of the Labor Department whether he was required to file a state complaint in order to preserve his federal rights. The DOL informed him that the Act did not require such a filing, and he relied on this advice in failing to file with a state agency. On March 7, 1977, after federal conciliation efforts had failed, the employee brought an action against the employer in federal court.

The employer moved to dismiss the complaint on the grounds that the state civil rights commission was empowered to remedy age discrimination in employment and that Section 14(b) of the Act[10] required resort to this state remedy before commencing the federal action.

The Supreme Court ruled that Section 14(b), like Section 706(b) of the Civil Rights Act of 1964,[11] requires a complainant to resort to appropriate state administrative proceedings before bringing a federal ADEA action, since both statutes share a common purpose—elimination of discrimination in the work-

---

[10]29 U.S.C. §633(b) (1984).
[11]42 U.S.C. §2000e-5(c) (1984).

place, and because the language and legislative history of the statutes support this interpretation.[12]

All state proceedings are superseded upon commencement of an ADEA action, under Section 14(a) of the Act.[13] However, this fact does not excuse complaining parties from the Section 14(b) requirement of filing a state administrative complaint at least 60 days before commencing the federal action, the Court added in *Oscar Mayer*.[14]

State agencies must be given at least some opportunity to solve problems of discrimination, the Court emphasized, otherwise Section 14(b) is stripped of all meaning. Although 60 days is a limited period for a state agency to act, the Court concluded, that was a decision for Congress to make.

The Court also interpreted Section 14(b)'s requirement that an age discrimination claimant must "commence" state proceedings before seeking relief under the ADEA as not requiring that the state proceedings be "commenced" within the time set forth by the appropriate state law, because:

(1) Use of the word "commence" strongly implies that the state limitations periods are irrelevant, since even time-barred actions may be "commenced" under the Federal Rules of Civil Procedure merely by filing a complaint;

(2) This implication is made express by the last sentence of Section 14(b) disregarding state requirements "other than a requirement of the filing of a written and signed statement of the facts upon which the proceeding is based;" and

(3) This construction is consistent both with the ADEA's remedial purposes and with purposes of Section 14(b).[15]

The Court concluded that the employee could comply with Section 14(b) by simply filing a signed complaint with the state FEP agency, and that the federal court action should be held in abeyance until either the state complaint is dismissed as untimely or 60 days pass without settlement. Suspending the federal court action is preferable to dismissal of the action with no leave to refile, it reasoned.[16]

Though failure to file a timely charge in a deferral state will not be fatal to an action under the ADEA,[17] the Second Circuit has ruled that an employee's failure to file an ADEA charge within the 300-day period allowed in deferral states was not subject to equitable tolling, since the employee was a well-educated attorney familiar with the law.[18] In many instances, the charge-filing requirements and their application will be determined on a fact-specific basis.

A district court found timely a charge filed with the EEOC 186 days after the employee's termination, even though the Florida Human Relations Commission did not have authority beyond a 180-day period to receive the em-

[12]Oscar Mayer v. Evans, 441 U.S. 750, 19 FEP 1167 (1979).

[13]29 U.S.C. §633(a) (1984).

[14]*Supra* note 12, 19 FEP at 1170.

[15]*Id.*

[16]*Id.*

[17]Clark v. American Home Prods. Corp., 34 FEP 813 (D Mass, 1982).

[18]Miller v. ITT Corp., 37 FEP 8 (CA 2, 1985).

ployee's charge, since the state commission had authority within the meaning of Section 14(b) of the ADEA to "grant or seek relief," in satisfaction of the requirement of Section 7(d)(2) for the extended filing period.[19]

Internal Agency Procedures

According to one agency official, 99 percent of all EEOC charges are filed by individuals and most charges are filed in person.[20] Under agency rules, charges must be signed and must indicate the date and description of the act complained of and the name of the company or union that allegedly committed the wrongful act. A letter meeting these requirements can be accepted as a charge.

When an ADEA charge is received and the agency determines that it meets these threshold requirements, the charge is assigned to an Equal Opportunity Specialist (EOS) for investigation. The EOS does not represent the charging party, but rather is an independent and trained investigator who is thoroughly familiar with the ADEA. The scope of the EOS' investigation will be determined by how the charge reads.

At this point the EEOC must make a "deferral" determination: whether to defer to the state FEP agency, if one exists, or to retain for EEOC action. This determination depends in large part on state or local law. The charge, if retained by the EEOC, will be assigned to either "rapid charge processing" (RCP) if it is relatively simple and pertinent case law is settled, or to "extended charge processing" (ECP) if it involves legally or factually complex problems. Examples of such problems include disparate impact, class actions, multiple respondents, or interpretations of collective bargaining agreements.[21] An attorney is assigned to an ECP claim and is present at all critical stages.

Rapid Charge Processing (RCP) emphasizes settlement, which has three distinct advantages to ECP:

(1) Resolution of problems arising from a simple lack of communication between the employer and the employee;
(2) The offer to the charging party of quick relief while avoiding the expense of protracted litigation to both parties; and
(3) The elimination of a backlog problem for the EEOC.

Management groups and civil rights organizations pressured the agency against using RCP, because that system appeared to encourage frivolous claims, discrimination was not eliminated, and the EEOC was becoming an agency for claims adjustment, rather than for civil rights enforcement.[22]

Consequently, since late 1983, the EEOC has required a fuller investigation of charges. In fiscal year 1982, 29 percent of all charges were settled before determination was made, while final determinations were rendered in 38 percent

---

[19]McKelvy v. Metal Container Corp., 37 FEP 270 (MD Fla, 1984).

[20]Interview with John D. Schmelzer, Legal Advisor to EEOC's Director of Program Operations, 132 DAILY LAB. REP. A-6 (BNA, July 10, 1985).

[21]Id.

[22]Id.

of all charges. By comparison, 20 percent of all charges were settled and 50 percent were decided by the EEOC in fiscal year 1984.[23]

EEOC Investigation of Charge. An EOS prepares an inventory plan for each charge identifying the basis of the charge (i.e., age discrimination), the issue involved (hiring, training, involuntary retirement), and whether the case involves disparate treatment or disparate impact. The EOS then conducts witness interviews and usually issues requests for information (RFIs) from the employer on prior disciplinary actions against the charging party or other employees. The RFI is similar to interrogatories in civil litigation. The agency is currently in the process of gathering a "Document Assembly System," which is designed to obtain standard information in many investigations.

The EOS also requests a position statement from the employer, and this is usually the most important submission the charged party can make. In close cases, the position statement should be drawn extremely carefully: if the employer proffers a reason for the disciplinary action that the agency regards as pretextual, the employer would have a difficult time asserting a different reason for taking the action at a later stage in the proceedings.[24]

The EOS also has discretion to undertake a fact-finding conference which is a relatively informal proceeding used to determine which issues are undisputed, to clarify disputed evidence, and to determine what additional evidence is necessary. Attendance is limited to those with first-hand knowledge, those with the authority to bind the parties, the charging party's representative, and the charged party's counsel. The charged party's counsel can only advise the charged party—cross examination of the charging party is not permitted, and parties cannot ask each other questions. The EOS controls the conference, and asks the parties step-by-step whether there is agreement.

If other investigative methods are unsuccessful, the EEOC will issue an administrative subpoena. Subpoenas are not issued at the demand of the charging party, but are generally issued by the agency district directors, after clearance with a regional attorney. (Only a commissioner may issue a subpoena under the Equal Pay Act.) Subpoenas may be issued if relevant to the charge and if the demand is not unduly burdensome to the charged party. Appeal procedures for the agency's decision to issue a subpoena are available under regulations promulgated under Title VII.[25]

However, one EEOC official said that he looked forward to litigation on the issue because "case law is so favorable to the government that it's an easy win for us."[26]

EEOC Action and Conciliation

Under Section 7(b), the EEOC can file a complaint in federal court against an employer, but the Act limits this power by stating:

---

[23]*Id.*
[24]*Id.*
[25]42 U.S.C. §2000e (1984).
[26]*Supra* note 20.

"Before instituting any action under this section, the Equal Employment Opportunity Commission shall attempt to eliminate the discriminatory practice or practices alleged, and to effect voluntary compliance with the requirements of this chapter through informal methods of conciliation, conference, and persuasion."[27]

The Act empowers the Commission to maintain an action in federal court, and courts have ruled that filing deadlines in deferral states and in federal court cannot operate to divest or deprive the EEOC of this authority. In one case, the discharged employees' failure to file a timely charge before the state FEP agency was found not to preclude the EEOC from seeking monetary relief on their behalf.[28] The district court also observed that the individual employees had not filed written consents to be represented by the EEOC, and were not named party plaintiffs in the original complaint, but it found these aspects of the case to be insufficient to overcome the clear language of the Act to empower the EEOC to bring actions on behalf of private parties. Analogies with the FLSA are inapposite, the court reasoned, since the FLSA provides for liquidated damages and the ADEA does not, and there is a significant difference between filing a private action and an agency action.[29]

On the issue of conciliation vis-à-vis timely filing, a district court in *EEOC v. Kansas* has ruled that the EEOC's ADEA action was not time-barred by the employee's failure to provide a notice of intent to sue within 180 days, as is required under Section 626(d). The court noted that the "only condition on a public enforcement action is the requirement of attempts to effect voluntary compliance (conciliation)."[30] The court defined "conciliation" as a "willingness" to consider "possible compromises" in a give-and-take situation:

"In the Tenth Circuit, if there has been any attempt at conciliation, the action cannot be dismissed for failure to attempt conciliation. *Marshall v. Sun Oil Co.,* 592 F.2d 563, 566, 18 FEP Cases 1632 (10th Cir. 1979); *Equal Employment Opportunity Commission v. Zia Co.,* 582 F.2d 527, 17 FEP Cases 1201 (10th Cir. 1978). Thus, in considering this motion, we need only look to see whether there is any correspondence which could be construed as an attempt to conciliate. The remedy for failure to conciliate in good faith is not dismissal; instead, if the EEOC has not conciliated in good faith, the proceedings are stayed for further conciliation efforts. The inquiry into good faith on the part of the EEOC is relevant to whether the court should entertain the claim or stay the proceedings, not to its power over the cause. *Equal Employment Opportunity Commission v. Zia Co., supra.*

Adequate conciliation has been described as informing the defendant of the nature and extent of the violations and of the relief sought, giving the defendant an opportunity to respond, and advising the defendant that if the informal methods fail, the case will be reviewed for possible legal action. *Marshall v. American Motors Corp.,* 475 F. Supp. 875, 878–879, 20 FEP Cases 575 (E.D. Mich. 1979). *See also, Marshall v. Sun Oil Co.,* 592 F.2d 563, 566–567, 18 FEP Cases 1632 (10th Cir. 1979); *Brennan v. Ace Hardware Corp.,* 495 F.2d 368, 374, 7 FEP Cases 657 (8th Cir. 1974). It involves a willingness on both sides to consider

---

[27]29 U.S.C. §626(b) (1984).
[28]EEOC v. Home Ins. Co., 553 F. Supp. 704, 30 FEP 841 (SD NY, 1982).
[29]*Id.,* 30 FEP at 849.
[30]EEOC v. Kansas, 28 FEP 1036, 1038 (D Kan, 1982).

possible compromises and settlements in a give and take situation. *Marshall v. B & O Railroad Co., supra*, 461 F. Supp. at 369."[31]

Another aspect of the requirement to engage in conciliation is that the limitations period is tolled during the duration of the conciliation under Section 7(e)(2) of the Act,[32] which provides that while the Secretary is attempting voluntary compliance through informal methods of conciliation, the limitations period under the Portal-to-Portal Act[33] should be tolled for up to one year. The court in *EEOC v. Kansas* initially determined that there was correspondence between the Commission and the defendant sufficient to frame a question of law to be resolved by the court. As to the employer's argument that the conciliation efforts must be made in "good faith" in order to toll the limitations period, the court simply observed that there were no requirements that attempts to effect voluntary compliance be made in good faith.[34] The court concluded that even if the Commission had failed to attempt to conciliate in good faith, the appropriate remedy would be a stay of the proceedings to permit further conciliation efforts, rather than outright dismissal.[35]

But the question may arise as to what effort is necessary to constitute "adequate" conciliation. Since the *Kansas* court established that good faith is not a prerequisite to finding conciliation under the Act, the degree of the effort is drawn into question. Another district court, hearing an EEOC action alleging classwide discrimination, has held that, at a minimum, adequate conciliation involves:

(1) Informing the violator of ways in which he can bring himself into compliance with the Act;

(2) Telling him that terminated employees may recover back pay;

(3) Notifying him that the Department of Labor may institute legal action; and

(4) Assuring him that he may respond to the violations in light of the possible remedy.[36]

The *Chrysler* court also added that, in view of the classwide action, the EEOC was attempting to correct a public wrong and the Act would not require individual documentation of conciliation attempts on behalf of all potential claimants: To do so would "reward the employer who discriminates on a large scale and undermine the legislative goal of obtaining voluntary compliance in these cases."[37]

Another district court was faced not with a claim of inadequate conciliation, or even conciliation lacking good faith. The employer had alleged a degree of bad faith in the EEOC's efforts, where the commission's second proposal was a partial reversal of an earlier position stated by an agency attorney, and that

---

[31]*Id.* at 1039. *See also* Marshall v. Chamberlain Mfg. Corp., 601 F.2d 100, 105, 20 FEP 147 (CA 3, 1979).

[32]29 U.S.C. §626(e)(2) (1984).

[33]29 U.S.C. §255 (1984).

[34]*Id.*, citing EEOC v. Zia Co., 582 F.2d 527, 17 FEP 1201 (CA 10, 1978).

[35]*Id.*

[36]EEOC v. Chrysler Corp., 546 F. Supp. 54, 29 FEP 285, 290 (ED Mich, 1982), citing Marshall v. Sun Oil Co., 605 F.2d 1331, 1334, 21 FEP 257 (CA 5), *reh'g denied*, 610 F.2d 818 (CA 5, 1979).

[37]*Id.*, 29 FEP at 290–291, citing Marshall v. Sun Oil, *supra* note 36.

attorney and his regional attorney were subsequently removed. The court rejected the employer's discovery request on the ground that the Commission is not bound by unauthorized representations made by its employees.[38] On motions for summary judgment, the court later ruled that the Act's statute of limitations was tolled only for the five-month period during which the agency actively sought conciliation; it rejected the Commission's claim that the tolling period ends only when the Commission sends a letter to the employer stating that otherwise conciliation has failed and that the tolling runs for an automatic one year after the conciliation begins.[39]

In the federal sector, the conciliation effort "must initially use exhaustive, affirmative action to attempt to achieve conciliation before legal action is begun" by the agency.[40]

Resort to State Authority

In *Oscar Mayer v. Evans*,[41] the Supreme Court established that the ADEA requires a claimant to resort to an appropriate state administrative proceeding, where one exists, before bringing an ADEA action. Many states have these EEOC-type agencies, usually created via some state fair employment practices statute. Typically, the states which have deemed it necessary to enact such statutes have borrowed heavily from the federal statutes and modified them where it felt modification was necessary.

Many states have also enacted local age discrimination in employment statutes, patterned after the federal ADEA. Though the federal ADEA contemplates concurrent jurisdiction with state courts,[42] few state laws have reciprocal provisions. The Louisiana Age Discrimination in Employment Act[43] was used successfully in a former employee's action alleging age discrimination, after the district court determined that the employer's extra-territorial activities precluded coverage by the federal ADEA.[44]

The Eleventh Circuit decided a complex statutory conflict in 1985 that involved the federal ADEA and the Tennessee employment discrimination statute.[45] At the state court level, the plaintiff and other former municipal employees who had been involuntarily retired from the Knoxville police force filed an action based on the state law claim, and the state and federal constitutions. The Chancery Court rejected their claims. Then, the plaintiffs filed age discrimination charges with the EEOC.

The district court held that the action was not barred under principles of *res judicata* or issue preclusion, and that the municipality had violated the federal ADEA by involuntarily retiring the plaintiff because of age.[46]

---

[38]EEOC v. Colgate-Palmolive Co., 34 FEP 1551 (SD NY, 1983).

[39]EEOC v. Colgate-Palmolive Co., 34 FEP 1749 (SD NY, 1984).

[40]Brennan v. Ace Hardware Corp., 495 F.2d 368, 7 FEP 657 (CA 8, 1974).

[41]441 U.S. 750, 19 FEP 1167 (1979).

[42]*Id.*, and see this chapter at "Concurrent Jurisdiction."

[43]LA. REV. STAT. ANN. §23:976 (1982).

[44]Belanger v. Keydril Co., 596 F. Supp. 823, 36 FEP 132 (ED La, 1984).

[45]TENN. CODE ANN. §§4-21-101 (1981).

[46]Whitfield v. City of Knoxville, 567 F. Supp. 1344, 32 FEP 1052 (ED Tenn, 1983). For a discussion of the difference between *res judicata* and collateral estoppel, *see* Migra v. Warren City School Dist. Bd. of Educ., 465 U.S. 75 n.1, 33 FEP 1345, 1346 (1984).

The appeals court examined the plaintiffs' federal ADEA claim, in light of what had transpired at the state court level on the state employment discrimination claim, and ruled that:

(1) An ADEA claim can be barred, if the circumstances warrant, where a state discrimination claim was adjudicated in the Tennessee courts and where the federal claim was not presented;

(2) Since the filing periods precluded the plaintiffs from raising the federal ADEA claim in the state court, the plaintiffs' federal claim is not barred by principles of *res judicata*;

(3) Provisions of the federal ADEA concerning the filing of a charge with the EEOC and filing with a state FEP agency are substantive limitations on the right to bring a suit that nonfederal courts must respect; and

(4) An individual is not required to wait the 60 days before filing with the state FEP agency before filing a state-court action simply so that the federal ADEA claim would be cognizable in that action.[47]

Federal Preemption

The concept of federal preemption is a well-established constitutional principle that can be paraphrased to mean that where the federal legislature has legislated in a certain area in an authoritative manner, the federal legislation is intended to preclude conflicting state legislation from controlling. The application of this principle can be clearly seen in a decision of the Third Circuit in *EEOC v. Altoona*.[48] The appeals court had to resolve a conflict between the federal ADEA and the Pennsylvania Civil Service Act.[49] The Civil Service Act required that any reduction in the number of firefighters for reasons of economy had to be made by retirement based on the pension eligibility of the oldest in age and service. However, the Third Circuit pointed out that mere eligibility for a pension is not a defense to a prima facie case of age discrimination.[50]

The appeals court reasoned that the state law demanded a reduction in force for economic considerations to be imposed on older employees, in order of their age. This is not permitted by the federal ADEA, it concluded, which "completely preempts" the state law.[51]

A memorandum of understanding between the EEOC and the Florida Commission on Human Relations concerning investigation of age discrimination charges did not deprive the state agency of its "authority to grant or seek relief" within the meaning of Section 14(b) of the federal ADEA, according

---

[47]Whitfield v. City of Knoxville, 37 FEP 288 (CA 6, 1985).

[48]33 FEP 888 (CA 3, 1983).

[49]PA. STAT. ANN. tit. 53 §39871 (Purdon 1957).

[50]*Supra* note 48, 33 FEP at 890, citing EEOC v. Baltimore & Ohio R.R. Co., 632 F.2d 1107, 1111, 23 FEP 1381 (CA 4, 1980), *cert. denied*, 454 U.S. 825, 26 FEP 1687 (1981).

[51]*Id.*, 33 FEP at 890.

to a district court in Florida.[52] Therefore, it reasoned, the extended 300-day period for filing with the EEOC was available to a discharged employee who filed a charge with the EEOC 186 days after his termination.[53]

Concurrent Jurisdiction

The federal ADEA contemplates jurisdiction over age claims concurrently with state courts, according to the Supreme Court in *Oscar Mayer v. Evans*.[54] The employer argued that ADEA claimants have the option to ignore state remedies, but the Court read Section 14(b) of the federal ADEA as requiring claimants to file with appropriate state agencies, concluding:

> "The ADEA permits concurrent rather than sequential state and federal administrative jurisdiction in order to expedite the processing of age discrimination claims. The premise for this difference is that the delay inherent in sequential jurisdiction is particularly prejudicial to the rights of 'older citizens to whom, by definition, relatively few productive years are left.' 113 CONG. REC. 7076 (1967) (remarks of Sen. Javits).
>
> "The purpose of expeditious disposition would not be frustrated were ADEA claimants required to pursue state and federal administrative remedies simultaneously. Indeed, simultaneous state and federal conciliation efforts may well facilitate rapid settlements. There is no reason to conclude, therefore, that the possibility of concurrent state and federal cognizance supports the construction of Section 14(b) that ADEA grievants may ignore state remedies altogether."[55]

---

[52] McKelvy v. Metal Container Corp., 37 FEP 270 (MD Fla, 1984).

[53] *Id.*

[54] 441 U.S. 750, 19 FEP 1167 (1979).

[55] *Id.*, 19 FEP at 1169.

Appendix A

Text of Age Discrimination
in Employment Act

(P.L. 90–202, effective June 12, 1968; as last amended by P.L. 98–369
and P.L. 98–459, effective January 1, 1985)

§ 621. Congressional statement of findings and purpose

[Sec. 2] (a) The Congress hereby finds and declares that—
(1) in the face of rising productivity and affluence, older workers find themselves disadvantaged in their efforts to retain employment, and especially to regain employment when displaced from jobs;
(2) the setting of arbitrary age limits regardless of potential for job performance has become a common practice, and certain otherwise desirable practices may work to the disadvantage of older persons;
(3) The incidence of unemployment, especially long-term unemployment with resultant deterioration of skill, morale, and employer acceptability is, relative to the younger ages, high among older workers; their numbers are great and growing; and their employment problems grave;
(4) the existence in industries affecting commerce of arbitrary discrimination in employment because of age burdens commerce and the free flow of goods in commerce.
(b) It is therefore the purpose of this Act to promote employment of older persons based on their ability rather than age; to prohibit arbitrary age discrimination in employment; to help employers and workers find ways of meeting problems arising from the impact of age on employment.

§ 622. Education and research program; recommendation
to Congress

[Sec. 3] (a) The Secretary of Labor shall undertake studies and provide information to labor unions, management, and the general public concerning the needs and abilities of older workers, and their potentials for continued employment and contribution to the economy. In order to achieve the purposes of this Act, the Secretary of Labor shall carry on a continuing program of education and information, under which he may, among other measures:
(1) undertake research, and promote research, with a view to reducing barriers to the employment of older persons, and the promotion of measures for utilizing their skills;
(2) publish and otherwise make available to employers, professional societies, the various media of communication and other interested persons the findings of studies and other materials for the promotion of employment;
(3) foster, through the public employment service system and through cooperative

effort, the development of facilities of public and private agencies for expanding the opportunities and potentials of older persons;

(4) sponsor and assist State and community informational and educational programs.

(b) Not later than six months after the effective date of this Act, the Secretary shall recommend to the Congress any measures he may deem desirable to change the lower or upper age limits set forth in section 12.

§ 623.   Prohibition of age discrimination

[Sec. 4] (a) It shall be unlawful for an employer—

(1) to fail or refuse to hire or to discharge any individual or otherwise discriminate against any individual with respect to his compensation, terms, conditions, or privileges of employment, because of such individual's age;

(2) to limit, segregate, or classify his employees in any way which would deprive or tend to deprive any individual of employment opportunities or otherwise adversely affect his status as an employee, because of such individual's age; or

(3) to reduce the wage rate of any employee in order to comply with this Act.

(b) It shall be unlawful for an employment agency to fail or refuse to refer for employment, or otherwise to discriminate against, any individual because of such individual's age, or to classify or refer for employment any individual on the basis of such individual's age.

(c) It shall be unlawful for a labor organization—

(1) to exclude or to expel from its membership or otherwise to discriminate against, any individual because of his age;

(2) to limit, segregate, or classify its membership, or to classify or fail or refuse to refer for employment any individual, in any way which would deprive or tend to deprive any individual of employment opportunities, or would limit such employment opportunities or otherwise adversely affect his status as an employee or as an applicant for employment, because of such individual's age;

(3) to cause or attempt to cause an employer to discriminate against an individual in violation of this section.

(d) It shall be unlawful for any employer to discriminate against any of his employees or applicants for employment, for an employment agency to discriminate against any individual, or for a labor organization to discriminate against any member thereof or applicant for membership, because such individual member, or applicant for membership, has opposed any practice made unlawful by this section, or because such individual, member, or applicant for membership has made a charge, testified, assisted, or participated in any manner in an investigation, proceeding, or litigation under this Act.

(e) It shall be unlawful for an employer, labor organization, or employment agency to print or publish, or cause to be printed or published, any notice or advertisement relating to employment by such an employer or membership in or any classification or referral for employment by such a labor organization, or relating to any classification or referral for employment by such an employment agency, indicating any preference, limitation, specification, or discrimination, based on age.

(f) It shall not be unlawful for an employer, employment agency, or labor organization—

(1) to take any action otherwise prohibited under subsection (a), (b), (c), or (e) of this section where age is a bona fide occupational qualification reasonably necessary to the normal operation of the particular business, or where the differentiation is based on reasonable factors other than age;

(2) to observe the terms of a bona fide seniority system or any bona fide employee

benefit plan such as retirement, pension, or insurance plan, which is not a subterfuge to evade the purpose of this Act, except that no such employee benefit plan shall excuse the failure to hire any individual, and no such seniority system or employee benefit plan shall require or permit the involuntary retirement of any individual specified by section 12(a) of this Act because of the age of such individual.

(3) to discharge or otherwise discipline an individual for good cause.

(g)(1) For purposes of this section, any employer must provide that any employee aged 65 through 69 and any employee's spouse aged 65 through 69 shall be entitled to coverage under any group health plan offered to such employees under the same conditions as any employee, and the spouse of such employee under age 65.

(2) For purposes of paragraph (1), the term "group health plan" has the meaning given to such term in section 162(i)(2) of the Internal Revenue Code of 1954.

§ 624. Study by Secretary of Labor; reports to President and Congress; scope of study; implementation of study; transmittal date of reports

[Sec. 5] (a)(1) The Secretary of Labor is directed to undertake an appropriate study of institutional and other arrangements giving rise to involuntary retirement, and report his findings and any appropriate legislative recommendations to the President and to the Congress. Such study shall include—

(A) an examination of the effect of the amendment made by section 3(a) of the Age Discrimination in Employment Act Amendments of 1978 in raising the upper age limitation established by section 12(a) of this act to 70 years of age;

(B) a determination of the feasibility of eliminating such limitation;

(C) a determination of the feasibility of raising such limitation above 70 years of age; and

(D) an examination of the effect of the exemption contained in section 12(c), relating to certain executive employees, and the exemption contained in section 12(d), relating to tenured teaching personnel.

(2) The Secretary may undertake the study required by paragraph (1) of this subsection directly or by contract or other arrangement.

(b) The report required by subsection (a) of this section, shall be transmitted to the President and to the Congress as an interim report not later than January 1, 1981, and in final form not later than January 1, 1982.

§ 625. Administration

[Sec. 6] The Secretary shall have the power—

(a) to make delegations, to appoint such agents and employees, and to pay for technical assistance on a fee-for-service basis, as he deems necessary to assist him in the performance of his functions under this Act;

(b) to cooperate with regional, State, local, and other agencies, and to cooperate with and furnish technical assistance to employers, labor organizations, and employment agencies to aid in effectuating the purposes of this Act.

§ 626. Recordkeeping, investigation, and enforcement

[Sec. 7] (a) The Secretary shall have the power to make investigations and require the keeping of records necessary or appropriate for the administration of this Act in accordance with the powers and procedures provided in sections 9 and 11 of the Fair Labor Standards Act of 1938, as amended (29 U.S.C. 209 and 211).

(b) The provisions of this Act shall be enforced in accordance with the powers, remedies, and procedures provided in sections 11(b), 16 (except for subsection (a) thereof), and 17 of the Fair Labor Standards Act of 1938, as amended (29 U.S.C. 211(b), 216, 217) and subsection (c) of this section. Any act prohibited under section 4 of this Act shall be deemed to be a prohibited act under section 15 of the Fair Labor Standards Act of 1938, as amended (29 U.S.C. 215). Amounts owing to an individual as a result of a violation of this Act shall be deemed to be unpaid minimum wages or unpaid overtime compensation for purposes of sections 16 and 17 of the Fair Labor Standards Act of 1938, as amended (29 U.S.C. 216, 217): *Provided*, That liquidated damages shall be payable only in cases of willful violations of this Act. In any action brought to enforce this Act the court shall have jurisdiction to grant such legal or equitable relief as may be appropriate to effectuate the purposes of this Act, including without limitation judgments compelling employment, reinstatement or promotion, or enforcing the liability for amounts deemed to be unpaid minimum wages or unpaid overtime compensation under this section. Before instituting any action under this section, the Secretary shall attempt to eliminate the discriminatory practice or practices alleged, and to effect voluntary compliance with the requirements of this Act through informal methods of conciliation, conference, and persuasion.

(c)(1) Any aggrieved individual may bring a civil action in any court of competent jurisdiction for such legal or equitable relief as will effectuate the purposes of this Act: *Provided*, That the right of any individual to bring such action shall terminate upon the commencement of an action by the Secretary to enforce the right of such individual under this Act.

(2) In an action brought under paragraph (1), a person shall be entitled to a trial by jury of any issue of fact in any such action for recovery of amounts owing as a result of a violation of this Act, regardless of whether equitable relief is sought by any party in such action.

(d) No civil action may be commenced by an individual under this section until 60 days after a charge alleging unlawful discrimination has been filed with the Secretary. Such a charge shall be filed—

(1) within 180 days after the alleged unlawful practice occurred; or

(2) in a case to which section 14(b) applies, within 300 days after the alleged unlawful practice occurred, or within 30 days after receipt by the individual of notice of termination of proceedings under State law, whichever is earlier.

Upon receiving such a charge, the Secretary shall promptly notify all persons named in such charge as prospective defendants in the action and shall promptly seek to eliminate any alleged unlawful practice by informal methods of conciliation, conference, and persuasion.

(e)(1) Sections 6 and 10 of the Portal-to-Portal Act of 1947 shall apply to actions under this Act.

(2) For the period during which the Secretary is attempting to effect voluntary compliance with requirements of this Act through informal methods of conciliation, conference, and persuasion pursuant to subsection (b), the statute of limitations as provided in section 6 of the Portal-to-Portal Act of 1947 shall be tolled, but in no event for a period in excess of one year.

§ 627.   Notices to be posted

[Sec. 8] Every employer, employment agency, and labor organization shall post and keep posted in conspicuous places upon its premises a notice to be prepared or approved by the Secretary setting forth information as the Secretary deems appropriate to effectuate the purposes of this Act.

§ 628.   Rules and regulations; exemptions

[Sec. 9] In accordance with the provisions of subchapter II of chapter 5 of title 5, United States Code, the Secretary of Labor may issue such rules and regulations as he may consider necessary or appropriate for carrying out this Act, and may establish such reasonable exemptions to and from any or all provisions of this Act as he may find necessary and proper in the public interest.

§ 629.   Criminal penalties

[Sec. 10] Whoever shall forcibly resist, oppose, impede, intimidate, or interfere with a duly authorized representative of the Secretary while he is engaged in the performance of duties under this Act shall be punished by a fine of not more than $500 or by imprisonment for not more than one year, or by both: *Provided*, however, That no person shall be imprisoned under this section except when there has been a prior conviction hereunder.

§ 630.   Definitions

[Sec. 11] For the purposes of this Act—(a) The term "person" means one or more individuals, partnerships, associations, labor organizations, corporations, business trusts, legal representatives, or any organized groups of persons.

(b) The term "employer" means a person engaged in an industry affecting commerce who has twenty or more employees for each working day in each of twenty or more calendar weeks in the current or preceding calendar year: *Provided*, That prior to June 30, 1968, employers having fewer than fifty employees shall not be considered employers. The term also means (1) any agent of such a person, and (2) a State or political subdivision of a State and any agency or instrumentality of a State or a political subdivision of a State, and any interstate agency but such term does not include the United States, or a corporation wholly owned by the Government of the United States.

(c) The term "employment agency" means any person regularly undertaking with or without compensation to procure employees for an employer and includes an agent of such a person; but shall not include an agency of the United States.

(d) The term "labor organization" means a labor organization engaged in an industry affecting commerce, and any agent of such an organization, and includes any organization of any kind, any agency, or employee representation committee, group, association, or plan so engaged in which employees participate and which exists for the purpose, in whole or in part, of dealing with employers concerning grievances, labor disputes, wages, rates of pay, hours, or other terms or conditions of employment, and any conference, general committee, joint or system board, or joint council so engaged which is subordinate to a national or international labor organization.

(e) A labor organization shall be deemed to be engaged in an industry affecting commerce if (1) it maintains or operates a hiring hall or hiring office which procures employees for an employer or procures for employees opportunities to work for an employer, or (2) the number of its members (or, where it is a labor organization composed of other labor organizations or their representatives, if the aggregate number of the members of such other labor organization) is fifty or more prior to July 1, 1968, or twenty-five or more on or after July 1, 1968, and such labor organization—

(1) is the certified representative of employees under the provisions of the National Labor Relation Act, as amended, or the Railway Labor Act, as amended; or

(2) although not certified, is a national or international labor organization or a local labor organization recognized or acting as the representative of employees of an employer or employers engaged in an industry affecting commerce; or

(3) has chartered a local labor organization or subsidiary body which is representing or actively seeking to represent employees of employers within the meaning of paragraph (1) or (2); or

(4) has been chartered by a labor organization representing or actively seeking to represent employees within the meaning of paragraph (1) or (2) as the local or subordinate body through which such employees may enjoy membership or become affiliated with such labor organization; or

(5) is a conference, general committee, joint or system board or joint council subordinate to a national or international labor organization, which includes a labor organization engaged in an industry affecting commerce within the meaning of any of the preceding paragraphs of this subsection.

(f) The term "employee" means an individual employed by an employer except that the term "employee" shall not include any person elected to public office in any State or political subdivision of any State by the qualified voters thereof, or any person chosen by such officer to be on such officer's personal staff, or an appointee on the policy-making level or an immediate adviser with respect to the exercise of the constitutional or legal powers of the office. The exemption set forth in the preceding sentence shall not include employees subject to the civil service laws of a State government, governmental agency, or political subdivision.

(g) The term "commerce" means trade, traffic, commerce, transportation, transmission, or communication among the several States, or between a State and any place outside thereof; or within the District of Columbia, or a possession of the United States, or between points in the same State but through a point outside thereof.

(h) The term "industry affecting commerce" means any activity, business, or industry in commerce or in which a labor dispute would hinder or obstruct commerce or the free flow of commerce and includes any activity or industry "affecting commerce" within the meaning of the Labor-Management Reporting and Disclosure Act of 1959.

(i) The term "State" includes a State of the United States, the District of Columbia, Puerto Rico, the Virgin Islands, American Samoa, Guam, Wake Island, the Canal Zone, and Outer Continental Shelf Lands defined in the Outer Continental Shelf Lands Act.

§ 631.   Age limits

[Sec. 12] (a) The prohibitions in this Act shall be limited to individuals who are at least 40 years of age but less than 70 years of age.

(b) In the case of any personnel action affecting employees or applicants for employment which is subject to the provisions of section 15 of this Act, the prohibitions established in section 15 of this Act shall be limited to individuals who are at least 40 years of age.

(c)(1) Nothing in this Act shall be construed to prohibit compulsory retirement of any employee who has attained 65 years of age but not 70 years of age, and who, for the two-year period immediately before retirement, is employed in a bona fide executive or a high policymaking position, if such employee is entitled to an immediate nonforfeitable annual retirement benefit from a pension, profitsharing, savings, or deferred compensation plan, or any combination of such plans, of the employer of such employee, which equals, in aggregate, at least $44,000.

(2) In applying the retirement benefit test of paragraph (1) of this subsection, if any such retirement benefit is in a form other than a straight life annuity (with no ancillary benefits), or if employees contribute to any such plan or make rollover contributions, such benefit shall be adjusted in accordance with regulations prescribed by the Sec-

retary, after consultation with the Secretary of the Treasury, so that the benefit is the equivalent of a straight life annuity (with no ancillary benefits) under a plan to which employees do not contribute and under which no rollover contributions are made.

§ 632. Annual report to Congress

[Sec. 13] The Secretary shall submit annually in January a report to the Congress covering his activities for the preceding year and including such information, data, and recommendations for further legislation in connection with the matters covered by this Act as he may find advisable. Such report shall contain an evaluation and appraisal by the Secretary of the effect of the minimum and maximum ages established by this Act, together with his recommendation to the Congress. In making such evaluation and appraisal, the Secretary shall take into consideration any changes which may have occurred in the general age level of the population, the effect of the Act upon workers not covered by its provisions, and such other factors as he may deem pertinent.

§ 633. Federal-state relationship

[Sec. 14] (a) Nothing in this Act shall affect the jurisdiction of any agency of any State performing like functions with regard to discriminatory employment practices on account of age except that upon commencement of an action under this Act such action shall supersede any State action.

(b) In the case of an alleged unlawful practice occurring in a State which has a law prohibiting discrimination in employment because of age and establishing or authorizing a State authority to grant or seek relief from such discriminatory practice, no suit may be brought under section 7 of this Act before the expiration of sixty days after proceedings have been commenced under the State law, unless such proceedings have been earlier terminated, provided that such sixty-day period shall be extended to one hundred and twenty days during the first year after the effective day of such State law. If any requirement for the commencement of such proceedings is imposed by a State authority other than a requirement of the filing of a written and signed statement of the facts upon which the proceeding is based, the proceeding shall be deemed to have been commenced for the purposes of this subsection at the time such statement is sent by registered mail to the appropriate State authority.

§ 633a. Nondiscrimination on account of age in Federal Government employment

[Sec. 15] (a) All personnel actions affecting employees or applicants for employment who are at least 40 years of age (except personnel actions with regard to aliens employed outside the limits of the United States) in military departments as defined in section 102 of title 5, in executive agencies as defined in section 105 of title 5 (including employees and applicants for employment who are paid from nonappropriated funds), in the United States Postal Service and the Postal Rate Commission, in those units in the government of the District of Columbia having positions in the competitive service, and in those units of the legislative and judicial branches of the Federal Government having positions in the competitive service, and in the Library of Congress shall be made free from any discrimination based on age.

(b) Except as otherwise provided in this subsection, the Equal Employment Opportunity Commission is authorized to enforce the provisions of subsection (a) of this section through appropriate remedies, including reinstatement or hiring of employees with or without backpay, as will effectuate the policies of this section. The Equal

Employment Opportunity Commission shall issue such rules, regulations, orders, and instructions as it deems necessary and appropriate to carry out its responsibilities under this section. The Equal Employment Opportunity Commission shall—

(1) be responsible for the review and evaluation of the operation of all agency programs designed to carry out the policy of this section, periodically obtaining and publishing (on at least a semiannual basis) progress reports from each department, agency, or unit referred to in subsection (a) of this section.

(2) consult with and solicit the recommendations of interested individuals, groups, and organizations relating to nondiscrimination in employment on account of age; and

(3) provide for the acceptance and processing of complaints of discrimination in Federal employment on account of age.

The head of each such department, agency, or unit shall comply with such rules, regulations, orders, and instructions of the Equal Employment Opportunity Commission which shall include a provision that an employee or applicant for employment shall be notified of any final action taken on any complaint of discrimination filed by him thereunder. Reasonable exemptions to the provisions of this section may be established by the Commission but only when the Commission has established a maximum age requirement on the basis of a determination that age is a bona fide occupational qualification necessary to the performance of the duties of the position. With respect to employment in the Library of Congress, authorities granted in this subsection to the Equal Employment Opportunity Commission shall be exercised by the Librarian of Congress.

(c) Any person aggrieved may bring a civil action in any Federal district court of competent jurisdiction for such legal or equitable relief as will effectuate the purposes of this chapter.

(d) When the individual has not filed a complaint concerning age discrimination with the Commission, no civil action may be commenced by any individual under this section until the individual has given the Commission not less than thirty days' notice of an intent to file such action. Such notice shall be filed within one hundred and eight days after the alleged unlawful practice occurred. Upon receiving a notice of intent to sue, the Commission shall promptly notify all persons named therein as prospective defendants in the action and take any appropriate action to ensure the elimination of any unlawful practice.

(e) Nothing contained in this section shall relieve any Government agency or official of the responsibility to assure nondiscrimination on account of age in employment as required under any provision of Federal law.

(f) Any personnel action of any department, agency, or other entity referred to in subsection (a) of this section shall not be subject to, or affected by, any provision of this chapter, other than the provisions of section 631(b) of this title and the provisions of this section.

(g)(1) The Equal Employment Opportunity Commission shall undertake a study relating to the effects of the amendments made to this section by the Age Discrimination in Employment Act Amendments of 1978, and the effects of section 631(b) of this title.

(2) The Equal Employment Opportunity Commission shall transmit a report to the President and to the Congress containing the findings of the Commission resulting from the study of the Commission under paragraph (1) of this subsection. Such report shall be transmitted no later than January 1, 1980.

[Sec. 16] [Deleted.]

§ 634. Authorization of appropriations

[Sec. 17] There are hereby authorized to be appropriated such sums as may be necessary to carry out this chapter.

Appendix B

Text of EEOC Regulations
on Enforcement of ADEA*

(29 CFR Sections 1625–1627, revised as of July 1, 1985)

***

Part 1625

Age Discrimination in Employment Act

Subpart A

Interpretations

§ 1625.1 Definitions

The Equal Employment Opportunity Commission is hereinafter referred to as the "Commission". The terms "person", "employer", "employment agency", "labor organization", and "employee" shall have the meanings set forth in Section 11 of the Age Discrimination in Employment Act of 1967, as amended, 29 U.S.C. 621 *et seq.*, hereinafter referred to as the "Act". References to "employers" in this part state principles that are applicable not only to employers but also to labor organizations and to employment agencies.

§ 1625.2 Discrimination between individuals protected by the Act

(a) It is unlawful in situations where this Act applies, for an employer to discriminate in hiring or in any other way by giving preference because of age between individuals within the 40–70 age bracket. Thus, if two people apply for the same position, and one is 42 and the other 52, the employer may not lawfully turn down either one on the basis of age, but must make such decision on the basis of some other factor.

(b) The extension of additional benefits, such as increased severance pay, to older employees within the protected age bracket may be lawful if an employer has a reasonable basis to conclude that those benefits will counteract problems related to age discrimination. The extension of those additional benefits may not be used as a means to accomplish practices otherwise prohibited by the Act.

---

*Appendix B includes the Proposed Rule Allowing Unsupervised Waiver of Rights Under ADEA (50 FR 40871, Sept. 17, 1985), appearing at p. 194.

§ 1625.3   Employment agency

(a) As long as an employment agency regularly procures employees for at least one covered employer, it qualifies under section 11(c) of the Act as an employment agency with respect to all of its activities whether or not such activities are for employers covered by the act.

(b) The prohibitions of section 4(b) of the Act apply not only to the referral activities of a covered employment agency but also to the agency's own employment practices, regardless of the number of employees the agency may have.

§ 1625.4   Help wanted notices or advertisements

(a) When help wanted notices or advertisements contain terms and phrases, such as "age 25 to 35," "young," "college student," "recent college graduate," "boy," "girl," or others of a similar nature, such a term or phrase deters the employment of older persons and is a violation of the Act, unless one of the exceptions applies. Such phrases as "age 40 to 50," "age over 65," "retired person," or "supplement your pension" discriminate against others within the protected group and, therefore, are prohibited unless one of the exceptions applies.

(b) The use of the phrase "state age" in help wanted notices or advertisements is not, in itself, a violation of the Act. But because the request that an applicant state his age may tend to deter older applicants or otherwise indicate discrimination based on age, employment notices or advertisements which include the phrase "state age," or any similar term, will be closely scrutinized to assure that the request is for a lawful purpose.

§ 1625.5   Employment applications

A request on the part of an employer for information such as "Date of Birth" or "State Age" on an employment application form is not, in itself, a violation of the Act. But because the request that an applicant state his age may tend to deter older applicants or otherwise indicate discrimination based on age, employment application forms which request such information will be closely scrutinized to assure that the request is for a permissible purpose and not for purposes proscribed by the Act. That the purpose is not one proscribed by the statute should be made known to the applicant, either by a reference on the application form to the statutory prohibition in language to the following effect: "The Age Discrimination in Employment Act of 1967 prohibits discrimination on the basis of age with respect to individuals who are at least 40 but less than 70 years of age," or by other means. The term "employment applications," refers to all written inquiries about employment or applications for employment or promotion including, but not limited to, résumés or other summaries of the applicant's background. It relates not only to written preemployment inquiries, but to inquiries by employees concerning terms, conditions, or privileges of employment as specified in section 4 of the Act.

§ 1625.6   Bona fide occupational qualifications

(a) Whether occupational qualifications will be deemed to be "bona fide" to a specific job and "reasonably necessary to the normal operation of the particular business," will be determined on the basis of all the pertinent facts surrounding each particular situation. It is anticipated that this concept of a bona fide occupational qualification will have limited scope and application. Further, as this is an exception to the Act it must be narrowly construed.

(b) An employer asserting a BFOQ defense has the burden of proving that (1) the age limit is reasonably necessary to the essence of the business, and either (2) that all or substantially all individuals excluded from the job involved are in fact disqualified, or (3) that some of the individuals so excluded possess a disqualifying trait that cannot be ascertained except by reference to age. If the employer's objective in asserting a BFOQ is the goal of public safety, the employer must prove that the challenged practice does indeed effectuate that goal and that there is no acceptable alternative which would better advance it or equally advance it with less discriminatory impact.

(c) Many State and local governments have enacted laws or administrative regulations which limit employment opportunities based on age. Unless these laws meet the standards for the establishment of a valid bona fide occupational qualification under section 4(f)(1) of the Act, they will be considered in conflict with and effectively superseded by the ADEA.

§ 1625.7   Differentiations based on reasonable factors other than age

(a) Section 4(f)(1) of the Act provides that

* * * it shall not be unlawful for an employer, employment agency, or labor organization * * * to take any action otherwise prohibited under paragraphs (a), (b), (c), or (e) of this section * * * where the differentiation is based on reasonable factors other than age * * *.

(b) No precise and unequivocal determination can be made as to the scope of the phrase "differentiation based on reasonable factors other than age." Whether such differentiations exist must be decided on the basis of all the particular facts and circumstances surrounding each individual situation.

(c) When an employment practice uses age as a limiting criterion, the defense that the practice is justified by a reasonable factor other than age is unavailable.

(d) When an employment practice, including a test, is claimed as a basis for different treatment of employees or applicants for employment on the ground that it is a "factor other than" age, and such a practice has an adverse impact on individuals within the protected age group, it can only be justified as a business necessity. Tests which are asserted as "reasonable factors other than age" will be scrutinized in accordance with the standards set forth at Part 1607 of this title.

(e) When the exception of "a reasonable factor other than age" is raised against an individual claim of discriminatory treatment, the employer bears the burden of showing that the "reasonable factor other than age" exists factually.

(f) A differentiation based on the average cost of employing older employees as a group is unlawful except with respect to employee benefit plans which qualify for the section 4(f)(2) exception to the Act.

§ 1625.8   Bona fide seniority systems

Section 4(f)(2) of the Act provides that

* * * It shall not be unlawful for an employer, employment agency, or labor organization * * * to observe the terms of a bona fide seniority system * * * which is not a subterfuge to evade the purposes of this Act except that no such seniority system * * * shall require or permit the involuntary retirement of any individual specified by section 12(a) of this Act because of the age of such individual. * * *

(In the case of employees covered by a collective bargaining agreement which was in effect on September 1, 1977, which was entered into by a labor organization (as defined by section 6(d)(4) of the Fair Labor Standards Act), the provisions of this section with respect to involuntary retirement of individuals between the ages of 65 and 70 were effective upon the termination of the collective bargaining agreement or January 1, 1980, whichever occurred first.) (See also § 1625.9 (d) (e), and (f).)

(a) Though a seniority system may be qualified by such factors as merit, capacity, or ability, any bona fide seniority system must be based on length of service as the primary criterion for the equitable allocation of available employment opportunities and prerogatives among younger and older workers.

(b) Adoption of a purported seniority system which gives those with longer service lesser rights, and results in discharge or less favored treatment to those within the protection of the Act, may, depending upon the circumstances, be a "subterfuge to evade the purposes" of the Act.

(c) Unless the essential terms and conditions of an alleged seniority system have been communicated to the affected employees and can be shown to be applied uniformly to all of those affected, regardless of age, it will not be considered a bona fide seniority system within the meaning of the Act.

(d) It should be noted that seniority systems which segregate, classify, or otherwise discriminate against individuals on the basis of race, color, religion, sex, or national origin, are prohibited under Title VII of the Civil Rights Act of 1964, where that Act otherwise applies. The "bona fides" of such a system will be closely scrutinized to ensure that such a system is, in fact, bona fide under the ADEA.

§ 1625.9   Prohibition of involuntary retirement

(a)(1) As originally enacted in 1967, section 4(f)(2) of the Act provided: "It shall not be unlawful * * * to observe the terms of a bona fide seniority system or any bona fide employee benefit plan such as a retirement, pension, or insurance plan, which is not a subterfuge to evade the purposes of this Act, except that no such employee benefit plan shall excuse the failure to hire any individual * * *." The Department of Labor interpreted the provision as "Authoriz[ing] involuntary retirement irrespective of age: *Provided*, That such retirement is pursuant to the terms of a retirement or pension plan meeting the requirements of section 4(f)(2)." *See* 29 CFR 860.110(a), 34 FR 9709 (June 21, 1969). The Department took the position that in order to meet the requirements of section 4(f)(2), the involuntary retirement provision had to be (i) contained in a bona fide pension or retirement plan, (ii) required by the terms of the plan and not optional, and (iii) essential to the plan's economic survival or to some other legitimate business purpose—i.e., the provision was not in the plan as the result of arbitrary discrimination on the basis of age.

(2) As revised by the 1978 amendments, section 4(f)(2) was amended by adding the following clause at the end: "and no such seniority system or employee benefit plan shall require or permit the involuntary retirement of any individual specified by section 12(a) of this Act because of the age of such individual * * *." The Conference Committee Report expressly states that this amendment is intended "to make absolutely clear one of the original purposes of this provision, namely, that the exception does not authorize an employer to require or permit involuntary retirement of an employee within the protected age group on account of age" (H.R. Rept. No. 95–950, p. 8).

(b)(1) The amendment applies to all new and existing seniority systems and employee benefit plans. Accordingly, any system or plan provision requiring or permitting involuntary retirement is unlawful, regardless of whether the provision antedates the 1967 Act or the 1978 amendments.

(2) Where lawsuits pending on the date of enactment (April 6, 1978) or filed thereafter challenge involuntary retirements which occurred either before or after that date, the amendment applies.

(c) The amendment protects all individuals covered by section 12(a) of the Act. Accordingly, before January 1, 1979 (the effective date of the amendment to section 12(a) which raised the upper age limit to 70), the amendment applied to individuals who were at least 40 years of age but less than 65 years of age. On and after that date it applies also to individuals who are at least 65 years of age but less than 70 years of age, unless otherwise exempt.

(d)(1) To allow time for the adjustment of collective bargaining agreements, the 1978 amendments provide that

* * * in the case of employees covered by a collective bargaining agreement which is in effect on September 1, 1977, which was entered into by a labor organization (as defined by section 6(d)(4) of the Fair Labor Standards Act of 1938), and which would otherwise be prohibited by the amendment (to section 12 of the Act), the amendment (to section 4(f)(2) of the Act) shall take effect upon the termination of such agreement or on January 1, 1980, whichever occurs first * * *

(Pub. L. 95–256, section 2(b), 92 Stat. 189)

(2) This delay of up to one year in the effective date of the amendment to section 4(f)(2) applies only to the protection afforded against involuntary retirement and affects only individuals who have attained 65 years of age but not 70 years of age on and after January 1, 1979. Such individuals may not be involuntarily retired unless (i) the retirement age specified in the plan is 65 or above; (ii) the retirement is authorized by the express terms of a bona fide seniority system or a bona fide employee benefit plan which is not a subterfuge to evade the purposes of the Act; and (iii) those terms have been adopted no later than September 1, 1977 and are pursuant to a collective bargaining agreement in effect on September 1, 1977. "Bona fide" shall have the same meaning as in § 860.120(b), as amended, 44 FR 30658 (May 25, 1979).

(3) Where a collective bargaining agreement expired prior to September 1, 1977, and a new agreement was signed subsequent to that date effective retroactively to the expiration date of the previous agreement, the exemption does not apply. The expressed congressional intent was to exempt only those agreements which had been "negotiated" before September 1, 1977 (see S. Rept. No. 95–493, 95th Cong., 1st Sess. (1977), p. 11; H.R. Rept. No. 95–527, Part 1, 95th Cong., 1st Sess. (1977), pp. 8–9).

(e) The exemption of up to one year is inapplicable after the expiration of the collective bargaining agreement in effect on September 1, 1977, whether or not the agreement is extended or renewed. The exemption is in no event applicable after January 1, 1980.

(f) Neither section 4(f)(2) nor any other provision of the Act makes it unlawful for a plan to permit individuals to elect early retirement at a specified age at their own option. Nor is it unlawful for a plan to require early retirement for reasons other than age.

§ 1625.10   Reserved for costs and benefits under employee benefit plans

For currently applicable interpretations, see 29 CFR 860.120.

§ 1625.11   Exemption for employees serving under a contract of unlimited tenure

(a)(1) Section 12(d) of the Act, added by the 1978 amendments, provides: "Nothing in this act shall be construed to prohibit compulsory retirement of any employee who has attained 65 years of age but not 70 years of age, and who is serving under a contract of unlimited tenure (or similar arrangement providing for unlimited tenure) at an institution of higher education (as defined by section 1201(a) of the Higher Education Act of 1965)."

(2) This exemption from the Act's protection of covered individuals took effect on January 1, 1979, and is repealed on July 1, 1982 (see sections 3(b)(1) and 3(b)(3) of the Age Discrimination in Employment Act Amendments of 1978, Pub. L. 95–256, 92 Stat. 189). Individuals who attain age 65 prior to July 1, 1982 and all of whose job duties and responsibilities cease prior to that date will not be considered outside the exemption merely because their contract (or similar arrangement) providing for unlimited tenure expires on or after July 1, 1982.

(b) Since section 12(d) is an exemption from the nondiscrimination requirements of the Act, the burden is on the one seeking to invoke the exemption to show that every element has been clearly and unmistakably met. Moreover, as with other exemptions from the ADEA, this exemption must be narrowly construed.

(c) Section 1201(a) of the Higher Education Act of 1965, as amended, and set forth in 20 U.S.C. 1141(a), provides in pertinent part:

> The term "institution of higher education" means an educational institution in any State which (1) admits as regular students only persons having a certificate of graduation from a school providing secondary education, or the recognized equivalent of such a certificate, (2) is legally authorized within such State to provide a program of education beyond secondary education, (3) provides an educational program for which it awards a bachelor's degree or provides not less than a two-year program which is acceptable for full credit toward such a degree, (4) is a public or other nonprofit institution, and (5) is accredited by a nationally recognized accrediting agency or association or, if not so accredited, (A) is an institution with respect to which the Commissioner has determined that there is satisfactory assurance, considering the resources available to the institution, the period of time, if any, during which it has operated, the effort it is making to meet accreditation standards, and the purpose for which this determination is being made, that the institution will meet the accreditation standards of such an agency or association within a reasonable time, or (B) is an institution whose credits are accepted, on transfer, by not less than three institutions which are so accredited, for credit on the same basis as if transferred from an institution so accredited.

The definition encompasses almost all public and private universities and two- and four-year colleges. The omitted portion of the text of section 1201(a) refers largely to one-year technical schools which generally do not grant tenure to employees but which, if they do, are also eligible to claim the exemption.

(d)(1) Use of the term "any employee" indicates that application of the exemption is not limited to teachers, who are traditional recipients of tenure. The exemption may also be available with respect to other groups, such as academic deans, scientific researchers, professional librarians and counseling staff, who frequently have tenured status.

(2) The Conference Committee Report on the 1978 amendments expressly states that the exemption does not apply to Federal employees covered by section 15 of the Act (H.R. Rept. No. 95–950, p. 10).

(e)(1) The phrase "unlimited tenure" is not defined in the Act. However, the almost universally accepted definition of academic "tenure" is an arrangement under which certain appointments in an institution of higher education are continued until retirement for age or physical disability, subject to dismissal for adequate cause or under extraordinary circumstances on account of financial exigency or change of institutional program. Adopting that definition, it is evident that the word "unlimited" refers to the duration of tenure. Therefore, a contract (or other similar arrangement) which is limited to a specific term (for example, one year or 10 years) will not meet the requirements of the exemption.

(2) The legislative history shows that Congress intended the exemption to apply only where the minimum rights and privileges traditionally associated with tenure are guaranteed to an employee by contract or similar arrangement. While tenure policies and practices vary greatly from one institution to another, the minimum standards set forth in the 1940 Statement of Principles on Academic Freedom and Tenure, jointly developed by the Association of American Colleges and the American Association of University Professors, have enjoyed widespread adoption or endorsement. The 1940 Statement of Principles on academic tenure provides as follows:

(a) After the expiration of a probationary period, teachers or investigators should have permanent or continuous tenure, and their service should be terminated only for adequate cause, except in the case of retirement for age, or under extraordinary circumstances because of financial exigencies.

In the interpretation of this principle it is understood that the following represents acceptable academic practice:

(1) The precise terms and conditions of every appointment should be stated in writing and be in the possession of both institution and teacher before the appointment is consummated.

(2) Beginning with appointment to the rank of full-time instructor or a higher rank, the probationary period should not exceed seven years, including within this period full-time service in all institutions of higher education; but subject to the proviso that when, after a term of probationary service of more than three years in one or more institutions, a teacher is called to another institution it may be agreed in writing that his new appointment is for a probationary period of not more than four years, even though thereby the person's total probationary period in the academic profession is extended beyond the normal maximum of seven years. Notice should be given at least one year prior to the expiration of the probationary period if the teacher is not to be continued in service after the expiration of that period.

(3) During the probationary period a teacher should have the academic freedom that all other members of the faculty have.

(4) Termination for cause of a continuous appointment, or the dismissal for cause of a teacher previous to the expiration of a term appointment, should, if possible, be considered by both a faculty committee and the governing board of the institution. In all cases where the facts are in dispute, the accused teacher should be informed before the hearing in writing of the charges against him and should have the opportunity to be heard in his own defense by all bodies that pass judgment upon his case. He should be permitted to have with him an advisor of his own choosing who may act as counsel. There should be a full stenographic record of the hearing available to the parties concerned. In the hearing of charges of incompetence the testimony should include that of teachers and other scholars, either from his own or from other institutions. Teachers on continuous appointment who are dismissed for reasons not involving moral turpitude should receive their salaries for at least a year from the date of notification of dismissal whether or not they are continued in their duties at the institution.

(5) Termination of a continuous appointment because of financial exigency should be demonstrably bona fide.

(3) A contract or similar arrangement which meets the standards in the 1940 Statement of Principles will satisfy the tenure requirements of the exemption. However, a tenure arrangement will not be deemed inadequate solely because it fails to meet these standards in every respect. For example, a tenure plan will not be deemed inadequate solely because it includes a probationary period somewhat longer than seven years. Of course, the greater the deviation from the standards in the 1940 Statement of Principles, the less likely it is that the employee in question will be deemed subject

to "unlimited tenure" within the meaning of the exemption. Whether or not a tenure arrangement is adequate to satisfy the requirements of the exemption must be determined on the basis of the facts of each case.

(f) Employees who are not assured of a continuing appointment either by contract of unlimited tenure or other similar arrangement (such as a state statute) would not, of course, be exempted from the prohibitions against compulsory retirement, even if they perform functions identical to those performed by employees with appropriate tenure.

(g) An employee within the exemption can lawfully be forced to retire on account of age at age 65 or above. In addition, the employer is free to retain such employees, either in the same position or status or in a different position or status: *Provided*, That the employee voluntarily accepts this new position or status. For example, an employee who falls within the exemption may be offered a nontenured position or part-time employment. An employee who accepts a nontenured position or part-time employment, however, may not be treated any less favorably, on account of age, than any similarly situated younger employee (unless such less favorable treatment is excused by an exception to the Act).

[44 FR 66799, Nov. 21, 1979; 45 FR 43704, June 30, 1980; 45 FR 51547, Aug. 4, 1980]

§ 1625.12 Exemption for bona fide executive or high policymaking employees

(a) Section 12(c)(1) of the Act, added by the 1978 amendments and as amended in 1984, provides: "Nothing in this Act shall be construed to prohibit compulsory retirement of any employee who has attained 65 years of age but not 70 years of age, and who, for the 2-year period immediately before retirement, is employed in a bona fide executive or a high policymaking position, if such employee is entitled to an immediate nonforfeitable annual retirement benefit from a pension, profit-sharing, savings, or deferred compensation plan, or any combination of such plans, of the employer of such employee which equals, in the aggregate, at least $44,000."

(b) Since this provision is an exemption from the non-discrimination requirements of the Act, the burden is on the one seeking to invoke the exemption to show that every element has been clearly and unmistakably met. Moreover, as with other exemptions from the Act, this exemption must be narrowly construed.

(c) An employee within the exemption can lawfully be forced to retire on account of age at age 65 or above. In addition, the employer is free to retain such employees, either in the same position or status or in a different position or status. For example, an employee who falls within the exemption may be offered a position of lesser status or a part-time position. An employee who accepts such a new status or position, however, may not be treated any less favorably, on account of age, than any similarly situated younger employee.

(d)(1) In order for an employee to qualify as a "bona fide executive," the employer must initially show that the employee satisfies the definition of a bona fide executive set forth in § 541.1 of this chapter. Each of the requirements in paragraphs (a) through (e) of § 541.1 must be satisfied, regardless of the level of the employee's salary or compensation.

(2) Even if an employee qualifies as an executive under the definition in § 541.1 of this chapter, the exemption from the ADEA may not be claimed unless the employee also meets the further criteria specified in the Conference Committee Report in the form of examples (see H.R. Rept. No. 95–950, p. 9). The examples are intended to make clear that the exemption does not apply to middle-management employees, no

matter how great their retirement income, but only to a very few top level employees who exercise substantial executive authority over a significant number of employees and a large volume of business. As stated in the Conference Report (H.R. Rept. No. 95–950, p. 9):

> Typically the head of a significant and substantial local or regional operation of a corporation [or other business organization], such as a major production facility or retail establishment, but not the head of a minor branch, warehouse or retail store, would be covered by the term "bona fide executive." Individuals at higher levels in the corporate organizational structure who possess comparable or greater levels of responsibility and authority as measured by established and recognized criteria would also be covered.
>
> The heads of major departments or divisions of corporations [or other business organizations] are usually located at corporate or regional headquarters. With respect to employees whose duties are associated with corporate headquarters operations, such as finance, marketing, legal, production and manufacturing (or in a corporation organized on a product line basis, the management of product lines), the definition would cover employees who head those divisions.
>
> In a large organization the immediate subordinates of the heads of these divisions sometimes also exercise executive authority, within the meaning of this exemption. The conferees intend the definition to cover such employees if they possess responsibility which is comparable to or greater than that possessed by the head of a significant and substantial local operation who meets the definition.

(e) The phrase "high policymaking position," according to the Conference Report (H.R. Rept. No. 95–950, p. 10), is limited to "* * * certain top level employees who are not 'bona fide executives' * * *." Specifically, these are:

> * * * individuals who have little or no line authority but whose position and responsibility are such that they play a significant role in the development of corporate policy and effectively recommend the implementation thereof.
>
> For example, the chief economist or the chief research scientist of a corporation typically has little line authority. His duties would be primarily intellectual as opposed to executive or managerial. His responsibility would be to evaluate significant economic or scientific trends and issues, to develop and recommend policy direction to the top executive officers of the corporation, and he would have a significant impact on the ultimate decision on such policies by virtue of his expertise and direct access to the decisionmakers. Such an employee would meet the definition of a "high policymaking" employee.

On the other hand, as this description makes clear, the support personnel of a "high policymaking" employee would not be subject to the exemption even if they supervise the development, and draft the recommendation, of various policies submitted by their supervisors.

(f) In order for the exemption to apply to a particular employee, the employee must have been in a "bona fide executive or high policymaking position," as those terms are defined in this section, for the two-year period immediately before retirement. Thus, an employee who holds two or more different positions during the two-year period is subject to the exemption only if each such job is an executive or high policymaking position.

(g) The Conference Committee Report expressly states that the exemption is not applicable to Federal employees covered by section 15 of the Act (H.R. Rept. No. 95–950, p. 10).

(h) The "annual retirement benefit," to which covered employees must be entitled, is the sum of amounts payable during each one-year period from the date on which such benefits first become receivable by the retiree. Once established, the annual period upon which calculations are based may not be changed from year to year.

(i) The annual retirement benefit must be immediately available to the employee to be retired pursuant to the exemption. For purposes of determining compliance, "immediate" means that the payment of plan benefits (in a lump sum or the first of a series of periodic payments) must occur not later than 60 days after the effective date of the retirement in question. The fact that an employee will receive benefits only after expiration of the 60-day period will not preclude his retirement pursuant to the exemption, if the employee could have elected to receive benefits within that period.

(j)(1) The annual retirement benefit must equal, in the aggregate, at least $44,000. The manner of determining whether this requirement has been satisfied is set forth in § 1627.17(c).

(2) In determining whether the aggregate annual retirement benefit equals at least $44,000, the only benefits which may be counted are those authorized by and provided under the terms of a pension, profit-sharing, savings, or deferred compensation plan. (Regulations issued pursuant to section 12(c)(2) of the Act, regarding the manner of calculating the amount of qualified retirement benefits for purposes of the exemption, are set forth in § 1627.17 of this chapter.)

(k)(1) The annual retirement benefit must be "nonforfeitable." Accordingly, the exemption may not be applied to any employee subject to plan provisions which could cause the cessation of payments to a retiree or result in the reduction of benefits to less than $44,000 in any one year. For example, where a plan contains a provision under which benefits would be suspended if a retiree engages in litigation against the former employer, or obtains employment with a competitor of the former employer, the retirement benefit will be deemed to be forfeitable. However, retirement benefits will not be deemed forfeitable solely because the benefits are discontinued or suspended for reasons permitted under section 411(a)(3) of the Internal Revenue Code.

(2) An annual retirement benefit will not be deemed forfeitable merely because the minimum statutory benefit level is not guaranteed against the possibility of plan bankruptcy or is subject to benefit restrictions in the event of early termination of the plan in accordance with Treasury Regulation 1.401–4(c). However, as of the effective date of the retirement in question, there must be at least a reasonable expectation that the plan will meet its obligations.

(Sec. 12(c)(1) of the Age Discrimination In Employment Act of 1967, as amended by Sec. 802(c)(1) of the Older Americans Act Amendments of 1984, Pub. L. 98–459, 98 Stat. 1792)

[44 FR 66800, Nov. 21, 1979; 45 FR 43704, June 30, 1980, as amended at 50 FR 2544, Jan. 17, 1985]

§ 1625.13   Apprenticeship programs

Age limitations for entry into bona fide apprenticeship programs were not intended to be affected by the Act. Entry into most apprenticeship programs has traditionally been limited to youths under specified ages. This is in recognition of the fact that apprenticeship is an extension of the educational process to prepare young men and women for skilled employment. Accordingly, the prohibitions contained in the Act will not be applied to bona fide apprenticeship programs which meet the standards specified in 521.2 and 521.3 of this chapter.

Subpart B

Substantive Regulations

Authority: 81 Stat. 602; 29 U.S.C. 621, 5 U.S.C. 301, Secretary's Order No. 10–68; Secretary's Order No. 11–68, and sec. 2; Reorg. Plan No. 1 of 1978, 43 FR 19807.

Source: 46 FR 47726, Sept. 29, 1981, unless otherwise noted.

§ 1625.20   Employer obligations under Section 4(g) of the Act

(a) *Employee Coverage under Section 4(g) of the Act.* (1) Employees aged 65 through 69, including disabled employees, shall be entitled to coverage under any group health plan(s) offered to employees under age 65 under the same terms and conditions. The standard of compliance with this requirement shall be one of benefit equivalence.

(2) Any employees encompassed by paragraph (a)(1) of this section shall be entitled to spousal coverage under any group health plan offered to such employees under the same terms and conditions as any employee under age 65. The standard of compliance with this requirement shall be one of equality of treatment with similarly situated younger employees. In the event that the employer's plan does not provide for spousal coverage the employer need not do so for employees aged 65 through 69.

(3) Employees aged 65 through 69 are covered by the requirements of Section 4(g) of the Act from the month in which they attain age 65 through the day on which they attain age 70.

(4) Retirees are not covered by the provisions of Section 4(g) of the Act.

(b) *Employer coverage under Section 4(g) of the Act.* (1) Any employers who meet the standards for coverage set forth in Section 11(b) of the Act are subject to the requirements of Section 4(g) of the Act and the regulations of this part. As to persons other than employers subject to the Act, the provisions of 29 CFR 860.120 shall continue to apply.

(2) Any employer meeting the standards for coverage set forth in paragraph (b)(1) of this section who provides health insurance coverage to its employees either in cooperation with a labor organization or indirectly through an agent of the employer is covered by the provisions of Section 4(g) of the Act.

(c) *Election of primary health care coverage.* (1) Each employee aged 65 through 69 must be offered the opportunity to elect in writing coverage under any group health plan offered by its employer. Every employer must communicate to each eligible employee in writing prior to the time of election in specific terms and conditions of all available health insurance plans. Every employer must notify each eligible employee that if the employer's plan(s) covers any of the same items and services covered by Medicare, the employer plan(s) is primary for those services and Medicare pays secondary benefits. Every employer must inform all eligible employees of the consequences of choosing any employer health plan and the extent to which benefits available under an employer plan can be anticipated to be supplemented by Medicare coverage. Similarly, eligible employees must be informed of the consequences of not choosing an employer plan(s). Every employer must also inform eligible employees that if the employer's plan(s) covers only non-Medicare covered items and services, such as dental care and prescription drugs, the employer plan(s) is liable for those non-Medicare covered items and services and Medicare is liable for Medicare-covered items and services such as hospitalization. Every employer should attempt to inform each eligible employee of the need to apply for Medicare coverage. Where the employer previously paid or contributed toward the Medicare Part B premium payment, the employer must notify each eligible employee if and under what circumstances it intends to discontinue Medicare Part B contributions. Such a notice should specifically inform each eligible employee of the penalty resulting from a lapse in Medicare Part B coverage.

(i) The election described in paragraph (c)(1) of this section above must be offered to all eligible employees and implemented within 90 days following the date of publication of these regulations.

(ii) An employer's existing health plan coverage must continue in effect until an election is made and implemented or until an earlier date as requested by the employee.

(iii) Employees aged 65 through 69 who were not eligible by reason of age for the election described in paragraph (c)(1) of this section at the time it was offered must be informed of the options specified in paragraph (c)(1) of this section at least 30 days prior to their first day of eligibility.

(iv) Employees aged 65 through 69 must be afforded the same opportunities to change their primary health insurance coverage as are offered to younger employees.

(d) *Employer contributions.* Contributory Plans. An employer must offer to all employees aged 65 through 69, at no additional cost, the same plan or plans that are offered to younger employees.

(e) *Group Health Care Plans Designed to Supplement Medicare.* (1) An employer may no longer offer to an employee aged 65 through 69 a group health plan whose terms make it a secondary payor to Medicare for services covered under either Medicare Part A or Medicare Part B.

(2) An employer who offers to its employees a health benefits plan covering only non-Medicare covered items and services shall offer such a plan to all employees through age 69 on an equal basis.

(3) An employer may not offer inducements to employees age 65 through 69 to elect not to be covered by an employer plan.

(f) *Construction.* (1) The Commission will strictly enforce the provisions of these rules to ensure that no employee aged 65 through 69 suffers a discriminatory reduction in health care benefits as a result of the enactment of Section 4(g) of the Act.

(2) Violations of these rules will be deemed willful and will subject an employer to liquidated damages as provided by the provisions of Section 7(b) of the ADEA.

(3) Health care benefits provided under this section may not be included by an employer under a "benefit package" approach.

(4) An employer is prohibited from making benefit reductions in violation of section 4(a)(3) of the ADEA.

[48 FR 26437, June 7, 1983]

Part 1626

Procedures

Age Discrimination in Employment Act

***

Authority: Sec. 9, 81 Stat. 605, 29 U.S.C. 628; Sec. 2, Reorg. Plan No. 1 of 1978, 3 CFR 321 (1979).
Source: 48 FR 140, Jan. 3, 1983, unless otherwise noted.

§ 1626.1   Purpose

The regulations set forth in this part contain the procedures established by the Equal Employment Opportunity Commission for carrying out its responsibilities in the administration and enforcement of the Age Discrimination in Employment Act of 1967, as amended.

§ 1626.2   Terms defined in the Age Discrimination in Employment Act of 1967, as amended

The terms "person," "employer," "employment agency," "labor organization," "employee," "commerce," "industry affecting commerce," and "State" as used herein shall have the meanings set forth in section 11 of the Age Discrimination in Employment Act, as amended.

§ 1626.3   Other definitions

For purpose of this part, the term "the Act" shall mean the Age Discrimination in Employment Act of 1967, as amended; the "Commission" shall mean the Equal Employment Opportunity Commission or any of its designated representatives; "charge" shall mean a statement filed with the Commission by or on behalf of an aggrieved person which alleges that the named prospective defendant has engaged in or is about to engage in actions in violation of the Act; "complaint" shall mean information received from any source, that is not a charge, which alleges that a named prospective defendant has engaged in or is about to engage in actions in violation of the Act; "charging party" means the person filing a charge; "complainant" means the person filing a complaint; and "respondent" means the person named as a prospective defendant in a charge or complaint, or as a result of a Commission-initiated investigation.

§ 1626.4   Information concerning alleged violations of the Act

The Commission may, on its own initiative, conduct investigations of employers, employment agencies and labor organizations, in accordance with the powers vested in it pursuant to sections 6 and 7 of the Act. The Commission shall also receive information concerning alleged violations of the Act, including charges and complaints, from any source. Where the information discloses a possible violation, the appropriate Commission office may render assistance in the filing of a charge. The identity of a complainant, confidential witness, or aggrieved person on whose behalf a charge was filed will ordinarily not be disclosed without prior written consent, unless necessary in a court proceeding.

§ 1626.5   Where to submit complaints and charges

Complaints and charges may be submitted in person, by telephone, or by mail to any of the District, Area or local Offices of the Commission, or at the Headquarters of the Commission at Washington, D.C., or with any designated representative of the Commission. The addresses of the Commission's District, Area and Local Offices appear at § 1610.4.

[48 FR 140, Jan. 3, 1983, as amended at 49 FR 13025, Apr. 2, 1984]

§ 1626.6   Form of charge

A charge shall be in writing and shall name the prospective respondent and shall generally allege the discriminatory act(s). Charges received in person or by telephone shall be reduced to writing.

§ 1626.7   Timeliness of charge

(a) Charges will not be rejected as untimely provided that they are not barred by the statute of limitations as stated in section 6 of the Portal to Portal Act of 1947.

(b) Potential charging parties will be advised that, pursuant to section 7(d) (1) and

(2) of the Act, no civil suit may be commenced by an individual until 60 days after a charge has been filed on the subject matter of the suit, and such charge shall be filed with the Commission or its designated agent within 180 days of the alleged discriminatory action, or, in a case where the alleged discriminatory action occurs in a state which has its own age discrimination law and authority administering that law, within 300 days of the alleged discriminatory action, or 30 days after receipt of notice of termination of State proceedings, whichever is earlier.

(c) For purposes of determining the date of filing with the Commission, the following applies:

(1) Charges filed by mail: (i) Date of postmark, if legible, (ii) Date of letter, if postmark is illegible, (iii) Date of receipt by Commission, or its designated agent, if postmark and letter date are illegible and/or cannot be accurately affixed;

(2) Written charges filed in person: Date of receipt;

(3) Oral charges filed in person or by telephone, as reduced to writing: Date of oral communication received by Commission.

§ 1626.8   Contents of charge; amendment of charge

(a) In addition to the requirements of § 1626.6, each charge should contain the following:

(1) The full name, address and telephone number of the person making the charge;

(2) The full name and address of the person against whom the charge is made;

(3) A clear and concise statement of the facts, including pertinent dates, constituting the alleged unlawful employment practices;

(4) If known, the approximate number of employees of the prospective defendant employer or members of the prospective defendant labor organization.

(5) A statement disclosing whether proceedings involving the alleged unlawful employment practice have been commenced before a State agency charged with the enforcement of fair employment practice laws and, if so, the date of such commencement and the name of the agency.

(b) Notwithstanding the provisions of paragraph (a) of this section, a charge is sufficient when the Commission receives from the person making the charge either a written statement or information reduced to writing by the Commission that conforms to the requirements of § 1626.6.

(c) A charge may be amended to clarify or amplify allegations made therein. Such amendments and amendments alleging additional acts which constitute unlawful employment practices related to or growing out of the subject matter of the original charge will relate back to the date the charge was first received. A charge that has been so amended shall not again be referred to the appropriate State agency.

§ 1626.9   Referral to and from State agencies; referral States

(a) The Commission may refer all charges to any appropriate State agency and will encourage State agencies to refer charges to the Commission in order to assure that the prerequisites for private law suits, as set out in section 14(b) of the Act, are met. Charges so referred shall be deemed to have been filed with the Commission in accordance with the specifications contained in § 1626.7(b). The Commission may process any charge at any time, notwithstanding provisions for referral to and from appropriate State agencies.

(b) States to which all ADEA charges may be referred: Alaska, California, Connecticut, Delaware, District of Columbia, Florida, Georgia, Guam, Hawaii, Idaho, Illinois, Iowa, Kentucky, Maryland, Massachusetts, Michigan, Minnesota, Montana, Nebraska, Nevada, New Hampshire, New Jersey, New Mexico, New York, Oregon,

Pennsylvania, Puerto Rico, South Carolina, Utah, Virgin Islands, West Virginia, and Wisconsin.

(c) States to which only specified classes of charges are referred: Arizona, Colorado, Kansas, Maine, Ohio, Rhode Island, South Dakota, and Washington.

§ 1626.10   Agreements with State or local fair employment practices agencies

(a) Pursuant to sections 6 and 7 of the ADEA and section 11(b) of the FLSA, the Commission may enter into agreements with state or local fair employment practices agencies to cooperate in enforcement, technical assistance, research, or public informational activities, and may engage the services of such agencies in processing charges assuring the safeguard of the federal rights of aggrieved persons.

(b) The Commission may enter into agreements with state or local agencies which authorize such agencies to receive charges and complaints pursuant to § 1626.5 and in accordance with the specifications contained in §§ 1626.7 and 1626.8.

(c) When a worksharing agreement with a State agency is in effect, the State agency will act on certain charges and the Commission will promptly process charges which the State agency does not pursue. Charges received by one agency under the agreement shall be deemed received by the other agency for purposes of § 1626.7.

§ 1626.11   Notice of charge

Upon receipt of a charge, the Commission shall promptly notify the respondent that a charge has been filed.

§ 1626.12   Conciliation efforts pursuant to section 7(d) of the Act

Upon receipt of a charge, the Commission shall promptly attempt to eliminate any alleged unlawful practice by informal methods of conciliation, conference and persuasion. Upon failure of such conciliation the Commission will notify the charging party. Such notification enables the charging party or any person aggrieved by the subject matter of the charge to commence action to enforce their rights without waiting for the lapse of 60 days.

§ 1626.13   Withdrawal of charge

Charging parties may request withdrawal of a charge. Because the Commission has independent investigative authority, see § 1626.4, it may continue any investigation and may secure relief for all affected persons notwithstanding a request by a charging party to withdraw a charge.

§ 1626.14   Right to inspect or copy data

A person who submits data or evidence to the Commission may retain or, on payment of lawfully prescribed costs, procure a copy or transcript thereof, except that a witness may for good cause be limited to inspection of the official transcript of his or her testimony.

§ 1626.15   Commission enforcement

(a) As provided in Sections 9, 11, 16 and 17 of the Fair Labor Standards Act of 1938, as amended (29 U.S.C. 209, 211, 216 and 217) (FLSA) and Sections 6 and 7 of this Act, the Commission and its authorized representatives may (1) investigate and gather data; (2) enter and inspect establishments and records and make transcripts thereof; (3) interview employees; (4) impose on persons subject to the Act appropriate recordkeeping and reporting requirements; (5) advise employers, employment agencies and labor organizations with regard to their obligations under the Act and any changes necessary in their policies, practices and procedures to assure compliance with the Act; (6) subpoena witnesses and require the production of documents and other evidence; (7) supervise the payment of amounts owing pursuant to section 16(c) of the FLSA, and (8) institute action under section 16(c) or section 17 of the FLSA or both to obtain appropriate relief.

(b) Whenever the Commission has a reasonable basis to conclude that a violation of the Act has occurred or will occur, it may commence conciliation under section 7(b) of the Act. The date of issuance of written notice to the respondent of the Commission's intent to begin or continue conciliation shall determine when the statute of limitations is tolled pursuant to section 7(e)(2) of the Act. Such notice will ordinarily be issued in the form of a letter of violation; provided, however, that failure to issue a written violation letter shall in no instance be construed as a finding of no violation. The Commission will ordinarily notify the respondent and aggrieved persons of its determination. In the process of conducting any investigation or conciliation under this Act, the identity of persons who have provided information in confidence shall not be disclosed except in accordance with § 1626.4. When the written notice prescribed above is issued, the statute of limitations shall be tolled for a period of one year unless a conciliation agreement is obtained earlier.

(c) Any agreement reached as a result of efforts undertaken pursuant to this section shall, as far as practicable, require the respondent to eliminate the unlawful practice(s) and provide appropriate affirmative relief. Such agreement shall be reduced to writing and will ordinarily be signed by the Commission's delegated representative, the respondent, and the charging party, if any. A copy of the signed agreement shall be sent to all the signatories thereto.

(d) Upon the failure of informal conciliation, conference and persuasion under section 7(b) of the Act, the Commission may initiate and conduct litigation.

(e) The District Directors and the Director of the Office of Program Operations or their designees, are hereby delegated authority to exercise the powers enumerated in § 1626.15(a) (1) through (7) and (b) and (c). The General Counsel or his/her designee is hereby delegated the authority to exercise the powers in paragraph (a) of this section and at the direction of the Commission to initiate and conduct litigation.

§ 1626.16   Subpoenas

(a) To effectuate the purposes of the Act the Commission shall have the authority to issue a subpoena requiring:

(1) The attendance and testimony of witnesses;

(2) The production of evidence including, but not limited to, books, records, correspondence, or documents, in the possession or under the control of the person subpoenaed; and

(3) Access to evidence for the purpose of examination and the right to copy.

(b) The power to issue subpoenas has been delegated by the Commission, pursuant to section 6(a) of the Act, to the General Counsel, the District Directors, the Director of the Office of Program Operations, or their designees. The subpoena shall state the name, address and title of the issuer, identify the person or evidence subpoenaed, the name of the person to whom the subpoena is returnable, the date, time and place that testimony is to be given or that documents are to be provided or access provided.

(c) A subpoena issued by the Commission or its designee pursuant to the Act is not subject to review or appeal.

(d) Upon the failure of any person to comply with a subpoena issued under this section, the Commission may utilize the provisions of sections 9 and 10 of the Federal Trade Commission Act, 15 U.S.C. 49 and 50, to compel compliance with the subpoena.

(e) Persons subpoenaed shall be entitled to the same fees and mileage that are paid witnesses in the courts of the United States.

§ 1626.17   Procedure for requesting an opinion letter

(a) A request for an opinion letter should be submitted in writing to the Chairman, Equal Employment Opportunity Commission, 2401 E Street, N.W., Washington, D.C. 20506, and shall contain:

(1) A concise statement of the issues on which an opinion is requested;

(2) As full a statement as possible of relevant facts and law; and

(3) The names and addresses of the person making the request and other interested persons.

(b) Issuance of an opinion letter by the Commission is discretionary.

(c) Informal Advice: When the Commission, at its discretion, determines that it will not issue an opinion letter as defined in § 1626.18, the Commission may provide informal advice or guidance to the requestor. An informal letter of advice does not represent the formal position of the Commission and does not commit the Commission to the views expressed therein. Any letter other than those defined in § 1626.18(a)(1) will be considered a letter of advice and may not be relied upon by any employer within the meaning of section 10 of the Portal to Portal Act of 1947, incorporated into the Age Discrimination in Employment Act of 1967 through section 7(e)(1) of the Act.

§ 1626.18   Effect of opinions and interpretations
of the Commission

(a) Section 10 of the Portal to Portal Act of 1947, incorporated into the Age Discrimination in Employment Act of 1967 through section 7(e)(1) of the Act, provides that:

> In any action or proceeding based on any act or omission on or after the date of the enactment of this Act, no employer shall be subject to any liability or punishment . . . if he pleads and proves that the act or omission complained of was in good faith in conformity with and in reliance on any written administrative regulations, order, ruling, approval or interpretation . . . or any administrative practice or enforcement policy of [the Commission].

The Commission has determined that only (1) a written document, entitled "opinion letter," signed by the Legal Counsel on behalf of and as approved by the Commission, or (2) a written document issued in the conduct of litigation, entitled "opinion letter," signed by the General Counsel on behalf of and as approved by the Commission, or (3) matter published and specifically designated as such in the FEDERAL REGISTER, may be relied upon by any employer as a "written regulation, order, ruling, approval or interpretation" or "evidence of any administrative practice or enforcement policy" of the Commission "with respect to the class of employers to which he belongs," within the meaning of the statutory provisions quoted above.

(b) An opinion letter issued pursuant to § 1626.18(a)(1) above, when issued to the specific addressee, has no effect upon situations other than that of the specific addressee.

(c) When an opinion letter, as defined in § 1626.18(a)(1), is requested, the procedure stated in § 1626.17 shall be followed.

§ 1626.19   Rules to be liberally construed

(a) These rules and regulations shall be liberally construed to effectuate the purposes and provisions of this Act and any other acts administered by the Commission.

(b) Whenever the Commission receives a charge or obtains information relating to possible violations of one of the statutes which it administers and the charge or information reveals possible violations of one or more of the other statutes which it administers, the Commission will treat such charges or information in accordance with all such relevant statutes.

(c) Whenever a charge is filed under one statute and it is subsequently believed that the alleged discrimination constitutes an unlawful employment practice under another statute administered and enforced by the Commission, the charge may be so amended and timeliness determined from the date of filing of the original charge.

Part 1627

Records to be Made or Kept Relating to Age; Notices to be Posted; Administrative Exemptions

***

Subpart A

General

§ 1627.1   Purpose and scope

(a) Section 7 of the Age Discrimination in Employment Act of 1967 (hereinafter referred to in this part as the Act) empowers the Commission to require the keeping of records which are necessary or appropriate for the administration of the Act in accordance with the powers contained in section 11 of the Fair Labor Standards Act of 1938. Subpart B of this part sets forth the recordkeeping and posting requirements which are prescribed by the Commission for employers, employment agencies, and labor organizations which are subject to the Act. Reference should be made to section 11 of the Act for definitions of the terms "employer", "employment agency", and "labor organization". General interpretations of the Act and of this part are published in Part 1625 of this chapter. This part also reflects pertinent delegations of the Commission's duties.

(b) Subpart C of this part sets forth the Commission's rules under section 9 of the Act providing that the Commission may establish reasonable exemptions to and from any or all provisions of the Act as it may find necessary and proper in the public interest.

(c) Subpart D of this part sets forth the Commission's regulations issued pursuant to section 12(c)(2) of the Act, providing that the Secretary of Labor, after consultation with the Secretary of the Treasury, shall prescribe the manner of calculating the amount of qualified retirement benefits for purposes of the exemption in section 12(c)(1) of the Act.

[44 FR 38459, July 2, 1979, as amended at 44 FR 66797, Nov. 21, 1979]

Subpart B

Records to be Made or Kept Relating to Age; Notices to be Posted

§ 1627.2   Forms of records

No particular order or form of records is required by the regulations in this Part 1627. It is required only that the records contain in some form the information specified. If the information required is available in records kept for other purposes, or can be obtained readily by recomputing or extending data recorded in some other form, no further records are required to be made or kept on a routine basis by this Part 1627.

§ 1627.3   Records to be kept by employers

(a) Every employer shall make and keep for 3 years payroll or other records for each of his employees which contain:

(1) Name;

(2) Address;

(3) Date of birth;

(4) Occupation;

(5) Rate of pay; and

(6) Compensation earned each week.

(b)(1) Every employer who, in the regular course of his business, makes, obtains, or uses, any personnel or employment records related to the following, shall, except as provided in paragraphs (b) (3) and (4) of this section, keep them for a period of 1 year from the date of the personnel action to which any records relate:

(i) Job applications, resumes, or any other form of employment inquiry whenever submitted to the employer in response to his advertisement or other notice of existing or anticipated job openings, including records pertaining to the failure or refusal to hire any individual;

(ii) Promotion, demotion, transfer, selection for training, layoff, recall, or discharge of any employee;

(iii) Job orders submitted by the employer to an employment agency or labor organization for recruitment of personnel for job openings;

(iv) Test papers completed by applicants or candidates for any position which disclose the results of any employer-administered aptitude or other employment test considered by the employer in connection with any personnel action;

(v) The results of any physical examination where such examination is considered by the employer in connection with any personnel action;

(vi) Any advertisements or notices to the public or to employees relating to job openings, promotions, training programs, or opportunities for overtime work.

(2) Every employer shall keep on file any employee benefit plans such as pension and insurance plans, as well as copies of any seniority systems and merit systems which are in writing, for the full period the plan or system is in effect, and for at least 1 year after its termination. If the plan or system is not in writing, a memorandum fully outlining the terms of such plan or system and the manner in which it has been communicated to the affected employees, together with notations relating to any changes or revisions thereto, shall be kept on file for a like period.

(3) In the case of application forms and other preemployment records of applicants for positions which are, and are known by applicants to be, of a temporary nature, every record required to be kept under paragraph (b)(1) of this section shall be kept for a period of 90 days from the date of the personnel action to which the record relates.

(4) When an enforcement action is commenced under section 7 of the Act regarding a particular applicant or employee, the Commission or its authorized representative may require the employer to retain any record required to be kept under paragraph (b) (1), (2), or (3) of this section which is relative to such action until the final disposition thereof.

(Pub. L. No. 96–511, 94 Stat. 2812 (44 U.S.C. 3501 et seq.))

[44 FR 38459, July 2, 1979, as amended at 46 FR 63268, Dec. 31, 1981]

§ 1627.4   Records to be kept by employment agencies

(a)(1) Every employment agency which, in the regular course of its business, makes, obtains, or uses, any records related to the following, shall, except as provided in paragraphs (a) (2) and (3) of this section, keep them for a period of 1 year from the date of the action to which the records relate:

(i) Placements;

(ii) Referrals, where an individual is referred to an employer for a known or reasonably anticipated job opening;

(iii) Job orders from employers seeking individuals for job openings;

(iv) Job applications, resumes, or any other form of employment inquiry or record of any individual which identifies his qualifications for employment, whether for a known job opening at the time of submission or for future referral to an employer;

(v) Test papers completed by applicants or candidates for any position which disclose the results of any agency-administered aptitude or other employment test considered by the agency in connection with any referrals;

(vi) Advertisements or notices relative to job openings.

(2) In the case of application forms and other preemployment records of applicants for positions which are, and are known by applicants to be, of a temporary nature, every record required to be kept under paragraph (a)(1) of this section shall be kept for a period of 90 days from the date of the making or obtaining of the record involved.

(3) When an enforcement action is commenced under section 7 of the Act regarding a particular applicant, the Commission or its authorized representative may require the employment agency to retain any record required to be kept under paragraph (a) (1) or (2) of this section which is relative to such action until the final disposition thereof.

(b) Whenever an employment agency has an obligation as an "employer" or a "labor organization" under the Act, the employment agency must also comply with the recordkeeping requirements set forth in § 1627.3 or § 1627.5, as appropriate.

(Pub. L. No. 96–511, 94 Stat. 2812 (44 U.S.C. 3501 et seq.))

[44 FR 38459, July 2, 1979, as amended at 46 FR 63268, Dec. 31, 1981]

§ 1627.5   Records to be kept by labor organizations

(a) Every labor organization shall keep current records identifying its members by name, address, and date of birth.

(b) Every labor organization shall, except as provided in paragraph (c) of this section, keep for a period of 1 year from the making thereof, a record of the name, address, and age of any individual seeking membership in the organization. An individual seeking membership is considered to be a person who files an application for membership or who, in some other manner, indicates a specific intention to be considered for membership, but does not include any individual who is serving for a stated limited probationary period prior to permanent employment and formal union membership. A person who merely makes an inquiry about the labor organization or, for example, about its general program, is not considered to be an individual seeking membership in a labor organization.

(c) When an enforcement action is commenced under section 7 of the Act regarding a labor organization, the Commission or its authorized representative may require the labor organization to retain any record required to be kept under paragraph (b) of this section which is relative to such action until the final disposition thereof.

(d) Whenever a labor organization has an obligation as an "employer" or as an "employment agency" under the Act, the labor organization must also comply with the recordkeeping requirements set forth in § 1627.3 or § 1627.4, as appropriate.

(Pub. L. No. 96–511, 94 Stat. 2812 (44 U.S.C. 3501 et seq.))

[44 FR 38459, July 2, 1979, as amended at 46 FR 63268, Dec. 31, 1981]

§ 1627.6   Availability of records for inspection

(a) *Place records are to be kept.* The records required to be kept by this part shall be kept safe and accessible at the place of employment or business at which the individual to whom they relate is employed or has applied for employment or membership, or at one or more established central recordkeeping offices.

(b) *Inspection of records.* All records required by this part to be kept shall be made available for inspection and transcription by authorized representatives of the Commission during business hours generally observed by the office at which they are kept or in the community generally. Where records are maintained at a central recordkeeping office pursuant to paragraph (a) of this section, such records shall be made available at the office at which they would otherwise be required to be kept within 72 hours following request from the Commission or its authorized representative.

(Pub. L. No. 96–511, 94 Stat. 2812 (44 U.S.C. 3501 et seq.))

[44 FR 38459, July 2, 1979, as amended at 46 FR 63268, Dec. 31, 1981]

§ 1627.7   Transcriptions and reports

Every person required to maintain records under the Act shall make such extension, recomputation or transcriptions of his records and shall submit such reports concerning actions taken and limitations and classifications of individuals set forth in records as the Commission or its authorized representative may request in writing.

(Pub. L. No. 96–511, 94 Stat. 2812 (44 U.S.C. 3501 et seq.))

[44 38459, July 2, 1979, as amended at 46 FR 63268, Dec. 31, 1981]

§§ 1627.8–1627.9   [Reserved]

§ 1627.10   Notices to be posted

Every employer, employment agency, and labor organization which has an obligation under the Age Discrimination in Employment Act of 1967 shall post and keep posted in conspicuous places upon its premises the notice pertaining to the applicability of the Act prescribed by the Commission or its authorized representative. Such a notice must be posted in prominent and accessible places where it can readily be observed by employees, applicants for employment and union members.

§ 1627.11   Petitions for recordkeeping exceptions

(a) *Submission of petitions for relief*. Each employer, employment agency, or labor organization who for good cause wishes to maintain records in a manner other than required in this part, or to be relieved of preserving certain records for the period or periods prescribed in this part, may submit in writing a petition to the Commission requesting such relief setting forth the reasons therefor and proposing alternative recordkeeping or record-retention procedures.

(b) *Action on petitions*. If, on review of the petition and after completion of any necessary or appropriate investigation supplementary thereto, the Commission shall find that the alternative procedure proposed, if granted, will not hamper or interfere with the enforcement of the Act, and will be of equivalent usefulness in its enforcement, the Commission may grant the petition subject to such conditions as it may determine appropriate and subject to revocation. Whenever any relief granted to any person is sought to be revoked for failure to comply with the conditions of the Commission, that person shall be notified in writing of the facts constituting such failure and afforded an opportunity to achieve or demonstrate compliance.

(c) *Compliance after submission of petitions*. The submission of a petition or any delay of the Commission in acting upon such petition shall not relieve any employer, employment agency, or labor organization from any obligations to comply with this part. However, the Commission shall give notice of the denial of any petition with due promptness.

Subpart C

Administrative Exemptions

§ 1627.15   Administrative exemptions; procedures

(a) Section 9 of the Act provides that, "In accordance with the provisions of subchapter II of chapter 5, of title 5, United States Code, the Secretary of Labor * * * may establish such reasonable exemptions to and from any or all provisions of this Act as he may find necessary and proper in the public interest."

(b) The authority conferred on the Commission by section 9 of the Act to establish reasonable exemptions will be exercised with caution and due regard for the remedial purpose of the statute to promote employment of older persons based on their ability rather than age and to prohibit arbitrary age discrimination in employment. Administrative action consistent with this statutory purpose may be taken under this section, with or without a request therefor, when found necessary and proper in the public interest in accordance with the statutory standards. No formal procedures have been prescribed for requesting such action. However, a reasonable exemption from the Act's provisions will be granted only if it is decided, after notice published in the FEDERAL REGISTER giving all interested persons an opportunity to present data, views, or arguments, that a strong and affirmative showing has been made that such exemption is in fact necessary and proper in the public interest. Request for such exemption shall be submitted in writing to the Commission.

§ 1627.16   Specific exemptions

(a) Pursuant to the authority contained in section 9 of the Act and in accordance with the procedure provided therein and in § 1627.15(b) of this part, it has been found necessary and proper in the public interest to exempt from all prohibitions of the Act all activities and programs under Federal contracts or grants, or carried out by the public employment services of the several States, designed exclusively to provide employment for, or to encourage the employment of, persons with special employment problems, including employment activities and programs under the Manpower Development and Training Act of 1962, as amended, and the Economic Opportunity Act of 1964, as amended, for persons among the long-term unemployed, handicapped, members of minority groups, older workers, or youth. Questions concerning the application of this exemption shall be referred to the Commission for decision.

(b) Any employer, employment agency, or labor organization the activities of which are exempt from the prohibitions of the Act under paragraph (a) of this section shall maintain and preserve records containing the same information and data that is required of employers, employment agencies, and labor organizations under §§ 1627.3, 1627.4, and 1627.5, respectively.

Subpart D

Statutory Exemption

§ 1627.17   Calculating the amount of qualified retirement benefits for purposes of the exemption for bona fide executives or high policymaking employees

(a) Section 12(c)(1) of the Act, added by the 1978 amendments and amended in 1984, provides: "Nothing in this Act shall be construed to prohibit compulsory retirement of any employee who has attained 65 years of age but not 70 years of age, and who, for the 2-year period immediately before retirement, is employed in a bona fide executive or a high policymaking position, if such employee is entitled to an immediate nonforfeitable annual retirement benefit from a pension, profit-sharing, savings, or deferred compensation plan, or any combination of such plans, of the employer of such employee, which equals, in the aggregate, at least $44,000." The Commission's interpretative statements regarding this exemption are set forth in § 1625 of this chapter.

(b) Section 12(c)(2) of the Act provides:

In applying the retirement benefit test of paragraph (a) of this subsection, if any such retirement benefit is in a form other than a straight life annuity (with no ancillary benefits), or if employees contribute to any such plan or make rollover contributions, such benefit shall be adjusted in accordance with regulations prescribed by the Commission, after consultation with the Secretary of the Treasury, so that the benefit is the equivalent of a straight life annuity (with no ancillary benefits) under a plan to which employees do not contribute and under which no rollover contributions are made.

(c)(1) The requirement that an employee be entitled to the equivalent of a $44,000 straight life annuity (with no ancillary benefits) is satisfied in any case where the employee has the option of receiving, during each year of his or her lifetime following retirement, an annual payment of at least $44,000, or periodic payments on a more frequent basis which, in the aggregate, equal at least $44,000 per year: *Provided*, however, that the portion of the retirement income figure attributable to Social Security, employee contributions, rollover contributions and contributions of prior employers is excluded in the manner described in paragraph (e) of this section. (A retirement benefit which excludes these amounts is sometimes referred to herein as a "qualified" retirement benefit.)

(2) The requirement is also met where the employee has the option of receiving, upon retirement, a lump sum payment with which it is possible to purchase a single life annuity (with no ancillary benefits) yielding at least $44,000 per year as adjusted.

(3) The requirement is also satisfied where the employee is entitled to receive, upon retirement, benefits whose aggregate value, as of the date of the employee's retirement, with respect to those payments which are scheduled to be made within the period of life expectancy of the employee, is $44,000 per year as adjusted.

(4) Where an employee has one or more of the options described in paragraphs (c)(1) through (3) of this section, but instead selects another option (or options), the test is also met. On the other hand, where an employee has no choice but to have certain benefits provided after his or her death, the value of these benefits may not be included in this determination.

(5) The determination of the value of those benefits which may be counted towards the $44,000 requirement must be made on the basis of reasonable actuarial assumptions with respect to mortality and interest. For purposes of excluding from this determination any benefits which are available only after death, it is not necessary to determine the life expectancy of each person on an individual basis. A reasonable actuarial assumption with respect to mortaility will suffice.

(6) The benefits computed under paragraphs (c)(1), (2) and (3) of this section shall be aggregated for purposes of determining whether the $44,000 requirement has been met.

(d) The only retirement benefits which may be counted towards the $44,000 annual benefit are those from a pension, profit-sharing, savings, or deferred compensation plan, or any combination of such plans. Such plans include, but are not limited to, stock bonus, thrift and simplified employee pensions. The value of benefits from any other employee benefit plans, such as health or life insurance, may not be counted.

(e) In calculating the value of a pension, profit-sharing, savings, or deferred compensation plan (or any combination of such plans), amounts attributable to Social Security, employee contributions, contributions of prior employers, and rollover contributions must be excluded. Specific rules are set forth below.

(1) *Social Security*. Amounts attributable to Social Security must be excluded. Since these amounts are readily determinable, no specific rules are deemed necessary.

(2) *Employee contributions*. Amounts attributable to employee contributions must be excluded. The regulations governing this requirement are based on section 411(c) of the Internal Revenue Code and Treasury Regulations thereunder (§ 1.411(c)–(1)), relating to the allocation of accrued benefits between employer and employee contributions. Different calculations are needed to determine the amount of employee contributions, depending upon whether the retirement income plan is a defined contribution plan or a defined benefit plan. Defined contribution plans (also referred to as individual account plans) generally provide that each participant has an individual account and the participant's benefits are based solely on the account balance. No set benefit is promised in defined contribution plans, and the final amount is a result not only of the actual contributions, but also of other factors, such as investment gains and losses. Any retirement income plan which is not an individual account plan is a defined benefit plan. Defined benefit plans generally provide a definitely determinable benefit, by specifying either a flat monthly payment or a schedule of payments based on a formula (frequently involving salary and years of service), and they are funded according to actuarial principles over the employee's period of participation.

(i) *Defined contribution plans*—(A) *Separate accounts maintained*. If a separate account is maintained with respect to an employee's contributions and all income, expenses, gains and losses attributable thereto, the balance in such an account represents the amount attributable to employee contributions.

(B) *Separate accounts not maintained*. If a separate account is not maintained with respect to an employee's contributions and the income, expenses, gains and losses attributable thereto, the proportion of the total benefit attributable to employee contributions is determined by multiplying that benefit by a fraction:

(1) The numerator of which is the total amount of the employee's contributions under the plan (less withdrawals), and

(2) The denominator of which is the sum of the numerator and the total contributions made under the plan by the employer on behalf of the employee (less withdrawals).

> *Example*: A defined contribution plan does not maintain separate accounts for employee contributions. An employee's annual retirement benefit under the plan is $40,000. The employee has contributed $96,000 and the employer has contributed $144,000 to the employee's individual account; no withdrawals have been made. The amount of the $40,000 annual benefit attributable to employee contributions is $40,000 × $96,000/$96,000 + $144,000 = $16,000. Hence the employer's share of the $40,000 annual retirement benefit is $40,000 minus $16,000, or $24,000—too low to fall within the exemption.

(ii) *Defined benefit plans*—(A) *Separate accounts maintained*. If a separate account is maintained with respect to an employee's contributions and all income, expenses, gains and losses attributable thereto, the balance in such an account represents the amount attributable to employee contributions.

(B) *Separate accounts not maintained*. If a separate account is not maintained with respect to an employee's contributions and the income, expenses, gains and losses attributable thereto, all of the contributions made by an employee must be converted actuarially to a single life annuity (without ancillary benefits) commencing at the age of forced retirement. An employee's accumulated contributions are the sum of all contributions (mandatory and, if not separately accounted for, voluntary) made by the employee, together with interest on the sum of all such contributions compounded annually at the rate of 5 percent per annum from the time each such contribution was made until the date of retirement. *Provided, however*, That prior to the date any plan became subject to section 411(c) of the Internal Revenue Code, interest will be credited at the rate (if any) specified in the plan. The amount of the employee's accumulated contribution described in the previous sentence must be multiplied by an "appropriate conversion factor" in order to convert it to a single life annuity (without ancillary benefits) commencing at the age of actual retirement. The appropriate conversion factor depends upon the age of retirement. In accordance with Rev. Rul. 76–47, 1976–2 C.B. 109, the following conversion factors shall be used with respect to the specified retirement ages:

Retirement age	Conversion factor percent
65 through 66	10
67 through 68	11
69	12

> *Example*: An employee is scheduled to receive a pension from a defined benefit plan of $50,000 per year. Over the years he has contributed $150,000 to the plan, and at age 65 this amount, when contributions have been compounded at appropriate annual interest rates, is equal to $240,000. In accordance with Rev. Rul. 76–47, 10 percent is an appropriate conversion factor. When the $240,000 is multiplied by this conversion factor, the product is $24,000, which represents that part of the $50,000 annual pension payment which is attributable to employee contributions. The difference—$26,000—represents the employer's contribution, which is too low to meet the test in the exemption.

(3) *Contributions of prior employers*. Amounts attributable to contributions of prior employers must be excluded.

(i) *Current employer distinguished from prior employers*. Under the section 12(c) exemption, for purposes of excluding contributions of prior employers, a prior employer is every previous employer of the employee except those previous employers which are members of a "controlled group of corporations" with, or "under common control" with, the employer which forces the employee to retire, as those terms are used in sections 414(b) and 414(c) of the Internal Revenue Code, as modified by section 414(h) (26 U.S.C. 414(b), (c) and (h)).

(ii) *Benefits attributable to current employer and to prior employers.* Where the current employer maintains or contributes to a plan which is separate from plans maintained or contributed to by prior employers, the amount of the employee's benefit attributable to those prior employers can be readily determined. However, where the current employer maintains or contributes to the same plan as prior employers, the following rule shall apply. The benefit attributable to the current employer shall be the total benefit received by the employee, reduced by the benefit that the employee would have received from the plan if he or she had never worked for the current employer. For purposes of this calculation, it shall be assumed that all benefits have always been vested, even if benefits accrued as a result of service with a prior employer had not in fact been vested.

(4) *Rollover contributions.* Amounts attributable to rollover contributions must be excluded. For purposes of § 1627.17(e), a rollover contribution (as defined in section 402(a)(5), 403(a)(4), 408(d)(3) and 409(b)(3)(C) of the Internal Revenue Code) shall be treated as an employee contribution. These amounts have already been excluded as a result of the computations set forth in § 1627.17(e)(2). Accordingly, no separate calculation is necessary to comply with this requirement.

(Sec. 12(c)(1) of the Age Discrimination In Employment Act of 1967, as amended by Sec. 802(c)(1) of the Older Americans Act Amendments of 1984, Pub. L. 98–459, 98 Stat. 1792)

[44 FR 66797, Nov. 21, 1979, as amended at 50 FR 2544, Jan. 17, 1985]

Proposed Rule Allowing Unsupervised Waiver of Rights Under ADEA

(50 FR 40871, Sept. 17, 1985)

Part 1627

[Amended]

1. The authority citation for 29 CFR Part 1627 would be revised to read as follows:
Authority: Sec. 7, 81 Stat. 604; 29 U.S.C. 626; Sec. 9, 81 Stat. 605; 29 U.S.C. 628; sec. 11, 52 Stat. 1066, as amended, 29 U.S.C. 211; sec. 2, Reorg. Plan No. 1 of 1978, 43 FR 19807.
2. By adding a new paragraph (c) to read as follows:

§ 1627.16 Specific exemptions

* * *

(c) Pursuant to the authority contained in section 9 of the Act and in accordance with the procedure provided therein and in § 1627.15(b) of this part, it has been found necessary and proper in the public interest to permit waivers or releases of claims under the Act without the Commission's supervision or approval, provided that such waivers or releases are knowing and voluntary. No such waivers or releases, however, shall affect the Commission's rights and responsibilities to enforce the Act.

* * *

Appendix C

Text of The Wage-Hour Administrator's Interpretation of the ADEA

Subchapter C

Age Discrimination in Employment

Part 860

Interpretations

***

Authority: 81 Stat. 602; 29 U.S.C. 620, 5 U.S.C. 301, Secretary's Order No. 10–68, and Secretary's Order No. 11–68.

§ 860.1 Purpose of this part

This part is intended to provide an interpretative bulletin on the Age Discrimination in Employment Act of 1967 like Subchapter B of this title relating to the Fair Labor Standards Act of 1938. Such interpretations of this Act are published to provide "a practical guide to employers and employees as to how the office representing the public interest in its enforcement will seek to apply it" (*Skidmore v. Swift & Co.*, 323 U.S. 134, 138). These interpretations indicate the construction of the law which the Department of Labor believes to be correct, and which will guide it in the performance of its administrative and enforcement duties under the Act unless and until it is otherwise directed by authoritative decisions of the Courts or concludes, upon reexamination of an interpretation, that it is incorrect.

[33 FR 9172, June 21, 1968]

§ 860.20 Geographical scope of coverage

The prohibitions in section 4 of the Act are considered to apply only to performance of the described discriminatory acts in places over which the United States has sovereignty, territorial jurisdiction, or legislative control. These include principally the geographical areas set forth in the definition of the term "State" in section 11(i). There, the term State is defined to include "a State of the United States, the District of Columbia, Puerto Rico, the Virgin Islands, American Samoa, Guam, Wake Island, the Canal Zone, and Outer Continental Shelf lands defined in the Outer Continental Shelf Lands Act." Activities within such geographical areas which are discriminatory against protected individuals or employees are within the scope of the Act even though the activities are related to employment outside of such geographical areas.

[34 FR 322, Jan. 9, 1969]

§ 860.30   Definitions

Considering the purpose of the proviso to section 7(c) of the Act as indicated in the reports of both the Senate and House Committees (see S. Rept. No. 723, 90th Cong. 1st Sess., and H. Rept. No. 805, 90th Cong., 1st Sess.) it was clearly the intent of Congress that the term "employee" in that proviso should apply to any person who has a right to bring an action under the Act, including an applicant for employment.

[34 FR 9708, June 21, 1969]

§ 860.31   "Employer"

Section 11(b) defines "employer" to mean "* * * a person engaged in an industry affecting commerce who has 25 or more employees for each working day in each of 20 or more calendar weeks in the current or preceding calendar year: * * * The term also means any agent of such a person, but such term does not include the United States, a corporation wholly owned by the Government of the United States, or a State or political subdivision thereof."

[37 FR 13345, July 7, 1972]

§ 860.35   "Employment agency"

(a) Section 11(c) defines "employment agency" to mean "any person regularly undertaking with or without compensation to procure employees for an employer and includes an agent of such a person; but shall not include an agency of the United States, or an agency of a State or political subdivision of a State, except that such term shall include the United States Employment Service and the system of State and local employment services receiving Federal assistance.

(b) As long as an employment agency regularly procures employees for at least one covered employer, it qualifies under section 11(c) as an employment agency with respect to all of its activities whether they be for covered or noncovered employers.

[37 FR 13345, July 7, 1972]

§ 860.36   Employment agencies—prohibitions

(a) Section 4(b) provides that "It shall be unlawful for an employment agency to fail or refuse to refer for employment, or otherwise to discriminate against, any individual because of such individual's age, or to classify or refer for employment any individual on the basis of such individual's age."

(b) Since a covered employment agency is subject to the prohibitions of the Act even when acting on behalf of noncovered employers (see § 860.35(b)), it may not discriminate contrary to the statute with respect to any referrals it makes.

(c) The prohibitions of section 4(b) apply not only to the referral activities of a covered employment agency but also to the agency's own employment practices, regardless of the number of employees the agency may have. This is so because section 4(b) makes it unlawful for a covered employment agency "otherwise to discriminate against" any individual between 40 and 65 because of age. To illustrate, a covered employment agency's use of an age preference of "not over 35" in an advertisement seeking employees for itself is unlawful since such preference discriminates against individuals in the 40 to 65 age bracket.

[37 FR 13345, July 7, 1972]

§ 860.50   "Compensation, terms, conditions, or privileges of employment * * *"

(a) Section 4(a)(1) of the Act specifies that it is unlawful for an employer "to fail or refuse to hire or to discharge any individual or otherwise discriminate against any individual with respect to his compensation, terms, conditions, or privileges of employment, because of such individual's age".

(b) The term "compensation" includes all types and methods of remuneration paid to or on behalf of or received by an employee for his employment.

(c) The phrase "terms, conditions, or privileges of employment" encompasses a wide and varied range of job-related factors including, but not limited to, job security, advancement, status, and benefits. The following are examples of some of the more common terms, conditions, or privileges of employment: The many and varied employee advantages generally regarded as being within the phrase "fringe benefits," promotion, demotion or other disciplinary action, hours of work (including overtime), leave policy (including sick leave, vacation, holidays), career development programs, and seniority or merit systems (which govern such conditions as transfer, assignment, job retention, layoff and recall). An employer will be deemed to have violated the Act if he discriminates against any individual within its protection because of age with respect to any terms, conditions, or privileges of employment, such as the above, unless a statutory exception applies.

[33 FR 12227, Aug. 30, 1968]

§ 860.75   Wage rate reduction prohibited

Section 4(a)(3) of the Act provides that where an age-based wage differential is paid in violation of the statute, the employer cannot correct the violation by reducing the wage rate of any employee. Thus, for example, in a situation where it has been determined that an employer has violated the Act by paying a 62-year-old employee a prohibited wage differential of 50 cents an hour less than he is paying a 30-year-old worker, in order to achieve compliance with the Act he must raise the wage rate of the older employee to equal that of the younger worker. Furthermore, the employer's obligation to comply with the statute cannot be avoided by transferring either the older or the younger employee to other work since the transfer itself would appear discriminatory under the particular facts and circumstances.

[34 FR 322, Jan. 9, 1969]

§ 860.91   Discrimination within the age bracket of 40–65

(a) Although section 4 of the Act broadly makes unlawful various types of age discrimination by employers, employment agencies, and labor organizations, section 12 limits this protection to individuals who are at least 40 years of age but less than 65 years of age. Thus, for example it is unlawful in situations where this Act applies, for an employer to discriminate in hiring or in any other way by giving preference because of age to an individual 30 years old over another individual who is within the 40–65 age bracket limitation of section 12. Similarly, an employer will have violated the Act, in situations where it applies, when one individual within the age bracket of 40–65 is given job preference in hiring, assignment, promotion or any other term, condition, or privilege of employment, on the basis of age, over another individual within the same age bracket.

(b) Thus, if two men apply for employment to which the Act applies, and one is

42 and the other 52, the personnel officer or employer may not lawfully turn down either one on the basis of his age; he must make his decision on the basis of other factors, such as the capabilities and experience of the two individuals. The Act, however, does not restrain age discrimination between two individuals 25 and 35 years of age.

[33 FR 9172, June 21, 1968]

§ 860.92   Help wanted notices or advertisements

(a) Section 4(e) of the Act prohibits "an employer, labor organization, or employment agency" from using printed or published notices or advertisements indicating any preference, limitation, specification, or discrimination, based on age.

(b) When help wanted notices or advertisements contain terms and phrases such as "age 25 to 35," "young," "boy," "girl," "college student," "recent college graduate," or others of a similar nature, such a term or phrase discriminates against the employment of older persons and will be considered in violation of the Act. Such specifications as "age 40 to 50," "age over 50," or "age over 65" are also considered to be prohibited. Where such specifications as "retired person" or "supplement your pension" are intended and applied so as to discriminate against others within the protected group, they too are regarded as prohibited, unless one of the exceptions applies.

(c) However, help wanted notices or advertisements which include a term or phrase such as "college graduate," or other education requirement, or specify a minimum age less than 40, such as "not under 18", or "not under 21," are not prohibited by the statute.

(d) The use of the phrase "state age" in help wanted notices or advertisements is not, in itself, a violation of the statute. But because the request that an applicant state his age may tend to deter older applicants or otherwise indicate a discrimination based on age, employment notices or advertisements which include the phrase "state age," or any similar term, will be closely scrutinized to assure that the request is for a permissible purpose and not for purposes proscribed by the statute.

(e) There is no provision in the statute which prohibits an individual seeking employment through advertising from specifying his own age.

[33 FR 9172, June 21, 1968, as amended at 34 FR 9708, June 21, 1969]

§ 860.95   Job applications

(a) The term "job applications," within the meaning of the recordkeeping regulations under the Act (Part 850 of this chapter), refers to all inquiries about employment or applications for employment or promotion including, but not limited to, resumes or other summaries of the applicant's background. It relates not only to preemployment inquiries but to inquiries by employees concerning terms, conditions, or privileges of employment as specified in section 4 of the statute. As in the case with help wanted notices or advertisements (see § 860.92), a request on the part of an employer, employment agency, or labor organization for information such as "Date of Birth" or "State Age" on an employment application form is not, in itself, a violation of the Age Discrimination in Employment Act of 1967. But because the request that an applicant state his age may tend to deter older applicants or otherwise indicate a discrimination based on age, employment application forms which request such information in the above, or any similar phrase, will be closely scrutinized to assure that the request is for a permissible purpose and not for purposes proscribed by the statute. That the purpose is not proscribed by the statute should be made known to the applicant, as by a reference on the application form to the statutory prohibition in language to the following effect: "The Age Discrimination in Employment Act of 1967 prohibits discrimination on the basis of age with respect to individuals who are at least 40 but less than 65 years of age."

(b) An employer may limit the active period of consideration of an application so long as he treats all applicants alike regardless of age. Thus, for example, if the employer customarily retains employment applications in an active status for a period of 60 days, he will be in compliance with the Act if he so retains those of individuals in the 40 to 65 age group for an equal period of consideration as those of younger persons. Further, there is no objection to the employer advising all applicants of the above practice by means of a legend on his application forms as long as this does not suggest any limitation based on age. If it develops, however, that such a legend is used as a device to avoid consideration of the applications of older persons, or otherwise discriminate against them because of age, there would then appear to be a violation of the Act. It should be noted that this position in no way alters the recordkeeping requirements of the Act which are set forth in Part 850 of this chapter.

[33 FR 12227, Aug. 20, 1968, as amended at 34 FR 9708, June 21, 1969]

§ 860.102   Bona fide occupational qualifications

(a) Section 4(f)(1) of the Act provides that "it shall not be unlawful for an employer, employment agency, or labor organization * * * to take any action otherwise prohibited under paragraphs (a), (b), (c), or (e) of this section where age is a bona fide occupational qualification reasonably necessary to the normal operation of the particular business * * *"

(b) Whether occupational qualifications will be deemed to be "bona fide" and "reasonably necessary to the normal operation of the particular business", will be determined on the basis of all the pertinent facts surrounding each particular situation. It is anticipated that this concept of a bona fide occupational qualification will have limited scope and application. Further, as this is an exception it must be construed narrowly, and the burden of proof in establishing that it applies is the responsibility of the employer, employment agency, or labor organization which relies upon it.

(c) The following are illustrations of possible bona fide occupational qualifications.

(d) Federal statutory and regulatory requirements which provide compulsory age limitations for hiring or compulsory retirement, without reference to the individual's actual physical condition at the terminal age, when such conditions are clearly imposed for the safety and convenience of the public. This exception would apply, for example, to airline pilots within the jurisdiction of the Federal Aviation Agency. Federal Aviation Agency regulations do not permit airline pilots to engage in carrier operations, as pilots, after they reach age 60.

(e) A bona fide occupational qualification will also be recognized in certain special, individual occupational circumstances, e.g., actors required for youthful or elderly characterization or roles, and persons used to advertise or promote the sale of products designed for, and directed to appeal exclusively to, either youthful or elderly consumers.

[33 FR 9172, June 21, 1968]

§ 860.103   Differentiations based on reasonable factors other than age

(a) Section 4(f)(1) of the Act provides that "It shall not be unlawful for an employer, employment agency, or labor organization * * * to take any action otherwise prohibited under paragraphs (a), (b), (c), or (e) of this section * * * where the differentiation is based on reasonable factors other than age; * * *''

(b) No precise and unequivocal determination can be made as to the scope of the phrase ''differentiation based on reasonable factors other than age.'' Whether such differentiations exist must be decided on the basis of all the particular facts and circumstances surrounding each individual situation.

(c) It should be kept in mind that it was not the purpose or intent of Congress in enacting this Act to require the employment of anyone, regardless of age, who is disqualified on grounds other than age from performing a particular job. The clear purpose is to insure that age, within the limits prescribed by the Act, is not a determining factor in making any decision regarding hiring, dismissal, promotion or any other term, condition or privilege of employment of an individual.

(d) The reasonableness of a differentiation will be determined on an individual, case by case basis, not on the basis of any general or class concept, with unusual working conditions given weight according to their individual merit.

(e) Further, in accord with a long chain of decisions of the Supreme Court of the United States with respect to other remedial labor legislation, all exceptions such as this must be construed narrowly, and the burden of proof in establishing the applicability of the exception will rest upon the employer, employment agency or labor union which seeks to invoke it.

(f) Where the particular facts and circumstances in individual situations warrant such a conclusion, the following factors are among those which may be recognized as supporting a differentiation based on reasonable factors other than age.

(1)(i) Physical fitness requirements based upon preemployment or periodic physical examinations relating to minimum standards for employment: *Provided, however*, That such standards are reasonably necessary for the specific work to be performed and are uniformly and equally applied to all applicants for the particular job category, regardless of age.

(ii) Thus, a differentiation based on a physical examination, but not one based on age, may be recognized as reasonable in certain job situations which necessitate stringent physical requirements due to inherent occupational factors such as the safety of the individual employees or of other persons in their charge, or those occupations which by nature are particularly hazardous: For example, iron workers, bridge builders, sandhogs, underwater demolition men, and other similar job classifications which require rapid reflexes or a high degree of speed, coordination, dexterity, endurance, or strength.

(iii) However, a claim for a differentiation will not be permitted on the basis of an employer's assumption that every employee over a certain age in a particular type of job usually becomes physically unable to perform the duties of that job. There is medical evidence, for example, to support the contention that such is generally not the case. In many instances, an individual at age 60 may be physically capable of performing heavy-lifting on a job, whereas another individual of age 30 may be physically incapable of doing so.

(2) Evaluation factors such as quantity or quality of production, or educational level, would be acceptable bases for differentiation when, in the individual case, such factors are shown to have a valid relationship to job requirements and where the criteria or personnel policy establishing such factors are applied uniformly to all employees, regardless of age.

(g) The foregoing are intended only as examples of differentiations based on reasonable factors other than age, and do not constitute a complete or exhaustive list or limitation. It should always be kept in mind that even in situations where experience has shown that most elderly persons do not have certain qualifications which are essential to those who hold certain jobs, some may have them even though they have attained the age of 60 or 64, and thus discrimination based on age is forbidden.

(h) It should also be made clear that a general assertion that the average cost of employing older workers as a group is higher than the average cost of employing younger workers as a group will not be recognized as a differentiation under the terms and provisions of the Act, unless one of the other statutory exceptions applies. To classify or group employees solely on the basis of age for the purpose of comparing costs, or for any other purpose, necessarily rests on the assumption that the age factor alone may be used to justify a differentiation—an assumption plainly contrary to the terms of the Act and the purpose of Congress in enacting it. Differentials so based would serve only to perpetuate and promote the very discrimination at which the Act is directed.

[33 FR 9173, June 21, 1968]

§ 860.104   Differentiations based on reasonable factors other than age—additional examples

(a) *Employment of Social Security recipients.* (1) It is considered discriminatory for an employer to specify that he will hire only persons receiving old age Social Security insurance benefits. Such a specification could result in discrimination against other individuals within the age group covered by the Act willing to work under the wages and other conditions of employment involved, even though those wages and conditions may be peculiarly attractive to Social Security recipients. Similarly, the specification of Social Security recipients cannot be used as a convenient reference to persons of sufficient age to be eligible for old age benefits. Thus, where two persons apply for a job, one age 56, and the other age 62 and receiving Social Security benefits, the employer may not lawfully give preference in hiring to the older individual solely because he is receiving such benefits.

(2) Where a job applicant under age 65 is unwilling to accept the number or schedule of hours required by an employer as a condition for a particular job, because he is receiving Social Security benefits and is limited in the amount of wages he may earn without losing such benefits, failure to employ him would not violate the Act. An employer's condition as to the number or schedule of hours may be "a reasonable factor other than age" on which to base a differentiation.

(b) *Employee testing.* The use of a validated employee test is not, of itself, a violation of the Act when such test is specifically related to the requirements of the job, is fair and reasonable, is administered in good faith and without discrimination on the basis of age, and is properly evaluated. A vital factor in employee testing as it relates to the 40–65-age group protected by the statute is the "test-sophistication" or "test-wiseness" of the individual. Younger persons, due to the tremendous increase in the use of tests in primary and secondary schools in recent years, may generally have had more experience in test taking than older individuals and, consequently, where an employee test is used as the sole tool or the controlling factor in the employee selection procedure, such younger persons may have an advantage over older applicants who may have had considerable on-the-job experience but who due to age, are further removed from their schooling. Therefore, situations in which an employee test is used as the sole tool or the controlling factor in the employee selection procedure will be carefully scrutinized to ensure that the test is for a permissible purpose and not for purposes prohibited by the statute.

(c) *Refusal to hire relatives of current employees.* There is no provision in the Act which would prohibit an employer, employment agency, or labor organization from refusing to hire individuals within the protected age group not because of their age but because they are relatives of persons already employed by the firm or organization involved. Such a differentiation would appear to be based on "reasonable factors other than age."

[34 FR 322, Jan. 9, 1969, as amended at 34 FR 9709, June 21, 1969]

§ 860.105   Bona fide seniority systems

Section 4(f)(2) of the Act provides that "It shall not be unlawful for an employer, employment agency, or labor organization * * * to observe the terms of a bona fide seniority system * * * which is not a subterfuge to evade the purposes of this Act * * *"

(a) Though a seniority system may be qualified by such factors as merit, capacity, or ability, any bona fide seniority system must be based on length of service as the primary criterion for the equitable allocation of available employment opportunities and prerogatives among younger and older workers. In this regard, it should be noted that a bona fide seniority system may operate, for example, on an occupational, departmental, plant, or company wide unit basis.

(b) Seniority systems not only distinguish between employees on the basis of their length of service, they normally afford greater rights to those who have the longer service. Therefore, adoption of a purported seniority system which gives those with longer service lesser rights, and results in discharge or less favored treatment to those within the protection of the Act, may, depending upon the circumstances, be a "subterfuge to evade the purposes" of the Act. Furthermore, a seniority system which has the effect of perpetuating discrimination which may have existed on the basis of age prior to the effective date of the Act will not be recognized as "bona fide."

(c) Unless the essential terms and conditions of an alleged seniority system have been communicated to the affected employees and can be shown to be applied uniformly to all of those affected, regardless of age, it will also be regarded as lacking the necessary bona fides to qualify for the exception.

(d) It should be noted that seniority systems which segregate, classify, or otherwise discriminate against individuals on the basis of race, color, religion, sex or national origin, are prohibited under Title VII of the Civil Rights Act of 1964, where that Act otherwise applies. Neither will such systems be regarded as "bona fide" within the meaning of section 4(f)(2) of the Age Discrimination in Employment Act of 1967.

[33 FR 12227, Aug. 30, 1968]

§ 860.106   Bona fide apprenticeship programs

Age limitations for entry into bona fide apprenticeship programs were not intended to be affected by the Act. Entry into most apprenticeship programs has traditionally been limited to youths under specified ages. This is in recognition of the fact that apprenticeship is an extension of the educational process to prepare young men and women for skilled employment. Accordingly, the prohibitions contained in the Act will not be applied to bona fide apprenticeship programs which meet the standards specified in §§ 521.2 and 521.3 of this chapter.

[34 FR 323, Jan. 9, 1969]

§ 860.110   Involuntary retirement before age 65

(a) Section 4(f)(2) of the Act provides that "It shall not be unlawful for an employer, employment agency, or labor organization * * * to observe the terms of * * * any bona fide employee benefit plan such as a retirement, pension, or insurance plan, which is not a subterfuge to evade the purposes of this Act, except that no such employee benefit plan shall excuse the failure to hire any individual * * *.'' Thus, the Act authorizes involuntary retirement irrespective of age, provided that such retirement is pursuant to the terms of a retirement or pension plan meeting the requirements of section 4(f)(2). The fact that an employer may decide to permit certain employees to continue working beyond the age stipulated in the formal retirement program does not, in and of itself, render an otherwise bona fide plan invalid insofar, as the exception provided in section 4(f)(2) is concerned.

(b) This exception does not apply to the voluntary retirement before 65 of employees who are not participants in the employer's retirement or pension program. It should be noted that section 5 of the Act directs the Secretary of Labor to undertake an appropriate study of institutional and other arrangements giving rise to involuntary retirement, and report his findings and any appropriate legislative recommendations to the President and to Congress.

[34 FR 9709, June 21, 1969]

§ 860.120   Costs and benefits under employee benefit plans

(a)(1) *General.* Section 4(f)(2) of the Act provides that it is not unlawful for an employer, employment agency, or labor organization ''to observe the terms of * * * any bona fide employee benefit plan such as a retirement, pension, or insurance plan, which is not a subterfuge to evade the purposes of this Act, except that no such employee benefit plan shall excuse the failure to hire any individual, and no such * * * employee benefit plan shall require or permit the involuntary retirement of any individual specified by section 12(a) of this Act because of the age of such individuals.'' The legislative history of this provision indicates that its purpose is to permit age-based reductions in employee benefit plans where such reductions are justified by significant cost considerations. Accordingly, section 4(f)(2) does not apply, for example, to paid vacations and uninsured paid sick leave, since reductions in these benefits would not be justified by significant cost considerations. Where employee benefit plans do meet the criteria in section 4(f)(2), benefit levels for older workers may be reduced to the extent necessary to achieve approximate equivalency in cost for older and younger workers. A benefit plan will be considered in compliance with the statute where the actual amount of payment made, or cost incurred, in behalf of an older worker is equal to that made or incurred in behalf of a younger worker, even though the older worker may thereby receive a lesser amount of benefits of insurance coverage. Since section 4(f)(2) is an exception from the general non-discrimination provisions of the Act, the burden is on the one seeking to invoke the exception to show that every element has been clearly and unmistakably met. The exception must be narrowly construed. The following sections explain three key elements of the exception: (i) What a ''bona fide employee benefit plan'' is; (ii) what it means to ''observe the terms'' of such a plan; and (iii) what kind of plan, or plan provision, would be considered ''a subterfuge to evade the purposes of [the] Act.'' There is also a discussion of the application of the general rules governing all plans with respect to specific kinds of employee benefit plans. For a discussion of the provisions in section 4(f)(2) forbidding the failure to hire any individual or the involuntary retirement of any individual, see § 860.110 of this chapter.

(2) *Relation of section 4(f)(2) to sections 4(a), 4(b) and 4(c).* Sections 4(a), 4(b) and 4(c) prohibit specified acts of discrimination on the basis of age. Section 4(a) in particular makes it unlawful for an employer to ''discriminate against any individual with respect to his compensation, terms, conditions, or privileges of employment,

because of such individual's age * * *.'' Section 4(f)(2) is an exception to this general prohibition. Where an employer under an employee benefit plan provides the same level of benefits to older workers as to younger workers, there is no violation of section 4(a), and accordingly the practice does not have to be justified under section 4(f)(2).

(b) *"Bona fide employee benefit plan."* Section 4(f)(2) applies only to bona fide employee benefit plans. A plan is considered "bona fide" if its terms (including cessation of contributions or accruals in the case of retirement income plans) have been accurately described in writing to all employees and if it actually provides the benefits in accordance with the terms of the plan. Notifying employees promptly of the provisions and changes in an employee benefit plan is essential if they are to know how the plan affects them. For these purposes, it would be sufficient under the ADEA for employers to follow the disclosure requirements of ERISA and the regulations thereunder. The plan must actually provide the benefits its provisions describe, since otherwise the notification of the provisions to employees is misleading and inaccurate. An "employee benefit plan" is a plan, such as a retirement, pension, or insurance plan, which provides employees with what are frequently referred to as "fringe benefits." The term does not refer to wages or salary in cash; neither section 4(f)(2) nor any other section of the Act excuses the payment of lower wages or salary to older employees on account of age. Whether or not any particular employee benefit plan may lawfully provide lower benefits to older employees on account of age depends on whether all of the elements of the exception have been met. An "employee-pay-all" employee benefit plan is one of the "terms, conditions, or privileges of employment" with respect to which discrimination on the basis of age is forbidden under section 4(a)(1). In such a plan, benefits for older workers may be reduced only to the extent and according to the same principles as apply to other plans under section 4(f)(2).

(c) *"To observe the terms"* of a plan. In order for a bona fide employee benefit plan which provides lower benefits to older employees on account of age to be within the section 4(f)(2) exception, the lower benefits must be provided in "observ[ance of] the terms of" the plan. As this statutory text makes clear, the section 4(f)(2) exception is limited to otherwise discriminatory actions which are actually prescribed by the terms of a bona fide employee benefit plan. Where the employer, employment agency, or labor organization is not required by the express provisions of the plan to provide lesser benefit to older workers, section 4(f)(2) does not apply. Important purposes are served by this requirement. Where a discriminatory policy is an express term of a benefit plan, employees presumably have some opportunity to know of the policy and to plan (or protest) accordingly. Moreover, the requirement that the discrimination actually be prescribed by a plan assures that the particular plan provision will be equally applied to all employees of the same age. Where a discriminatory provision is an optional term of the plan, it permits individual, discretionary acts of discrimination, which do not fall within the section 4(f)(2) exception.

(d) *"Subterfuge."* In order for a bona fide employee benefit plan which prescribes lower benefits for older employees on account of age to be within the section 4(f)(2) exception, it must not be "a subterfuge to evade the purposes of [the] Act." In general, a plan or plan provision which prescribes lower benefits for older employees on account of age is not a "subterfuge" within the meaning of section 4(f)(2), provided that the lower level of benefits is justified by age-related cost considerations. (The only exception to this general rule is with respect to certain retirement plans. See paragraph (f)(4) of this section.) There are certain other requirements that must be met in order for a plan not to be a subterfuge. These requirements are set forth below.

(1) *Cost data—general.* Cost data used in justification of a benefit plan which provides lower benefits to older employees on account of age must be valid and

reasonable. This standard is met where an employer has cost data which show the actual cost to it of providing the particular benefit (or benefits) in question over a representative period of years. An employer may rely in cost data for its own employees over such a period, or on cost data for a larger group of similarly situated employees. Sometimes, as a result of experience rating or other causes, an employer incurs costs that differ significantly from costs for a group of similarly situated employees. Such an employer may not rely on cost data for the similarly situated employees where such reliance would result in significantly lower benefits for its own older employees. Where reliable cost information is not available, reasonable projections made from existing cost data meeting the standards set forth above will be considered acceptable.

(2) *Cost data—Individual benefit basis and "benefit package" basis.* Cost comparisons and adjustments under section 4(f)(2) must be made on a benefit-by-benefit basis or on a "benefit package" basis, as described below.

(i) *Benefit-by-benefit basis.* Adjustments made on a benefit-by-benefit basis must be made in the amount or level of a specific form of benefit for a specific event or contingency. For example, higher group term life insurance costs for older workers would justify a corresponding reduction in the amount of group term life insurance coverage for older workers, on the basis of age. However, a benefit-by-benefit approach would not justify the substitution of one form of benefit for another, even though both forms of benefit are designed for the same contingency, such as death. See § 860.120(f)(1) of this section.

(ii) *"Benefit package" basis.* As an alternative to the benefit-by-benefit basis, cost comparisons and adjustments under section 4(f)(2) may be made on a limited "benefit package" basis. Under this approach, subject to the limitations described below, cost comparisons and adjustments can be made with respect to section 4(f)(2) plans in the aggregate. This alternative basis provides greater flexibility than a benefit-by-benefit basis in order to carry out the declared statutory purpose "to help employers and workers find ways of meeting problems arising from the impact of age on employment." A "benefit package" approach is an alternative approach consistent with this purpose and with the general purpose of section 4(f)(2) only if it is not used to reduce the cost to the employer or the favorability to the employees of overall employee benefits for older employees. A "benefit package" approach used for either of these purposes would be a subterfuge to evade the purposes of the Act. In order to assure that such a "benefit package" approach is not abused and is consistent with the legislative intent, it is subject to the limitations described in § 860.120(f), which also includes a general example.

(3) *Cost data—five-year maximum basis.* Cost comparisons and adjustments under section 4(f)(2) may be made on the basis of age brackets of up to 5 years. Thus a particular benefit may be reduced for employees of any age within the protected age group by an amount no greater than that which could be justified by the additional cost to provide them with the same level of the benefit as younger employees within a specified five-year age group immediately preceding theirs. For example, where an employer chooses to provide unreduced group term life insurance benefits until age 60, benefits for employees who are between 60 and 65 years of age may be reduced only to the extent necessary to achieve approximate equivalency in costs with employees who are 55 to 60 years old. Similarly, any reductions in benefit levels for 65 to 70 year old employees cannot exceed an amount which is proportional to the additional costs for their coverage over 60 to 65 year old employees.

(4) *Employee contributions in support of employee benefit plans—(i) As a condition of employment.* An older employee within the protected age group may not be required as a condition of employment to make greater contributions than a younger employee in support of an employee benefit plan. Such a requirement would be in effect a

mandatory reduction in take-home pay, which is never authorized by section 4(f)(2), and would impose an impediment to employment in violation of the specific restrictions in section 4(f)(2).

(ii) *As a condition of participation in a voluntary employee benefit plan.* An older employee within the protected age group may be required as a condition of participation in a voluntary employee benefit plan to make a greater contribution than a younger employee only if the older employee is not thereby required to bear a greater proportion of the total premium cost (employer-paid and employee-paid) than the younger employee. Otherwise the requirement would discriminate against the older employee by making compensation in the form of an employer contribution available on less favorable terms than for the younger employee and denying that compensation altogether to an older employee unwilling or unable to meet the less favorable terms. Such discrimination is not authorized by section 4(f)(2). This principle applies to three different contribution arrangements as follows:

(A) *Employee-pay-all plans.* Older employees, like younger employees, may be required to contribute as a condition of participation up to the full premium cost for their age.

(B) *Non-contributory ("employer-pay-all") plans.* Where younger employees are not required to contribute any portion of the total premium cost, older employees may not be required to contribute any portion.

(C) *Contributory plans.* In these plans employers and participating employees share the premium cost. The required contributions of participants may increase with age so long as the *proportion* of the total premium required to be paid by the participants does not increase with age.

(iii) *As an option in order to receive an unreduced benefit.* An older employee may be given the option, as an individual, to make the additional contribution necessary to receive the same level of benefits as a younger employee (provided that the contemplated reduction in benefits is otherwise justified by section 4(f)(2)).

(5) *Forfeiture clauses.* Clauses in employee benefit plans which state that litigation or participation in any manner in a formal proceeding by an employee will result in the forfeiture of his rights are unlawful insofar as they may be applied to those who seek redress under the Act. This is by reason of section 4(d) which provides that it is unlawful for an employer, employment agency, or labor organization to discriminate against any individual because such individual "has made a charge, testified, assisted, or participated in any manner in an investigation, proceeding, or litigation under this Act."

(6) *Refusal to hire clauses.* Any provision of an employee benefit plan which requires or permits the refusal to hire an individual specified in section 12(a) of the Act on the basis of age is a subterfuge to evade the purposes of the Act and cannot be excused under section 4(f)(2).

(7) *Involuntary retirement clauses.* Any provision of an employee benefit plan which requires or permits the involuntary retirement of any individual specified in section 12(a) of the Act on the basis of age is a subterfuge to evade the purpose of the Act and cannot be excused under section 4(f)(2).

(e) *Benefits provided by the Government.* An employer does not violate the Act by permitting certain benefits to be provided by the Government, even though the availability of such benefits may be based on age. For example, it is not necessary for an employer to provide health benefits which are otherwise provided to certain employees by Medicare. However, the availability of benefits from the Government will not justify a reduction in employer-provided benefits if the result is that, taking the employer-provided and Government-provided benefits together, an older employee is entitled to a lesser benefit of any type (including coverage for family and/or dependents) than a similarly situated younger employee. For example, the availability of certain benefits to an older employee under Medicare will not justify denying an older employee a benefit which is provided to younger employees and is not provided to the older employee by Medicare.

(f) *Application of section 4(f)(2) to various employee benefit plans.* (1) *Benefit-by-benefit approach.* This portion of the interpretation discusses how a benefit-by-benefit approach would apply to four of the most common types of employee benefit plans.

(i) *Life insurance.* It is not uncommon for life insurance coverage to remain constant until a specified age, frequently 65, and then be reduced. This practice will not violate the Act (even if reductions start before age 65), provided that the reduction for an employee of a particular age is no greater than is justified by the increased cost of coverage for that employee's specific age bracket encompassing no more than five years. It should be noted that a total denial of life insurance, on the basis of age, would not be justified under a benefit-by-benefit analysis. However, it is not unlawful for life insurance coverage to cease at age 70 or upon separation from service, whichever occurs first.

(ii) *Health insurance.* Ordinarily, health insurance coverage has not varied significantly with age up to age 65. The great variety of health insurance plans makes it difficult to offer a general guideline as to when, if ever, reductions in coverage might be justified by increased costs. Such reductions may not, however, be concentrated on certain items so as to make coverage less attractive to older workers.

(A) With respect to employees eligible for Medicare, it is not unlawful for an employer to "carve-out" from its own health insurance plan those benefits actually paid for by Medicare. Under such a "carve-out" approach, Medicare assumes primary responsibility for health care expenses under the employer's regular health insurance plan; the regular plan pays only for those expenses it insures against which are not actually paid for by Medicare. It is also not unlawful for an employer to place employees eligible for Medicare in a separate health insurance plan which supplements Medicare, *provided* (*1*) that the cost to the employer for such a supplemental plan is not less than the cost which would be expended to include such individuals in the regular health plan (with a Medicare "carve-out") and (2) that the supplemental plan provides benefits which are no less favorable than an employee eligible for Medicare benefits would receive under the employer's regular health insurance plan.

(B) An employer may not assume that eligible employees have taken advantage of available Medicare coverage, unless the employer informs each eligible employee of the need to apply for Medicare coverage and provides any necessary assistance for making an application for benefits. Furthermore, where the employer's regular health plan requires no employee contribution or an employee contribution less than that required for Medicare "Part B" coverage, the employer must pay or contribute toward the "Part B" contribution so as to make the total benefits available on terms which are no less favorable for employees over 65 than for employees under 65. However, the employer's total contribution for "Part B" and the "carve-out" or supplemental plan would not have to be greater than the employer's highest contribution for health benefits for employees of any age under 65.

(C) As a result of the savings to employers when benefits are available through Medicare, reductions in total health benefits for employees age 65 to 70 will generally not be justified. The total denial on the basis of age of employer-provided health benefits for older employees not eligible for Medicare would never be justified. It is not unlawful, however, for health insurance coverage to cease at age 70 or upon separation from service, whichever occurs first.

(iii) *Long-term disability.* It has been common in the past to cut off long-term disability benefits for all disabled employees and long-term disability coverage for all active employees at age 65. Since the Act protects employees and their expectations of employment from discrimination up to age 70, this practice can no longer be justified under a benefit-by-benefit approach. Under such an approach, where employees who are disabled at younger ages are entitled to long-term disability benefits, there is no cost-based justification for denying such benefits altogether, on the basis of age, to employees who are disabled at older ages. It is not unlawful to cut off long-term disability benefits and coverage on the basis of some non-age factor, such as recovery from disability. Nor is it unlawful to terminate benefits or coverage, on the basis of age, at age 70. Reductions on the basis of age before age 70 in the level or duration of benefits available for disability are justifiable only on the basis of age-related cost considerations as set forth elsewhere in this section. An employer which provides long-term disability coverage to all employees until the age of 70 may avoid any increases in the cost to it that such coverage for older employees would entail by reducing the level of benefits available to older employees. An employer may also avoid such cost increases by reducing the duration of benefits available to employees who become disabled at older ages, without reducing the level of benefits. In this connection, the Department would not assert a violation where the level of benefits is not reduced and the duration of benefits is reduced in the following manner:

(A) With respect to disabilities which occur at age 60 or less, benefits cease at age 65.

(B) With respect to disabilities which occur after age 60, benefits cease 5 years after disablement or at age 70, whichever occurs first. Cost data may be produced to support other patterns of reduction as well.

(iv) *Retirement plans*—(A) *Participation.* No employee hired prior to normal retirement age may be excluded from a defined contribution plan. With respect to defined benefit plans not subject to the Employee Retirement Income Security Act (ERISA), Pub. L. 93–406, 29 U.S.C. 1001, 1003 (a) and (b), an employee hired at an age more than 5 years prior to normal retirement age may not be excluded from such a plan unless the exclusion is justifiable on the basis of cost considerations as set forth elsewhere in this section. With respect to defined benefit plans subject to ERISA, such an exclusion would be unlawful in any case. An employee hired less than 5 years prior to normal retirement age may be excluded for a defined benefit plan, regardless of whether or not the plan is covered by ERISA. Similarly, any employee hired after normal retirement age may be excluded from a defined benefit plan.

(B) *Benefits.* In addition to the requirements as set forth elsewhere in this section, the following special rules apply to benefits provided under a retirement plan.

(*1*) A defined contribution plan may provide for the cessation of employer contributions after the normal retirement age of any participant in the plan. A defined contribution plan may also provide that no employer contributions shall be made on behalf of an employee who is hired after normal retirement age. However, these provisions apply only with respect to plans which are not "supplemental." Any defined contribution plan is deemed "supplemental" with respect to any employee who is a participant in it as well as in a defined benefit plan maintained by the employer. Where an employer has no defined benefit plan but two or more defined contribution plans, all but one of the defined contribution plans are "supplemental" with respect to those employees who are participants in them. The one defined contribution plan which is not "supplemental" could provide for the cessation of employer contributions after normal retirement age. The employer can designate which one of the defined contributions plans is not "supplemental".

(*2*) In a defined contribution plan, investment gains and losses and employee termination forfeitures are typically allocated to individual accounts instead of being used to reduce employer contributions. Where this is done, the allocations shall not be made less favorably on the basis of age to older employees (including those continuing to work past normal retirement age) than to younger employees. This rule shall apply regardless of whether or not the defined contribution plan is "supplemental."

(3) A defined benefit plan may fail to credit, for purposes of benefit accrual, service which occurs after an employee's normal retirement age.

(4) A defined benefit plan need not adjust actuarially the benefit accrued as of normal retirement age for an employee who continues to work beyond that age. (A defined contribution plan would have to pay the balance in the individual account.)

(5) A defined benefit plan need not provide for the accrual of benefits for an employee who continues to work after normal retirement age.

(6) A defined benefit plan may provide, and may be amended to provide, that retirement benefits will commence at the actual date of retirement rather than at normal retirement age for employees who choose to work beyond normal retirement age. Employees receiving long-term disability benefits as a salary replacement may be deemed not to have "actually retired" and therefore need not be simultaneously provided with retirement benefits.

(7) A defined benefit plan need not take into account salary increases and benefit improvements under the plan which take place after an employee reaches the normal retirement age specified in the plan with respect to those employees continuing their employment beyond that age. However, benefit improvements for retirees may not be denied to such employees who do not receive the advantage of benefit accruals and increases given younger employees.

(8) A defined benefit plan which includes offsets for Social Security and which ceases benefit accruals or any other increases at the normal retirement age specified in the plan may not offset the benefit receivable by such employees at actual retirement with the amount of Social Security benefit receivable at that time if the amount is greater than it was at the cessation of accruals. The total retirement benefit must be calculated on the basis of a Social Security benefit no greater than that receivable at the time when benefit accruals ceased under the employer's plan.

(2) *"Benefit package" approach*. A "benefit package" approach to compliance under section 4(f)(2) offers greater flexibility than a benefit-by-benefit approach by permitting deviations from a benefit-by-benefit approach so long as the overall result is no lesser cost to the employer *and* no less favorable benefits for employees. As previously noted, in order to assure that such an approach is used for the benefit of older workers and not to their detriment, and is otherwise consistent with the legislative intent, it is subject to limitations as set forth below:

(i) *A benefit package approach shall apply only to employee benefit plans which fall within section 4(f)(2).*

(ii) *A benefit package approach shall not apply to a retirement or pension plan.* The 1978 legislative history sets forth specific and comprehensive rules governing such plans, which have been adopted above. These rules are not tied to actuarially significant cost considerations but are intended to deal with the special funding arrangements of retirement or pension plans. Variations from these special rules are therefore not justified by variations from the cost-based benefit-by-benefit approach in other benefit plans, nor may variations from the special rules governing pension and retirement plans justify variations from the benefit-by-benefit approach in other benefit plans.

(iii) *A benefit package approach shall not be used to justify reductions in health benefits greater than would be justified under a benefit-by-benefit approach.* Such benefits appear to be of particular importance to older workers in meeting "problems arising from the impact of age" and were of particular concern to Congress. Therefore, the "benefit package" approach may not be used to reduce health insurance benefits by more than is warranted by the increase in the cost to the employer of those benefits alone. Any greater reduction would be a subterfuge to evade the purpose of the Act.

(iv) *A benefit reduction greater than would be justified under a benefit-by-benefit approach must be offset by another benefit available to the same employees.* No employees may be deprived because of age of one benefit without an offsetting benefit being made available to them.

(v) *Employers who wish to justify benefit reductions under a benefit package approach must be prepared to produce data to show that those reductions are fully justified.* Thus employers must be able to show that deviations from a benefit-by-benefit approach do not result in lesser cost to them or less favorable benefits to their employees. A general example consistent with these limitations may be given. Assume two employee benefit plans, providing Benefit "A" and Benefit "B." Both plans fall within section 4(f)(2), and neither is a retirement or pension plan subject to special rules. Both benefits are available to all employees. Age-based cost increases would justify a 10% decrease in both benefits on a benefit-by-benefit basis. The affected employees would, however, find it more favorable—that is, more consistent with meeting their needs—for no reduction to be made in Benefit "A" and a greater reduction to be made in Benefit "B." This "trade-off" would not result in a reduction in health benefits. The "trade-off" may therefore be made. The details of the "trade-off" depend on data on the relative cost to the employer of the two benefits. If the data show that Benefit "A" and Benefit "B" cost the same, Benefit "B" may be reduced up to 20% if Benefit "A" is unreduced. If the data show that Benefit "A" costs only half as much as Benefit "B", however, Benefit "B" may be reduced up to only 15% if Benefit "A" is unreduced, since a greater reduction in Benefit "B" would result in an impermissible reduction in total benefit costs.

(g) *Relation of ADEA to State laws.* The ADEA does not preempt State age discrimination in employment laws. However, the failure of the ADEA to preempt such laws does not affect the issue of whether section 514 of the Employee Retirement Income Security Act (ERISA) preempts State laws which related to employee benefit plans.

[44 FR 30658, May 25, 1979]

Appendix D

Text of
Proposed Model Jury Instructions on Issue of
"Age as a Factor" in Determining Liability
In ADEA Cases*

Draft Proposed

Instruction on Age as a Factor

(1st, 2d, 4th, 7th, 9th, and 10th Circuits)

Plaintiff has the ultimate burden of proving age discrimination. In order to satisfy this burden, plaintiff need not show that age was the sole or exclusive factor in the defendant employer's decision [to discharge, demote, etc.]. The defendant's decision may have been motivated by more than one factor. Plaintiff is entitled to recover if he/she proves by a preponderance of the evidence that age was a determining factor in deciding whether he should be [discharged, demoted, etc.]. In other words, plaintiff must prove that "but for" the defendant's motive to discriminate against him/her because of his/her age, he/she would not have been [discharged, demoted, etc.].

[The following instructions, though not expressly stated in the cases cited below, may also be given consistent with the above standard.]

Thus, if you find that "but for" the defendant's motive to discriminate against plaintiff because of his/her age, plaintiff would not have been [discharged, demoted, etc.], then plaintiff is entitled to a verdict on the issue of liability, even if there were other reasons that motivated the defendant to [discharge, demote etc.].

On the other hand, if you find that the plaintiff would have been [discharged, demoted etc.] even if the defendant had not been motivated to discriminate against plaintiff because of his/her age, then defendant is entitled to a verdict on this issue.

Loeb v. Textron, Inc., 600 F.2d 1003 (1st Cir. 1979).

Hagelthorn v. Kennecott Corp., 710 F.2d 76 (2d Cir. 1983); *Bentley v. Stromberg-Carlson Corp.*, 638 F.2d 9 (2d Cir. 1981); *Geller v. Markham*, 635 F.2d 1027 (2d Cir. 1980), *cert. denied*, 451 U.S. 945 (1981).

Spagnuolo v. Whirlpool Corp., 641 F.2d 1109 (4th Cir.), *cert. denied*, 454 U.S. 860 (1981); *Cline v. Roadway Express, Inc.*, 689 F.2d 481 (4th Cir. 1982).

Golomb v. Prudential Ins. Co., 688 F.2d 547 (7th Cir. 1982); *Kephart v. Institute of Gas Technology*, 630 F.2d 1217 (7th Cir., 1980), *cert. denied*, 450 U.S. 959 (1981).

*Reprinted by permission, Lawrence Ashe, Jury Trials Subcommittee, Employment and Labor Relations Law Committee, Litigation Section, American Bar Association.

Criswell v. Western Airlines, Inc., 709 F.2d 544 (9th Cir. 1983), *cert. granted,—* U.S. —, 105 S. Ct. 80 (1984); *Cancellier v. Federated Dept. Stores*, 672 F.2d 1312 (9th Cir.), *cert. denied*, 459 U.S. 859 (1982); *Kelly v. American Standard, Inc.*, 640 F.2d 974 (9th Cir. 1981).

Perrell v. FinanceAmerica Corp., 726 F.2d 654 (10th Cir. 1984).

Draft Proposed

Instruction on Age as a Factor

(3d, 5th, 6th, 8th, 11th, and D.C. Circuits)

Plaintiff has the ultimate burden of proving age discrimination. In order to satisfy this burden, plaintiff is not required to show that age was the sole or exclusive factor in the defendant employer's decision [to discharge, demote, etc.]. The defendant's decision may have been motivated by more than one factor. Plaintiff is entitled to recover if he/she proves by a preponderance of the evidence that age was a determining factor in the defendant's decision. In other words, plaintiff must show that one of the factors considered was his/her age and that age made a difference in determining whether to [discharge, demote, etc.].

[The following instructions, though not expressly stated in the cases cited below, may also be given consistent with the above standard.]

Thus, if you find that age was a factor which made a difference in the defendant's decision to [demote, discharge, etc.] plaintiff, then plaintiff is entitled to a verdict on the issue of liability, even if there were other reasons that motivated the defendant. If, on the other hand, you find that age was not a factor which made a difference in the decision to [discharge, demote, etc.] plaintiff, then defendant is entitled to a verdict in this issue.

Smithers v. Bailar, 629 F.2d 892 (3d Cir. 1980).

Haring v. CPC Int'l, Inc., 664 F.2d 1234 (5th Cir. 1981).

Blackwell v. Sun Elec. Corp., 696 F.2d 1176 (6th Cir. 1983); *Laugesen v. Anaconda Co.*, 510 F.2d 307 (6th Cir. 1975).

Tribble v. Westinghouse Elec. Corp., 669 F.2d 1193 (8th Cir. 1982), *cert. denied*, 460 U.S. 1080 (1983). The court in *Tribble* said that under the ADEA, the ultimate burden shouldered by a plaintiff is to show that age was a determining factor in the employer's decision. The court did not elaborate, but cited to *Laugesen v. Anaconda Co.*, 510 F.2d 307 (6th Cir. 1975), which sets forth the standard embraced in the instruction above. This standard was also adopted by a Fifth Circuit district court in *Carolan v. Central Freight Lines, Inc.*, 489 F. Supp. 941 (E.D. Tex. 1980).

Anderson v. Savage Laboratories, Inc., 675 F.2d 1221 (11th Cir. 1982).

Coburn v. Pan Am. World Airways, Inc., 711 F.2d 339 (D.C. Cir.), *cert. denied,—* U.S. —, 104 S. Ct. 488 (1983).

Cuddy v. Carmen, 694 F.2d 853 (D.C. Cir. 1982).

Draft Proposed

Instruction on Willfulness

The Court instructs you that the Age Discrimination in Employment Act allows a successful plaintiff the benefit of a three-year Statute of Limitations and to recover liquidated damages in an amount equal to the backpay award damages if he/she proves by a preponderance of the evidence that the defendant has willfully violated the Act. A violation of the ADEA is "willful" if the defendant knew its conduct was prohibited by the ADEA or showed a reckless disregard for whether or not it was so prohibited. A violation of the ADEA is not willful if the defendant simply knew of the potential applicability of the Act.

Thus, for you to find a willful violation of the Act, you must find that the defendant knew its conduct was prohibited by the Act or showed a reckless disregard for whether or not it was so prohibited.

Trans World Airlines, Inc. v. Thurston, — U.S. —, 105 S. Ct. 613 (1985).

Table of Cases

Cases presented in text or partial text are in italic type. Other cases—those discussed or merely cited—are in roman type. References are to pages.

Index

About the Author

Joseph E. Kalet, a former cryptologist/interpreter for the U.S. Navy, is a Senior Legal Editor with The Bureau of National Affairs, Inc., Washington, D.C. Mr. Kalet is an Honors Graduate from the State University of New York at Binghamton, N.Y., and an Honors Graduate from the Foreign Service Institute, Washington, D.C. He received his Juris Doctor from the George Washington University-National Law Center, Washington, D.C.

Mr. Kalet is a frequent speaker on labor law before such organizations as the National Association of Attorneys General and the National Labor Relations Board. He has written for the *American Bar Association Journal,* the *Arbitration Journal,* and other professional publications. He is a member of the National Labor Panel of the American Arbitration Association. He also is a member of the District of Columbia and Pennsylvania Bars.